T0322632

'In precise and sharp language, *Malevolent Republic* takes readers on a terrifying and yet illuminating journey through the rapidly transforming political, social, and religious landscape of Modi's India.'

Rafia Zakaria, *The Times Literary Supplement*

'[E]loquent on the subject of religious tolerance, communal harmony and human decency, all of which appear to be in harrowingly short supply among the acolytes who surround Modi.'

The Times

'Resembles VS Naipaul ... an invaluable primer for anyone trying to comprehend the "new India".'

Jon P. Dorschner, *American Diplomacy*

'Kapil Komireddi is one of the most thoughtful and thorough journalists writing today. His range of interests is impressive in its breadth and cosmopolitanism; his is a rare voice that can comment on global affairs from a truly comparative perspective.'

Amitav Ghosh

'Kapil Komireddi ranks high among the wisest, most astute, and most humane observers of modern India.'

David Frum, Senior Editor, *The Atlantic*

'Kapil Komireddi is a writer of flair, originality and, above all, an absolute independence of mind. His ability to see through posturing and prejudice makes his work both distinctive and compelling. This book deserves to be widely read within India and beyond.'

Ramachandra Guha

'Here lies an important trick of the book: its language, twinned with detail. Komireddi is master of pithy sentences... For someone like this reviewer who has lived through almost the entire time period covered in this book, I was struck by how it was able to keep me engaged.'

Nilanjan Sarkar, Deputy Director, South Asia Centre,
London School of Economics

'[I]ntensely readable ... a robust primer of the political history of modern India.'

Sidharth Bhatia, *The Wire*

'Devastating'

Priya Ramani, *Mint Lounge*

'[E]ven if you recoil from the full blast of Komireddi's anger, read *Malevolent Republic*. It's a reminder that India is a righteous project mishandled and let down, as the Hindutva brigade says, by the pseudo-seculars. India will, as a result, have to be reclaimed from those who now have the mandate to undo it.'

Shougat Dagupta, *India Today*

'What makes Komireddi's narrative interesting, and more importantly fair, is the care he's taken to look at all leaders from Nehru to Modi in equal light... The book ... merits a wider audience. Here, for a change, is a critic of the present order who is fair-handed even if he is a bit harsh in his anger at the political evolution of independent India.'

Siddharth Singh, *Open*

'Conservatives should consider picking up a copy of K.S. Komireddi's fierce (and fine) polemic, *Malevolent Republic*, which has the goods on India's long, sad decline into tyranny.'

Bill Myers, *Washington Examiner*

'The diagnosis is clinical and in prose that is hard to put down ... written in a style that makes it one of the most fascinating non-fiction books this writer has read.'

Nilanjan Mukhopadhyay, *Business Standard*

'It's difficult to accommodate more than 70 years of a country's history in 200 pages. The challenge is even more difficult when the work in question attempts to create a genealogy of how India turned into a "malevolent republic" ... But for anyone trying to understand the transformation, K.S. Komireddi's [book] is a must read.'

Kaushik Das Gupta, *The Indian Express*

'Well-documented and highly readable. All discerning Indians and their well-wishers should read it, reflect on the issues raised in it, and if possible act on them.'

P. Radhakrishnan, *The Hindu*

'Komireddi dispassionately deals with the violence the Hindutva supremacists engage in and the support it has garnered among a significant section of people ... a welcome addition to an analysis of post-Independence India'

Subhash Gatade, *The Telegraph*

MALEVOLENT REPUBLIC

K.S. KOMIREDDI

Malevolent Republic

A Short History of the New India

HURST & COMPANY, LONDON

First published in the United Kingdom in 2019 by
C. Hurst & Co. (Publishers) Ltd.,
41 Great Russell Street, London, WC1B 3PL
This paperback edition first published in 2024 by
C. Hurst & Co. (Publishers) Ltd.,
New Wing, Somerset House, Strand, London, WC2R 1LA
© K.S. Komireddi, 2024
All rights reserved.
Printed in the United Kingdom

The right of K.S. Komireddi to be identified as the author of
this publication is asserted by him in accordance with the
Copyright, Designs and Patents Act, 1988.

A Cataloguing-in-Publication data record for this book
is available from the British Library.

ISBN: 9781911723288

This book is printed using paper from registered sustainable
and managed sources.

www.hurstpublishers.com

It would be a boon to democracy if one of the great nations of the world … proves that it is possible to provide a good living for everyone without surrendering to a dictatorship of either the 'right' or 'left' … India is a tremendous force for peace and non-violence, at home and abroad. It is a land where the idealist and the intellectual are yet respected. We should want to help India preserve her soul and thus help to save our own.

Dr Martin Luther King, Jr., 1959

CONTENTS

To my mother
and
to my father

The Publisher acknowledges with thanks the kind permission granted by Mendonca Chogle, Kalpana Chogle, and Elkana Ezekiel to republish poems by the late Nissim Ezekiel

CHRONOLOGY OF EVENTS

1947   India wins freedom from British rule and becomes an independent dominion in the British Commonwealth of Nations. Parts of northwestern and eastern India are carved out to create Pakistan. Jawaharlal Nehru is sworn in as the first prime minister of the Dominion of India.

1948   Mahatma Gandhi, the Father of the Nation, is assassinated by the Hindu supremacist Nathuram Godse.

1948   Pakistan attempts an invasion of Kashmir, a sovereign kingdom with a Hindu ruler and a popular pro-India Muslim leader. Kashmir accedes to India in October 1947 in return for New Delhi's help against Pakistan. India pushes back the invaders but a part of Kashmir falls into Pakistani hands. India takes the matter to the United Nations, which calls on Pakistan to vacate its troops from the occupied territory to facilitate a referendum to determine Kashmir's status.

1950   The Constitution of India is adopted. India proclaims itself a liberal democratic republic.

1962	India and China go to war over a border dispute in eastern India. China wins.
1964	Nehru dies, and is succeeded by Lal Bahadur Shastri, who dies a year later.
1966	Indira Gandhi becomes the third prime minister of India.
1969	Indira Gandhi is expelled from the Congress Party for undermining internal democracy and violating party discipline. She forms a rival front. An overwhelming majority of senior Congress Party members switch to her side.
1971	India goes to war to halt the genocide in East Pakistan (now Bangladesh) at the hands of Pakistan's military dictatorship. India, aided by Bengali freedom fighters, liberates East Pakistan in days. The Pakistan constituted in 1947 ceases effectively to exist. Bangladesh is born.
1974	India stages a successful nuclear bomb test.
1975	Indira Gandhi's election to parliament is declared void by a court on technical grounds. She declares a state of internal emergency, suspends civil liberties, curtails the press, and jails her political opponents. The first spell of dictatorship begins.
1975	Indira Gandhi's younger son, Sanjay, enforces a mass sterilisation programme in which millions of Indians are forcibly mutilated.
1977	Indira Gandhi terminates the Emergency and calls a general election. The ideologically varied opposition forms a united front. Indira Gandhi and the Congress Party lose the general election. Morarji Desai becomes the prime minister.

1980	Early elections are called. Indira Gandhi and the Congress Party emerge victorious.
1984	Indira Gandhi authorises Indian special forces to storm the Akal Takht, the temporal seat of Sikhism located inside the Golden Temple Complex, to flush out militants holed up inside. The success of Operation Blue Star, led by Sikh officers, is accompanied by a tremendous loss of life and property.
1984	Indira Gandhi reinstates her Sikh bodyguards, after they are deemed a potential threat and reassigned by her office, by citing Indian secularism. She is assassinated by the same Sikh bodyguards. An anti-Sikh pogrom erupts in Delhi.
1984	Rajiv Gandhi, Indira Gandhi's elder son, is sworn in as prime minister before being elected in a landslide victory the same year.
1985	Shah Bano Begum, a divorced Muslim woman, is awarded full alimony by the Supreme Court of India, which affirms the supremacy of civil law over Muslim personal laws. Muslim men stage violent protests against the decision. Rajiv Gandhi forces through a bill in parliament nullifying the Supreme Court's judgement. Arif Mohammad Khan, one of the leading Muslim members of the Congress Party, resigns from Rajiv Gandhi's cabinet and leaves the party in solidarity with Muslim women.
1986	To pacify Hindus incensed by the Shah Bano saga, Rajiv Gandhi opens the medieval Babri Mosque in Ayodhya—the site of a bitter dispute between Muslims and Hindus—to Hindu worshippers.

1987 India deploys troops in Sri Lanka.

1988 To calm Muslim sentiments inflamed by his decision to open Babri, Rajiv Gandhi imposes an indirect ban on Salman Rushdie's novel *The Satanic Verses*.

1989 Rajiv Gandhi opens his campaign for the general elections from the vicinity of Ayodhya, pledging to recreate the rule of the Hindu god Rama. Congress is defeated.

1991 Rajiv Gandhi is assassinated by a suicide bomber of Sri Lanka's Liberation Tigers of Tamil Eelam. PV Narasimha Rao is sworn in as prime minister and appoints Manmohan Singh, a bureaucrat, as his finance minister. Together, they launch an ambitious liberalisation of India's partially closed economy.

1992 Hindu supremacists demolish the Babri Mosque in Ayodhya. Religious riots break out across the country.

1997 PV Narasimha Rao's coalition government is defeated at the polls. No party receives a full mandate. A period of political instability follows. The Hindu-first Bharatiya Janata Party emerges as the frontrunner.

1998 India conducts nuclear tests and declares itself a nuclear power, provoking international condemnation and sanctions.

1999 The National Democratic Alliance, led by the Bharatiya Janata Party, forms the government. Atal Bihari Vajpayee, having served two short spells as prime minister, is sworn in for the third time.

1999 Pakistan's army stages a covert operation to

invade Kashmir. Indian troops expel them in the ensuing battle.

2001   Narendra Modi, a full-time evangelist of Hindu nationalism, is appointed chief minister of Gujarat.

2002   A train carrying Hindu pilgrims from Ayodhya catches fire in Godhra, Gujarat. Fifty-six charred bodies are recovered from it. Before the cause of the arson can be investigated, Narendra Modi calls it an act of terrorism. The state is engulfed by days of anti-Muslim violence. There is a complete breakdown of law and order. Prime Minister Vajpayee considers firing Modi but is overruled by his colleagues.

2004   The Congress-led United Progressive Alliance wins a surprise victory in the general elections. Sonia Gandhi, Rajiv Gandhi's Italian-born widow, declines the premiership. Manmohan Singh becomes the prime minister.

2008   Mumbai, India's financial capital, is besieged by terrorists from Pakistan. More than 160 people are killed. Jews are targeted and killed for the first time in India's history.

2014   Narendra Modi becomes the prime minister of India following the BJP's decisive victory in the general elections, bringing to an end a three-decade-long tradition of government by coalition.

2015   Mohammed Akhlaq is lynched to death by a Hindu mob in Uttar Pradesh, India's largest state, for allegedly storing beef in his house. Yogi Adityanath, a priest and BJP politician in UP, demands police action against the deceased's family.

2016   Modi imposes an abrupt ban on high-value currency notes. The move plunges India into chaos.

2017   Modi appoints Yogi Adityanath as the chief minister of Uttar Pradesh.

2017   Rahul Gandhi, a fourth-generation Gandhi dynast, is made president of the Congress Party.

2018   Urjit Patel, handpicked by the government to run the Reserve Bank of India, resigns.

2019   The BJP is re-elected in a landslide. Modi returns as the prime minister for a second term.

2019   The government revokes Article 370, the basis of Kashmir's statehood-autonomous status, and abolishes the state of Jammu and Kashmir.

2019   Modi launches a project to redevelop the administrative heart of Delhi, converting Parliament House into a museum.

2020   The Citizenship (Amendment) Act, passed by parliament the previous year, comes into force. The law threatens to introduce a religious test of citizenship by stealth. Large-scale protests, initially led by Muslims but eventually drawing Indians of all faiths, materialise across India. Elderly women stage a prolonged sit-in in Delhi's Shaheen Bagh.

2020   Sectarian riots flare up in Delhi for the first time in more than three decades. More than fifty people, mostly Muslims, are killed.

2020   Covid-19 marches into India. Modi declares a nationwide lockdown with four hour's notice and seeks a directive from the Supreme Court requiring the press to self-censor. An exodus on foot of millions of workers from cities to small towns and villages across India begins.

2020	Modi launches an opaque new private trust—christened the Prime Minister's Citizen Assistance and Relief in Emergency Situations Fund, or 'PM CARES'—to raise money to fight Covid. Millions flow into the fund.
2021	Modi declares victory against Covid in a virtual speech to the World Economic Forum in January. In February, the BJP passes a resolution praising Modi's 'leadership for introducing India to the world as a proud and victorious nation in the fight against COVID-19' and asserting that India 'defeated COVID-19 under the able, sensitive, committed, and visionary leadership of Prime Minister Narendra Modi.'
2021	In March, the government announces that India is 'in the endgame' of the pandemic.
2021	By the close of April, India becomes the global epicentre of the second wave of the Covid pandemic. Hospitals run out of oxygen. The health system breaks down. Corpses float in rivers. India's Covid death toll is subsequently estimated by the World Health Organization to be 4.7 million.
2021	In May, the government sets a deadline for the completion of a new official residence for Modi in the heart of Delhi.
2020–2021	Farmers' protests erupt against a triad of agricultural reforms forced through by the government.
2022	India celebrates its 75th Independence Day, marking 75 years since its independence from British rule.
2023	Narendra Modi opens the new Parliament building.

January, 2024   A Hindu temple opens on the site of the razed Babri mosque in Ayodhya. Narendra Modi attends the ceremony.

PROLOGUE

RUPTURE

We noticed nothing as we went,
A straggling crowd of little hope,
Ignoring what the thunder meant …

Nissim Ezekiel

Saare jahaan se achhaa, Hindositaan hamaraa. 'Better than all the world is our India.' My days began with those words when I was a child. I chanted them, in a school assembly of a hundred or so boys, facing the Indian flag, every morning for four months. The author of this unabashed ode to India, the great poet Iqbal, had not actually seen the world beyond the subcontinent when he published it at the beginning of the twentieth century; and, after a brief sojourn abroad, had recoiled from the song's pan-Indian timbre and reinvented himself as an exponent of ruinous ethno-religious nationalism, the spiritual father of the idea of religious segregation that culminated in the Partition of India and the birth of Pakistan. But we did not know this then. And so, at one of the first schools I attended, which was really a madrassa, an Islamic seminary, we recited every morning of the week, in the shade of the mosque that soared behind the flagpole, Iqbal's verses exalting India's specialness. 'We are Indian,' we sang in chorus. 'India is our homeland.'

The mosque, which lent grandeur to the school, looked so majestic that I thought the Taj Mahal must have been modelled on it. For a while, I thought it *was* the Taj. At noon, the boys, led by an elderly man with a soft beard and thick black glasses, went there to pray. The only non-Muslim pupil, I was left on my own. I was sitting alone in the classroom when a man walked in and asked me why I wasn't at prayer. He was tall and slender, with a pencil-thin moustache and black eyes lined with kohl. I had seen him before, always in a loose-fitting kurta standing at the back of the assembly, almost an adult. I wasn't allowed to, I said. 'O, *you* are that boy,' he said excitedly, as though he had just confirmed some improbable rumour. He walked over and sat next to me. 'No one is prohibited from praying,' he said. 'Ask your father to buy you a cap. I'll take you to the mosque.' He then offered me his protection: 'If anyone gives you trouble, let me know. Ask for Murad.'

He was beside himself with laughter when he saw me walking up to him a few days later with my cap on. What I was wearing was a Nehru topi, not the taqiyah, the Islamic prayer cap. My father, who had deposited me at this madrassa for a lofty reason—to inoculate me against sectarian temptations in later life—did not know the difference, and had bought me a hat made popular by India's notoriously godless founding Prime Minister.

But no matter. Any head covering would do, Murad said. We stood beneath the imposing dome that afternoon, and I, after rinsing my hands and feet, mimicked his motions, while repeating, under my breath, the only words I discerned in the call to prayer that radiated from the loudspeakers affixed to the mosque's minarets: *Allahu Akbar Allah*.

We fell in together after that. A bond formed over afternoons of sharing lunch, praying, and playing cricket. He was the first person I accepted, consciously, as a friend. He called me his brother and invited me to his house. On a Friday, when classes finished early, we rode a packed green double-decker bus to the old quarter of Hyderabad where he lived. Murad held my hand and led me through the crowds. We walked under grand identical arches that were like gateways to a fabled city, flanked on either side by carts piled with fruit and jewellery shops canopied with stacked columns of red and green glass bangles suspended from their lintels, and stopped at Charminar, a stupendous hazel-hued mosque with four minarets but no dome, the architectural gem of the old city, built four decades before the Taj Mahal, slummy and chaotic now, but a few generations ago the resplendent seat of the Nizam, the ruler of Hyderabad, the richest man in the world. Unexpectedly, at the base of one of its minarets, was a Hindu temple.

I had driven past this place before. But now we walked, making our way through the late afternoon traffic of motorbikes, buses and yellow auto-rickshaws, past butcher shops with fly-blown hunks of beef and mutton hanging from hooks behind rusting grilles, exotic birds in cages, women examining saris splayed out on the floors of carpeted shops, a man outside a chemist's pouring water into his mouth from a steel pitcher and gurgling and spitting it on the road.

Murad's house, on the first floor of a dilapidated building, was really a small room that opened out on to the corridor, with one naked bulb and no furniture, painted green and partitioned by an old sari. There was a small cot with a thin mattress on it and calendars on the wall with pictures of Mecca. His mother, who opened the door, invited me in warmly and asked me to sit on the bed. She gave me hot milk in a small steel tumbler. Murad told his mother and sister, who sat in a corner and never spoke, that I had mastered the *namaz*. He was proud of me. His family seemed amused by it all. And then it was time for me to go.

I asked Murad where his father was. He didn't know. They had a nicer, bigger house when he was small and his father worked in the Gulf, he said. But then his father stopped sending money and abandoned the family. The room I had seen belonged to his uncle. Murad, I discovered, wasn't just a student at the madrassa; he also did odd jobs there. He was thirteen, and his family depended upon him. His mother was asking him to quit school and take up work near their house. I had no means then to understand the precariousness of his life.

Murad had never seen a hundred-rupee note, or sat in a car, or been to the cinema. But he thought my life was grim when I told him that my family never celebrated Diwali, the Hindu festival of lights, because my father thought it was vulgar. When once I pleaded with him to let me buy fireworks as we were driving home on or before Diwali, my father parked the car and took me for a walk. He gestured at the crush of people sleeping on the pavements under the smoky black sky illuminated by festive flares and thrust a hundred-rupee note into my hand. *It will be less insulting to these people if you burn this right now*, he said. Diwali was dead for me.

Murad said this was unfair and smuggled a bag of fireworks into the school a few weeks later. And in the courtyard of the mosque, I, prompted by him, celebrated Diwali as we both thought it ought to be. Then, with a stone, he chiselled our names in Urdu into the wall of the mosque.

We parted very shortly after that.

The madrassa was never intended as a proper education— only a primer in Indian pluralism. I was shipped off mid-term to boarding school: a different world, a thousand miles from home, miserable and forbidding at first. There were bands and gangs, and seniors smoked pot in the woods. I thought about Murad; we hadn't said goodbye before I was abruptly plucked out and put on a train to Delhi. I spent spare, unsupervised afternoons in the library. I played cricket and chess, and learnt to ride and to swim. I moved on. Among my new friends were the scions of a Nepalese political dynasty and expatriate Afghans. Nobody discussed religion.

A year into this life, my father, determined to grant me 'exposure' to new experiences, began making arrangements to send me to the Indian school in Afghanistan. The Taliban's successes foiled those plans. But after straying interminably from school to school and spending a year studying drama in a Himalayan village, I was sent away, in my mid-teens, to England. My mind, which had begun in Delhi to dislodge Murad, secreted memories of the madrassa in some remote fold of my consciousness in London, where, coming of age in the aftermath of 9/11, I was overcome by a crippling admixture of pride and awkwardness about this past. I never thought to look him up.

It was Murad who found me.

Almost a quarter of a century had passed since the day he carved our names into the wall of the school's mosque when I received a call from my father. 'A man is here to see you. He says he is your friend.' I was in Hyderabad, on a break from travelling in India. I did not recognise him at first. He wore a crimson plaid shirt and faded blue jeans. The skullcap was gone. His scalp, balding, was covered with a red baseball cap. His eyes, still lined with kohl, were just as intense. 'Forgotten me already, boss?,' he said in Urdu and embraced me. He limped as we climbed down the stairs, a man who had aged beyond his years.

I thought he reappeared to ask for help. We went for tea to an Iranian cafe. It was owned by a Muslim family originally from Tehran, but its Sanskrit name, *Panchsheel*—the five principles of peaceful coexistence Nehru had negotiated in the 1950s with China—memorialised an epoch that had long ago vanished. Castigating Nehru was now a national pastime. Votes were being cast across India to elect a new government, and people complained, wherever I went, that Nehru had destroyed the country. An age was ending, and the aggrieved voice of a suppressed nation within a nation whose existence we, asserting our claim on India by reciting Iqbal, were oblivious to was closing in on us. We sat in a place that was a reliquary of a disappeared era, conceived as a tribute to the achievement of a man now despised.

But just when our own world was in jeopardy, Murad and I found ourselves searching for a common vocabulary. A great gulf had opened up between us. He had come looking for me over the years, he told me, but was told each time that I was away. He found my email address and wrote to me, but there was no answer.

He dropped out of the madrassa not long after I left, and took up a job. His uncle owed money to the shop owner, so Murad took nothing home; he was repaying his uncle's debts. The old man had been attempting for years to marry off Murad's sister to a man in the Gulf. His mother, astonishingly for a woman in such a helpless condition, had put up resistance. But the uncle was unrelenting, and threatened to push the family out of their room if they did not consent. His sister agreed to settle for the marriage, and the family kept the roof over their heads. The groom who came to take her away was much older than they had anticipated, almost elderly, and his teenaged sister, after going through the wedding rituals, poisoned herself. To Murad's trauma was added shame: he was the only male in his immediate family, and there was nothing he could do.

A year after I left Hyderabad, violence between Muslims and Hindus engulfed Murad's part of the city. The spark was supplied by the storming, in distant Ayodhya, of the medieval Babri masjid by mobs who, led by the Hindu-nationalist Bharatiya Janata Party, claimed that the mosque had been erected by the founder of the Mughal empire on the birthplace of the Hindu god-king Rama. The BJP was launched in 1980 as the political arm of the Rashtriya Swayamsevak Sangh, the mother ship of Hindu nationalism. Founded in the city of Nagpur in 1925 by a physician whose family had fled religious persecution in Muslim-ruled Hyderabad, the RSS ascribed India's history of conquests by Muslims and Europeans to the weakness of Hindus. The source of the weakness was attributed to caste, the most oppressive apparatus of segregation ever devised by man, which compartmentalised Hindus into four hereditary categories—priests, warriors, merchants, labour—while keeping multitudes, the so-called 'untouchables', wholly locked out of the system. The fact that the bulk of India's Muslims were descendants of converts from the outcastes was a source of shame for Hindu nationalists. The RSS built on the doctrine of Hindutva—'Hinduness'—formulated in 1923 by an atheist called Vinayak Savarkar. To be an Indian, Savarkar wrote in his foundational text on Hindu nationalism, one had first to be a Hindu—and Savarkar's Hinduness was an elastic category, open to all: the price of admission to it was allegiance to India, the secular deity of Hindus. But because India was also the *sacred* land of the Hindus, Muslims—practisers of an Arab faith—were precluded from membership of it.[1] To become Indian, they had to undergo 'purification' rituals and 'reconvert' to the Hindu faith their forebears had relinquished. The growth of Hinduism as a political identity was inseparable from the sense of having been wronged by history. The self-definition was anchored in an awareness of the self's inadequacy: shame was the basis of its foundation. The RSS fused Western ideas of individualism with the aggression it descried in Islam and committed itself to the creation of a muscular Hindu nation. For most of its early existence, it did not have a market beyond upper-caste Hindu men, and its leaders remained virtually unknown to most Indians. In 1948, the RSS was banned for a year after one its former members—a protégé of Savarkar's—gunned down Mahatma Gandhi for having allowed India to be Partitioned by Muslim nationalists the previous year. Banished from the centre of power by the secular establishment in the early decades after Independence, the RSS pullulated out of sight and announced itself as a force in the 1980s. To its swollen ranks, Babri's obliteration was the first step in healing the wounds inflicted upon Hindus by history.

Two hundred people died in the rioting that ensued in Hyderabad. A majority of them were Hindus, the dominant religious community in the city as a whole but a minority in its old quarter. The authorities were by and large impartial as they stamped out the fighting—there were curfews, and rumours of an imminent shoot-at-sight order were circulated to deter crowds from forming—and their neutrality is perhaps what accounted for the uneven distribution of deaths. Hindus, being exhorted by the BJP to unite as a *nation*, began to seethe: their coreligionists had to die because they had the misfortune of living under a state that, calling itself 'secular', deserted the majority.

In 1990, when the streets ran with blood, Murad, in spite of his family's extreme poverty and physical proximity to the bloodletting, felt detached from it all. His sense of security, naive in retrospect, was an aspect of his unspoken faith in what he believed to be Indian 'secularism'.

The word signified something. It helped him navigate and form an idea of himself in relation to the world around him. It implied that he belonged despite being a Muslim, practitioner of a faith in whose name India had been mutilated with a wrenching finality. It guaranteed his position as a full citizen of a state that, vehemently rejecting religion as a valid determinant of nationalism even after Pakistan had been hacked out from it as the homeland of India's Muslims, committed itself to upholding an ecumenical secularity in public life.

It was a perilously audacious experiment from the outset. The future of the state was mortgaged to the presumption that Indians would continue to respond to history's unresolved knots with the same self-possession as the Republic's founders. It was a project floated on the supposition that democracy would contain rather than intensify the yearnings for consolidation among India's Hindus who, for the first time in history, would be an enfranchised majority in a politically united India devoid of a foreign master. It gave Indians an outstanding Constitution without, as Ardeshir Palkhivala put it, 'the ability to keep it'.

India did not always work for Murad and his family. It extended them rights without fostering the conditions for their exercise. What it did *not* do, however, is question their Indianness. So in 1990, when riots erupted on his doorstep because Hindu mobs had entered the Babri mosque, he was confident, despite the history of the city he lived in, that he would be all right. But two years later, when Hindu militias razed the Babri mosque, he felt endangered. He had seen, or heard from someone who had seen, footage of policemen spectating as hundreds of Hindus scaled the domes of Babri and, working only with poleaxes and hammers for several hours, levelled the mosque that had stood there for half a millennium. P.V. Narasimha Rao, the Prime Minister of India when the mosque was pulled down, grew up in a village not far from Hyderabad. Murad still felt wounded by the betrayal of 'our man'.

The elders in the old city convened a meeting after Babri's destruction. The police could no longer be trusted. Muslims would have to organise their own security. Murad was now treated as an asset by people who had been content to see him and his family fall apart. Patrols were formed. Women were instructed to stay inside. Men were given knives. Then there was a long wait. Miraculously, the violence never touched them directly. This upset a few men who wanted to burn down the houses of the destitute Hindus who lived cheek-by-jowl with them. The elders vetoed the idea and everybody went home.

But a rupture had occurred. What was the position of Muslims in India? Were they wanted or not? Where else could they go?

These questions had an extra special relevance for Hyderabad, the only region of southern India—the more developed and peaceable half of the country—to become embroiled in the parricidal bloodshed that attended the Partition of India. The clamour for India's division originated in the anxieties and prejudices of the subcontinent's decaying Muslim elites. Having lost their privileges after India fell to the British, they pitched for a state of their own as Britain's exit from the subcontinent loomed. If Muslims remained in a democratic India, Muhammad Ali Jinnah, the founder of Pakistan, told a meeting of his co-religionists in 1940, they would be responsible for the 'complete destruction of what is most precious in Islam'. Jinnah had begun his political career as a proponent of interfaith collaboration in India's struggle against British colonial rule. But cruelly thwarted on the nationalist stage by Gandhi, he morphed into the classical demagogue Abe Lincoln had warned against almost exactly a century before Jinnah picked up the baton of Muslim nationalism: 'Distinction will be his paramount object, and although he would as willingly, perhaps more so, acquire it by doing good as harm ... that opportunity being past, and nothing left to be done in the way of building up, he would set boldly to the task of pulling down.'[2]

Insisting that Muslims and Hindus were two distinct 'nations' inhabiting one land, Jinnah demanded the amputation of the subcontinent along religious lines to invent 'Pakistan', *Land of the Pure*. Muslims who regarded their faith as one aspect of their composite Indian identity turned in horror from his agitation. But Jinnah could not be reasoned with: ethno-religious nationalism, worn in the beginning as an expedient mask, had progressively devoured his face. Diagnosed with terminal lung disease, he kept his illness hidden from his followers and incited religious passions he knew he would not be able to contain. 'India divided or India destroyed' was Jinnah's ultimatum to the British as they prepared to leave: civil war and scission were the choices before Indians.

On 15 August 1947, Britain formally withdrew from its most lucrative colonial possession, India attained independence, and Pakistan, carved from the eastern and western flanks of the subcontinent, was inaugurated as a state for its Muslims. A complete negation of the very notion of human multiplicity, Pakistan was, on its own terms, a monument to majoritarian bigotry and chauvinism. But its creation also dramatically validated every Hindunationalist trope about Muslim treachery. India had extended its hospitality to believers of all faiths for thousands of years: only the followers of Islam, they said, saw themselves as a people apart by virtue of their religion, refused to become assimilated into it, and dismembered its difficultly achieved unity.

Within days began the transfer of populations. More than half a million people were killed as Indians, suddenly uprooted in the name of religion, exploded with irrepressible fury. Trainloads of corpses travelled in both directions. It was the largest—and possibly the bloodiest—exodus in human history. Jinnah died just over a year after Pakistan's birth. His only daughter, forbidden by her once-secular father from marrying outside the faith, remained in India.

After Partition, the hundreds of so-called 'princely states' governed indirectly by London had the choice of acceding either to India or to Pakistan. Hyderabad's Muslim ruler dreamt of making his overwhelmingly non-Muslim dominion, located in the centre of India, an exclave of Pakistan. His capital was one of the best endowed cities in India. But the dry country that formed the bulk of his kingdom was a theatre of ancient horrors. Its human cast was composed of the Nizam's vassals—implacably sadistic feudal lords belonging to the Reddi and Velama castes—and landless serfs emaciated by centuries of servitude. A form of bondage that was slavery in every sense flourished there.

There are foreigners who have written books in which the Nizam's court is a setting for taboo romance. The starveling peasants whose labour underwrote the opulence of Hyderabad do not appear in these exotic amphigories, which continue the literary tradition inaugurated by Kipling's *William the Conqueror*, in which a famine in southern India furnishes the backdrop for a British love story. There are Indians who have mourned the passing of the Nizam's rule. No matter that, in addition to slavery, the Nizam presided over a system of rigid religious segregation.

Refusing to see himself as a native of the land ruled by his dynasty for centuries, the Nizam used the taxes extracted from his etiolated subjects to advance a generous subvention to the insolvent government of Pakistan, which might otherwise have collapsed within days of its inception. He ordered a halt on the export of metals to the rest of India and banned Indian currency in Hyderabad. The British warned the Nizam not to test the resolve of India, reminding him that their successor state in Delhi 'was immensely powerful, and still possessed one of the biggest armies in the world'.[3] But the old man had by then lost touch with reality. He squandered millions of dollars on 400 tons of weapons purchased from the European black market with the assistance of an Australian arms dealer. His mujahideen, meanwhile, led by a man called Kasim Rizvi and calling themselves Razakars, rampaged through towns and villages terrorising civilians.

After exhaustive attempts to parley with the Nizam failed, India ordered in its forces in September 1948. It would have been inexpressibly cathartic for the people exposed to the Razakars' ravages had India, upon liberating Hyderabad, placed the Nizam on trial. Instead, it pensioned him off. His band of holy warriors was permitted to emigrate to Pakistan. And the Muslim–Hindu collaboration that had bolstered the uprising against the Nizam dissolved in a bloodbath in which 40,000 Muslims were slaughtered.

The secular Indian state's arrival in Hyderabad began with three irremediable mistakes. First, the failure to hold the Nizam and his government accountable for their crimes against humanity; second, the failure to protect Muslim civilians; third, the suppression of the official report commissioned by Nehru which chronicled in chilling detail the subsequent massacres of Muslims. Integration into the Indian union was dyed with bitter disappointment for virtually every party in Hyderabad.

Thousands of Hyderabadi Muslims resettled in Pakistan. The many thousands more who remained, who refused to vacate the hell that was Hyderabad despite the blandishments of paradise in Pakistan, voted for India with their lives. India's Hindus never had to make that choice. Its Muslims did. Consider the view from the eyes of an ordinary Muslim family: encircled by the violence precipitated by Partition, their coreligionists were fleeing in the millions to Pakistan; Muslim businesses were being plundered and burnt to the ground; Hindu and Sikh fanatics were hunting Muslims for slaughter and rape; the possibility of being betrayed by neighbours and friends was very far from remote; families were permanently fracturing; powerful functionaries in the government were openly hostile to Muslims—hostility which no doubt would have been seen by many Hindus as tacit endorsement of their savagery.

In spite of all this, millions of Muslims remained.

In the 1940s, Congress—the dominant secular party that led India to independence from Britain, and was assailed by both Jinnah and the RSS—heroically withstood the demand of aggrieved Hindus to respond to Pakistan's birth by turning India into a Hindu state. Nehru, as India's first Prime Minister, frequently raced to scenes of communal clashes on his own, often chasing vengeful Hindu and Sikh refugees expelled from Pakistan without regard for his personal safety. 'If you harm one single hair on the head of one Muslim,' he told a mob plotting a massacre of Muslims, 'I will send in a tank and blast you to bits.'[4]

In the 1990s, Nehru was being recast by the ascendant Hindu nationalists as a deracinated interloper. Congress, once the revered engine of India's freedom movement, was in the late stage of its slow metamorphosis into a sump for Nehru's parasitical progeny to luxuriate in. The party's commitment to secularism had long ago ceased to be a conviction. And half a century after placing everything on the line to hold on to India, Muslims were being told by Hindu nationalists—just as they had been told by the Muslim segregationist Jinnah—that they could not be Muslim *and* Indian.

This was the milieu in which the bitterness and anger provoked by the destruction of the Babri mosque, finding no productive release, festered. And the old city, forsaken by India, degenerated into a fertile recruitment field for Pakistani spies. There was a surfeit of angry young men in Hyderabad, and Pakistani operatives materialised to marshal them into militancy. Claiming to be emancipators of Muslims besieged by unbelievers, they lured their prey with invocations of religious solidarity. The wretched reality of Muslims made them especially susceptible to such plain manipulation. Political victories by Hindu nationalists, heightening Muslim insecurity, made it easier for Pakistan to exploit them; and Pakistan's penetration into India lent credence to the Hindu-nationalist claim that Muslims were a fifth column. As always, Muslim nationalism and Hindu nationalism, two sides of the same sectarian coin, fortified each other.

Hyderabad became a hotspot of anti-terror operations.

Murad stayed out of trouble, but around him men disappeared. There were whispers in his community that some of those captured or killed by the authorities had fallen under the spell of the ISI, Pakistan's spy-ops agency. The prospect of losing their children made parents vigilant. The elders who once encouraged the young to carry arms now beseeched them to stay loyal to India. Edicts enjoining Muslims to abjure violence flowed from the mosques. Indian democracy, congregants were told, had adequate mechanisms to redress their grievances.

Just as Hyderabad began attracting international attention as India's Silicon Valley in the 1990s, the old city gained notoriety in the intelligence community as an entrepot of Pakistan-sponsored radicalism. Respectable newspapers published reports that said Osama bin Laden had scouted the city in 1998, two years before Bill Clinton paid it a presidential visit.

By the new millennium, there were two Hyderabads, and they were increasingly immiscible. The new Hyderabad swirled with entrepreneurial energy, full of promise and opportunity. Its sobriquet was 'Cyberabad', a name that conveyed its status as the poster child for an impatient post-socialist India. The old Hyderabad was a suppurating ruin. People privately called it mini Pakistan. At dinner parties, its backwardness was ascribed by Hyderabad's newly rich caste of software entrepreneurs to the benightedness of its inhabitants. Others, who owed their place at the table to old money and considered themselves progressive in the Nehruvian mould, protested meekly that this was a 'communal' way of looking at things. Everyone, in the end, projected their ideas on to the old city. Nobody, it seemed, really knew the place. It was a no-go area: no one wanted to go there. It was, beyond its much-fetishised façade, inaccessible. They did not admit it, but they felt threatened by it. The party that now governed the old city, that exerted total control over it, was a new avatar of the party once commanded by Kasim Rizvi. The distance between the two Hyderabads appeared unbridgeable.

In India, complains a character in Upamanyu Chatterjee's novel *English, August*, 'from washing your arse to dying, an ordinary citizen is up against the government'. Delhi is zealously interventionist. For all the grumbling it arouses, this has not always been such a bad thing. Being harried by the state has had a civilising effect in many places where Indians have been forced to forgo barbaric customs sanctioned by religion.

But things have worked differently for Muslims. The state bypassed the people of the old city in the crucial decades after Independence, in part because it was inhibited by its own secular credo, which required it to abide the stagnation of Muslim communities for fear of offending the leaders of those communities. Murad's mother lived in penury because, as a Muslim woman, she was barred by the law from seeking alimony from her ex-husband. Islam, said the men who claimed to be scholars of the faith, conferred upon husbands the right to cast aside their wives without providing for them; and the government, by recognising and defending the rights vested in Muslim men by their faith, was proving its secularity.

This interpretation of secularism could express itself in perverse ways. When the Bangladeshi authoress Taslima Nasreen appeared in Hyderabad, elected leaders of Rizvi's political party assaulted her on camera and threatened to assassinate her. She was to them a blasphemer, deserving of death. When the police staged token arrests, a close relative of mine immediately offered to dispatch a team of lawyers to defend the assailants. The relative abhorred what had been done to Nasreen. But the only way he knew to uphold the 'secularism' he had internalised in his youth was by deferring to people who claimed to be tribunes of their religious communities. Hadn't Gandhi taught us that Muslims and Hindus must always 'respect each other's religion and religious feelings'? Sure. But wasn't the second half of that particular moral that we must 'always refrain from violence'? The relative shrugged. He was not condoning violence. He was helping to contain it by rising to defend 'community leaders'.

Striving to buy communal harmony in this way, India left its Muslims behind while forcing its Hindus to modernise. A staggering social disparity has arisen between Muslims and Hindus, as the results of a survey commissioned by the government in 2010 show.[5] Only 4 per cent of all Indian Muslims are graduates, 5 per cent have public employment, and a majority of Muslims remain locked out of public institutions. The ghettoes of the old city, when I drove with Murad one afternoon in 2014, looked as much like a memorial to the failures of Indian secularism as the detritus of the Babri mosque.

Murad felt stifled by this strange new city of multiplying glass-and-steel buildings bearing the names of Western corporations but diminishing chances for people like him. His mother begged him to get married and go away. But he stayed to look after her. He sold computer accessories out of a shack. It was hard work, and he was giving more in bribes to the police than he took home. At the mosque, someone introduced him to a man who said he could find him a job in the Gulf. At a time when newspapers in the West were acclaiming India as the next great success story of globalisation, and Indian commentators were proclaiming the country a superpower in waiting, Murad, unable to access the prosperity that was percolating down to well-heeled people around him, was looking for ways to flee India. Arabia always had a need for Indian labour, and India was always able to meet the need. Murad began putting together money to resettle in Muscat or Kuwait.

Catastrophe struck just when escape became available.

In the summer of 2007, Mecca Masjid, the magnificent granite mosque in the old city that had taken thousands of workers in the seventeenth century almost fifty years to complete, became a scene of carnage. Ten thousand men were saying the afternoon prayer when an improvised explosive, lodged in the area where worshippers performed ablutions, went off. It's a marvel that only eleven people were killed in the blast.

Within a day, the blame for the atrocity was assigned to Islamic detachments operating from Bangladesh and Pakistan. The first instinct of the authorities who long ago wrote off the old city was to swamp the place and cart away 200 random Muslim men for what they euphemistically called 'interrogation'. Murad, ill-fated from an early age, was among them. There was no record of his detention. Nobody knew where he had been until after he was freed. He could not walk or sit or eat for days. He was broken from the inside. As horror stories of torture chambers spread, his mother, cursing herself for being alive, grabbed his legs and sobbed and asked him to go away.

A year after the blast at Mecca Masjid, twenty-one Muslim men were put up for criminal prosecution. It was reported that they had been taking orders from a Pakistani outfit. Their handler, a man called Shahid Bilal, was later shot dead by the police. India's news media welcomed the 'breakthrough'. It is 'a fallacy to believe that there are rogue cells of the ISI at work operating beyond the pale of the Pakistani establishment,' India's largest English-language newsmagazine told its readers. The assault on Mecca Masjid, it assured readers, was part of the Pakistani government's 'newest game plan to target religious places and foment communal unrest' in India.[6]

Such comforting certitudes were upended only a few years later when a repentant Hindu priest, captured by India's National Investigation Agency, volunteered a shattering confession: that the attack at Mecca Masjid had been one of several staged by a militant *Hindu* group which, he said, was intimately connected with the parent body of the BJP. The organisation counted among its members, the swami disclosed, an officer of the Indian Army.[7]

Pundits immediately began conducting cautious enquiries on television. Did this revelation mean that India was now under attack by 'Hindu terrorism'?

The question landed like a whip on the wounds being nursed by the tortured men in Hyderabad. Graphic videos of atrocities against Muslims across India now began circulating in the old city. And late one evening, after prayers, dozens of people assembled to watch a documentary on the riots in Gujarat in 2002. Until then, Gujarat was something people talked about without fully knowing what had actually happened there. The film gave them a glimpse. The audience in the old city saw and heard testimonies of survivors of the violence. Wombs of pregnant Muslim women were sliced open with knives and their foetuses tossed out. Women were raped by gangs of Hindu men and then killed. Muslim houses were splashed with kerosene and set on fire. Truckloads of corpses of Muslims were dumped in mass graves. All of this happened over the course of several days. India watched. No help was sent. How much of this was true? It almost didn't matter as long as some of it was.

Narendra Modi was the newly appointed chief minister of Gujarat when this happened. He was asked by a foreign reporter if he had any regrets. Yes, he told her. He wished he had handled the news media better. The man on whose watch the murders and rapes and arsons by Hindus raged was, if not criminally complicit, then criminally negligent. If not criminally negligent, then he was, at the very minimum, the most incompetent administrator in India at the time. His political career should have come to an end in that moment. Instead, in 2014, a dozen years after the riots in Gujarat, Modi was the top contender for India's highest political office; and, agonisingly for those with vivid memories of Gujarat, he was being applauded as a *competent* leader. Twenty-two years after the demolition of

Babri, butchering Muslims—or failing to intervene and stop them from being butchered—was not a disqualification in Indian politics. It was a prelude to success.

How, after this, could India call upon Muslims to believe that they were of India, that India was theirs? I could scarcely object when Murad told me he was leaving the country.

A few days before he went away, we drove to the place where we had first met as children. The madrassa was gone: the ground it once stood upon was now prime real estate. The mosque remained, but what had appeared so sublime to me as a child now looked squalid. The dome was a shrunken mound. I had expected to find a grand building. This was a ramshackle affair of brick and concrete. We couldn't find our names on its walls.

Earlier in the day, Murad had invited me for a meal of authentic beef biryani. I demurred; I had been a vegetarian for most of my life. Now, sitting on plastic chairs under the shade of a tree in the deserted courtyard of the mosque where we first celebrated Diwali, refreshing my memory of those days when he taught me to pray and took me to his house, he advanced a theory. I was mutinying, he said, against my 'secular' upbringing with my belated obeyance of Hindu dietary laws. I wanted to reply, in a spirit of mischief, that I'd gladly eat beef if he would eat pork. But he was the wrong audience for such a joke. So I told him the truth. My time at the madrassa, though fleeting, had become a formative experience for me. I had over the years been to more mosques—Badshahi in Lahore, Al Aqsa in Jerusalem, Umayyad in Damascus, the Tatar mosque in Minsk—than Hindu temples, and I never felt like a stranger in any of them. I felt strengthened now by my perforated memory of this place.

Beyond the compound of the mosque, the city proliferated; the rebars and heavy construction machines for as far as the eye could see were evidence of Hyderabad's new wealth and importance. On the horizon, buildings were draped in sheets of white scaffolding. A huge billboard next to them displayed a poster of

Narendra Modi. The sound of the traffic grew louder as the nearby construction work stopped. The smell of burned diesel wafted in the breeze. We heard snatches of conversation. Then the small rusty gate opened and boys in neat white kurta-pyjamas and prayer caps with gold embroidery acknowledged our presence with a nod and walked into the mosque. That's when Murad said: 'I seriously thought about becoming a terrorist.' He could have, he said. The old city swarmed with agents fishing for recruits. And there were times when he wanted to join them.

More than his own torture, he said, it was the torment of others that made him restless. He could not for some reason expunge from his mind the face of a little girl in the documentary about Gujarat who reminded him of his own sister. He could not make sense of the lack of remorse among Gujarati Hindus. He felt deceived. 'I never thought I could, but I really hated all Hindus. I wanted to kill them all. I had no emotions left inside me.' But memories intruded. What I let myself forget in London, he, who grew up without being befriended by another Hindu, held on to in Hyderabad. 'I remembered that your father sent you to this school to study with us.' There must be other Hindus who are like me, he thought to himself. '*Aap ki yaad ne mujhe rok diya,*' he said. 'It is the memory of you that stopped me.'

I did not have a response.

We had met as unformed children, strangers to prejudice, open to difference. Now we were men with asymmetrical dispositions.

Having entered and retreated from his world as if it were an adventure, I thought he had come all these years later to ask for help. This is what he had come to tell me. India had irreparably smashed his innocent faith in it. It had violated his elemental humanity. He had somehow pulled himself from the depths of despair. But he was done with India: he was not of it, and it was not his. He was leaving with the hope that he would never have to return.

The sun had almost disappeared when the muezzin's melancholy call to prayer suffused the air. Murad pulled up his jeans and folded his shirt sleeves and washed his hands and feet and went inside. I sat outside in the chair. It was dark when we walked to the car. The billboard displaying Modi's poster was now lit up brightly with floodlights. The caption in bold lettering next to his smiling face said: 'Good days are about to come.'

PART ONE

ANTECEDENTS

1

EROSION

India is Indira, Indira is India.
Dev Kant Barooah

'Save your penis.' That was the cry heard across northern India during the darkest months of dictatorial rule that engulfed the world's most populous democracy between 1975 and 1977. The man who suppressed a country as diverse as India, dislodged entire communities, and condemned millions of men to surgical mutilations was then just twenty-eight years old. Measured purely by his excesses, Sanjay Gandhi was in many respects India's Ceausescu. Emotionally bruised, intellectually arid, a failure at everything he attempted in a family that typified success, Sanjay effectively took over the Indian government for two years as his criminally indulgent mother suspended the Constitution, declared a state of internal emergency, terminated civil liberties, censored the press, banished her political opponents to prison, and presided over the protracted detrition of the Republic founded by her own father.

When Jawaharlal Nehru, India's first Prime Minister, died on 27 May 1964, the ground shifted beneath Delhi. Buildings swayed. An earthquake was registered on the seismograph.[1] Yet

25

where blood had always attended the end of great epochs, there was sorrow but no savagery in sight. The tranquil transition that ensued in Delhi, occurring against the backdrop of almost universal anxiety about India's fate, was perhaps the truest measure of Nehru's achievement.

Within two hours of Nehru's death, Gulzarilal Nanda was sworn in as his interim successor. And possibly for the first time in living memory, the Indian who wielded the greatest clout was not a priest or a sage or a prince or a soldier, but a lower-caste Tamil politician called K. Kamaraj Nadar. Leaders with large constituencies and lofty lineages lined up for his attention and favour. The source of Kamaraj's king-making authority was his job. He was the president of the Congress Party. And he who controlled Congress controlled India.

Originating in 1885 as a forum for the airing of native political aspirations in British India, Congress metamorphosed, under Mahatma Gandhi's supervision, into the engine of India's agitation for independence from British rule. Claiming to speak for all of India, it spread its presence to the remotest regions of the subcontinent: by the 1930s, Congress was the only organisation that could match the British administration's reach. A decade later, when the British transferred power to the natives and left, it was the largest political machine in Asia. As its leaders entered their inheritance—the elaborate apparatus of governance constructed over two centuries of Indo-British collaboration—Congress established itself as the paramount power in India, its unrivalled organisational capability burnished by its undisputed claim to be the party that led India to freedom. Mahatma Gandhi, repelled by the authoritarian temptations supplied by the exalted position it occupied in the Indian imagination, called for Congress's immediate disbandment after Independence. He was ignored.

After Gandhi's exit, untrammelled authority was Nehru's for the taking. But Nehru had long displayed a profound awareness of power's potential to deform idealists. In 1937, a year after he was elected president of Congress for a second time, a Calcutta magazine carried a widely-circulated article urging Indians to be wary of Nehru. 'Men like Jawaharlal,' it warned, 'are unsafe in democracy.' Nehru, the piece cautioned, 'calls himself a democrat and a socialist, and no doubt he does so in all earnestness, but every psychologist knows that the mind is ultimately a slave to the heart and logic can always be made to fit in with the desires and irrepressible urges of a person. A little twist and Jawaharlal might turn a dictator sweeping aside the paraphernalia of a slow-moving democracy.' The author of this remarkable essay, published under a pseudonym, was none other than Nehru himself.[2]

As India's first Prime Minister, Nehru saw himself as a preceptor and strove to become a model of democratic leadership in a post-colonial landscape yielding rapidly to dictatorships. He dutifully attended parliament, conferred with the cabinet as first among equals, and deferred unfailingly to the judiciary. On the day of Nehru's demise, Congress under Kamaraj conducted itself with a maturity that cloaked the extreme youth of the Republic it governed: it was not yet twenty.

In less than two weeks of his death, a full-time successor to Nehru was installed in office. Lal Bahadur Shastri, an experienced member of the cabinet, was not an instantly arresting figure. When Zulfi Bhutto, Pakistan's ambitious foreign minister, flew to Delhi as Islamabad's representative at Nehru's funeral, so unimpressed was he by Shastri that he returned home and pressed his boss, Field Marshal Ayub Khan, for mischief in Kashmir. Nehru had come so thoroughly to define India to outsiders that without him, Zulfi felt, India was ready for conquest.[3]

Incidents along the border quickly escalated. A few months later, Shastri flew to Karachi for an informal meeting with Ayub. As difficult discussions ranged, the mighty dictator, dressed in evening suit, considered his democratic counterpart—sandal-strapped, dhoti-clad, diminutive, frail, vegetarian—and concluded that Shastri was a weakling incapable of putting up a fight.[4] It was a big mistake. When Pakistani troops stormed Kashmir in 1965, Shastri went for the jugular. He ordered the Indian Army to seize Lahore, capital of Pakistan's most important province. Ayub, crippled by the absence of reliable intelligence in a dictatorial dispensation devoid of honest deliberation, was staggered.[5]

Shastri was aggrieved for other reasons. The characterisation of the war in the foreign press as a clash between Muslims, apparently represented by Pakistan, and 'Hindu' India appalled him. He regarded such a depiction as a denial of Indian secularism, which, along with democracy, socialism, and non-alignment in foreign affairs, constituted the essence of Congress's—and, therefore, the country's—ideological self-conception. Mobilising Indians in the name of religion, when memories of India's dismemberment to accommodate the demands of Muslim nationalism were still tender, would probably have been easier and politically more rewarding. But Shastri, like Nehru before him, believed in and subordinated himself to the higher ideals of the Republic. Addressing a large public meeting in Delhi, he emphatically affirmed India's ecumenical character, reminding everyone that the ongoing conflagration between India and Pakistan was an international, not an interreligious, matter. 'This is the difference between India and Pakistan,' Shastri told the crowd, name-checking luminaries of the Republic's numerous religious communities who were in attendance: 'Whereas Pakistan proclaims herself to be an Islamic State and uses religion as a political factor, we Indians have the freedom to follow whatever religion we may choose … So far as politics is concerned, each of us is as much an Indian as the other.'[6]

Pakistan eventually sued for peace. Bhutto, not for the last time in his baleful career, detected the hidden hand of Jews behind the outcome.[7] For India, which under Nehru had failed to thwart a Chinese invasion, the war with Pakistan afforded an opportunity for redemption and self-renewal. As Ayub landed in Uzbekistan to parley with Shastri under Soviet auspices for the return of precious Pakistani territory seized by India, the world's largest democracy demonstrated, to itself more than to the world, that its institutions—Congress, parliament, cabinet, military—and ideals could do more than merely survive epochal change of guard at home. They could withstand and prevail against foreign belligerence. After magnanimously relinquishing control of Pakistani lands, Shastri—an abler and more decisive administrator than Nehru—died unexpectedly. Ayub had come to venerate the Indian premier's integrity and despise his own foreign minister. Remorseful, he offered himself as a pallbearer.

This moment of poignant vindication for India, containing within it the seed of reconciliation in South Asia, was tragically fleeting. A battle for succession began in Delhi before the plane carrying Shastri's body took off from Tashkent. Kamaraj, overlooking a host of more qualified candidates, decided to back Indira Gandhi, Nehru's daughter and a junior minister in Shastri's cabinet. The methuselahs in Congress went along in the belief that she could easily be manipulated: a 'dumb doll', they called her. It was one of history's costliest misjudgements.

A year after becoming Prime Minister, Indira had a revealing exchange with an American journalist. 'Do you think any of them,' she said, referring to her colleagues in Congress, 'could hold this thing together?' By 'this thing', did the Prime Minister mean the Congress Party, inquired the interviewer. 'I mean India,' she replied.[8] In her haughty self-regard and easy contempt for others, Indira was typically Nehruvian. For the duration of her reign, Indian citizens became a shackled audience to a squalid family drama, impuissant lab rats immolated to validate the vanities of what had once been a wandering clan of gifted Kashmiri Brahmins.

Before they became Indian nationalists, the Nehrus were perfect specimens of prosperous anglophile natives in British

India. Governesses imported from England tended to the children in Anand Bhavan—*house of happiness*—the palatial Nehru residence in Allahabad. Motilal, the Nehru paterfamilias, had his suits tailored in London. His heir, Jawaharlal Nehru, was educated at Harrow and Cambridge, and called to the Bar in London. On the subject of marriage, however, Motilal proved to be obstinately orthodox in outlook: his son would have to endure an arranged match. Kamala Kaul, the bride selected for Jawaharlal, was exquisitely beautiful but possessed none of the refinement prized by her in-laws. It was a disastrous union. Immersed in nationalist politics, Jawaharlal cruelly neglected her. His sisters mercilessly mocked her. Indira, the only child Kamala bore, grew up bitterly resenting her father's family.

Once the Nehrus, magnetised by the saintly spell of Mahatma Gandhi, started renouncing their material comforts for the country's sake, Anand Bhavan, ceasing to be a private residence, morphed into an informal headquarters of the Congress Party. Kamala, lonely in the crowded palace, found comfort in the companionship of a young freedom fighter called Feroze Gandhi. Their closeness sparked rumours of an affair. Nehru felt injured, but was scarcely in a position to demand fidelity from his wife. Kamala, in any case, soon died of tuberculosis and Feroze transferred his affections to Indira. Repressing his own personal feelings and disregarding the vitriol of Hindu puritanists who pressed him to reject Feroze because of his Parsi faith, Nehru blessed their marriage. Feroze's family name, suggesting a link to Mahatma Gandhi that did not exist, certainly did not injure his prospects.

Celebrities in the freedom movement, the Nehrus came increasingly to regard themselves as a native nobility. 'The Nehrus had become so much a part of our national history,' Indira's aunt, Krishna, wrote in her memoir, 'that the Indian people seemed to feel that we belonged to them, which in a sense we did.'[9] Indira's father, for all his obvious detachments, was not immune to this peculiar family conceit. For much of his life, Nehru believed that he was fated to lead India to its destiny. His own ascendancy in Congress was studiously choreographed by his wealthy father, with a helping hand eagerly extended by Mahatma Gandhi who, exuding a fatherly affection for the young socialist, deployed his moral authority to decapitate Nehru's more accomplished rivals. Trailed by a phalanx of liveried workers, Nehru rode a white horse to the Congress Party's 1929 convention in Lahore, where his elderly father, incumbent president of the organisation, stepped down and placed his son on the throne. 'Long live Jawaharlal Nehru, the uncrowned king of India,' screamed the crowds.[10]

The Nehrus injected dynasticism into the Congress Party's genetic makeup decades before the advent of the Indian Republic. And Jawaharlal Nehru—the original beneficiary of the custom of hereditary succession in colonial India's pre-eminent democratic movement—can hardly be absolved of the charge of instituting dynasticism in democratic India's ruling party. Nehru's closest colleagues in Congress, from Kamaraj to Shastri, openly acknowledged that he was grooming Indira to be his successor.[11] Yet Nehru, posthumously divinised by establishment intellectuals, received no reproval on this subject from his contemporaries. When the prominent editor Frank Moraes asserted in 1960 that 'there is no question of Nehru's attempting to create a dynasty of his own,'[12] Indira had already spent a year as president of the Congress Party. What exactly qualified her for the job once held by Mahatma Gandhi, Abdul Kalam Azad, Sarojini Naidu, and Dadabhai Naoroji? Nobody asked. But if Nehru, in deference to whom more competent candidates refrained from challenging his daughter, believed that it was anything other than her connection to him, he was in the grip of a delusion.

The man who in the colonial period had observed that 'logic can always be made to fit in with the desires and irrepressible urges of a person' was, in the republican era, capable of rationalising frequent departures from his avowed beliefs. The principled anti-imperialist and acolyte of Mahatma Gandhi who never tired of dispensing prelections about peace to foreign leaders had few misgivings about utilising disproportionate force against people he claimed as his own. In Kerala in the south, he engineered the overthrow of a democratically elected Communist government. In Kashmir in the north, he presided over an anti-democratic farce. In Nagaland to the east, he authorised the bombing of Christians who had had the temerity to demand from India what India had sought from the British. The Armed Forces (Special Powers) Act, an extraordinarily repressive piece of legislation enacted by parliament in 1958 to grant impunity to agents of the state dispatched to stamp out insurgencies in India's peripheries, embodied Nehru's ruthless resolve to preserve the Indian union at any expense.

The authoritarianism in Nehru existed alongside and was tempered by a genuine aversion to dictatorship and rigid adherence to democratic procedure: he did not always get his way, and he accepted the outcome when he did not.

Nehru encouraged Indira to move into his official residence once her marriage began to fall apart. Her two sons, Rajiv and Sanjay, were torn from their father. Sanjay, who was closer to Feroze, was deeply damaged by the separation. And when Feroze died, just before Sanjay's fourteenth birthday, Indira and Nehru compensated for his loss by coddling him.[13] Sanjay never did finish school. All he talked about was cars. So he was sent away in 1964 to England to apprentice at the Rolls-Royce factory in Crewe. It was a three-year programme. Sanjay dropped out in the second year. When he returned to India, in 1966, Nehru and Shastri were gone, and his mother was India's Prime Minister.

Sanjay's rise in the Congress Party replicated Indira's own trajectory under her father's reign. But the self-moderating complexities present in Nehru seemed to attenuate with each generation in his bloodline. Indira was animated most of all by despotic impulses; in Sanjay, there wasn't even a residue of democratic inclination. Congress was the laboratory in which

Indira tested the limits of her power. If she could make Congress bend to her will, she could subjugate India.

And so when it came time to elect a new president of India, in 1969, she prompted her party's elected lawmakers—who made up the bulk of the electoral college—to vote against Congress's official candidate because he was not *her* choice. Having lost the democratic vote within the party, she called for 'conscience voting' to tame those who defied her.[14] Wizened leaders attempted futilely to explain to Indira that her father, twice defeated in the party on the question of the presidency, had acquiesced on both occasions.

Indira was not her father, as she was fond of reminding everybody. She refused to relent and proceeded to discredit colleagues who canvassed the opposition—which included Hindu nationalists—as agents of 'communal and Rightist forces' in the country.[15] The president of the Congress Party recorded mournfully in his diary that, having been 'brought up by a father who was always grooming her for the prime ministership', Indira was incapable of tolerating dissent.[16] Indira's man ultimately prevailed in the presidential election; the candidate nominated by her own party lost by a narrow margin.

If Congress was to survive as a democratic entity, Indira would have to be sacked. By the time the old men arrayed against her contrived to act, however, Indira had consolidated her position. When handed a notice of expulsion from Congress, she engineered a split in the party and expelled the so-called 'old guard' represented by a chastened Kamaraj and his cronies.

There was now no countervailing force left in the party. Congress—which had survived the rivalries between Nehru and Sardar Patel, and between Nehru and Bose; contained within it, and reflected proudly, the ideological, linguistic, cultural and religious variety of India; and was viewed as a model by aspiring democrats everywhere in the decolonising world—now belonged to Indira. And since the country belonged, as it were, to Congress, it belonged also, by extension, to the Nehrus.

They did not betray a hint of remorse as they eviscerated it.

For years, India had been considering plans to build an affordable indigenous car. It would be a gigantic undertaking, requiring real expertise and hundreds of millions of dollars. But where previous proposals had stalled after passing through layers of scrutiny, Sanjay's application to open a car factory, buttressed by a grotesque 'prototype' rigged up in a backyard garage, was expedited by his mother's cabinet with astonishing celerity in a command economy where private enterprises with substantial records were made to sweat for years for a licence to trade. Four hundred and fifty acres of fertile land were secured for Sanjay's car-manufacturing plant in 1970. Families scratching a living from them were displaced. Sanjay promised to produce 50,000 small cars within a year. Five years later, he hadn't delivered even one. Instead, once the private capital raised by his family network was exhausted, the banks nationalised by his mother were raided for unsecured loans. India's credit policy was being undermined. But bank bosses who protested were swiftly supplanted with yes-men.[17]

Indira then got to work on the judiciary. The last remnant of autonomy in the government, the Supreme Court had repeatedly hindered her efforts to disfigure the Constitution. In 1973, shredding convention, she appointed a junior (and pliant) judge as the chief justice of India. The gravest attack to date on the independence of the highest court in the country, the decision provoked protests in every major city. India's maiden solicitor general emerged from retirement to decry the 'blackest day in the history of democracy'.[18] But the Prime Minister could survive the backlash: she had come to be revered, since defeating Pakistan in 1971, as a semi-divine figure.

The war itself had been swift. That year, the Pakistani state, invented explicitly to safeguard Muslims, staged the worst atrocities ever committed against a predominantly Muslim population. Three million people in East Pakistan were butchered, ten million displaced, and more than 400,000 women coerced into sexual servitude.[19] It was a holocaust precipitated by West Pakistan's unwillingness to honour the results of the first free election, swept by East Pakistan, in the Islamic Republic's history. Zulfi Bhutto, the loser in the vote, refused to accept the outcome—and the army, egged on by the feudal megalomaniac, went on a murderous splurge. America, dependent on Pakistan to make inroads into Mao's China, ignored the piling dead bodies and warned India to keep out. Indira, to her credit, spat at Nixon and Kissinger, and aided the Bengali rebels. In December, the Pakistani air force inexplicably offered India a casus belli by launching a series of pre-emptive strikes on Indian targets. Indira ordered her generals to punch into Pakistan. Within two weeks, Pakistan was vanquished and Bangladesh born.

'War is not a game woman can play,' Radio Pakistan had blared in the run-up to hostilities.[20] Now Bhutto, who took over the western rump that continued absurdly to call itself Pakistan even after a majority of its citizens had subtracted themselves from it, abjectly begged Indira for an audience. Portraits of her went up in the homes of Indians of every faith. The painter M.F. Husain rendered her as the deity Durga riding a tiger. Even Hindu nationalists conceded that Indira was the ruler of *India*, not just of Congress. Pakistani generals blamed an 'Indo-Zionist' plot for their defeat. Newspapers in the Islamic state, echoing Bhutto's characteristically self-pitying lamentations, bemoaned that this was the first time in a thousand years that Hindus had won against Muslims.[21] This summation would have struck the officers whom Indira sent into battle as odd—because none of them was a Hindu. The head of India's Air Force in the northern sector, Idris Latif, was a Hyderabadi Muslim; the commander of its ground forces in East Pakistan, J.S. Aurora, was a Sikh; the chief of the Indian armed forces, Sam Maneckshaw, was a Parsi; and J.F.R. Jacob, the brilliant strategist who captured Dhaka and forced Pakistan to surrender, was Jewish. As democracy shrank, the war of 1971 put on shimmering display that other sacred conviction of Congress: secularism. And Indira's commitment to it could not be faulted.

The Prime Minister, having received a renewed mandate in 1971 on the slogan 'abolish poverty', made no use of her political capital after the war to improve life for the poor. Rather than bleach Congress of the corrosive influence of the country's tiny elite—industrialists in the cities, landowners in the countryside—she increased its dependency on them. By the mid 1970s, the party's finances came almost entirely from 'rich industrialists, the rich traders and … the richest smugglers'.[22] At the same time rural India, replete with stupefied skeletal figures surviving on watery gruel, devolved into a theatre of inexpressible wretchedness. Urban India sought comfort in atavistic fantasies. Travelling in Delhi, Ved Mehta was met with 'constant talk about the glories of ancient India—about how the Hindus in Vedic times travelled around in "flying machines", talked to each other on "skyphones", and constructed "bridges of stones" spanning oceans'.[23]

Indira's re-election was by no means a foregone conclusion.

Just as her term in office was nearing its end, a lower court, in Allahabad, announced that it was going to pronounce its decision on an election petition involving the Prime Minister that had been dragging on for years. Its gravamen was that Indira Gandhi had violated election codes in her own constituency during the general elections. The court agreed with the plaintiff, effectively annulling Indira's election to parliament and imperilling her job as Prime Minister. Before the decision was read out, the presiding judge was offered half a million rupees and promised a seat on the Supreme Court. Officers from the Intelligence Bureau harassed him and his staff. Astonishingly, no inducement or threat worked.[24] The violations were trivial and the judgement, a flickering asseveration of the rule of law, would in all likelihood have been reversed on appeal. For now, however, Indira would have to step down.

Sanjay intervened.

Mother and son shared the experience of traumatic upbringings. Now they sought strength and reinforcement in their mutual grievances. In the court's decision, and in the extraordinary public outcry directed at their collective abuse of power, they espied a combination of foreign plotting and personal hatred for their family. The Supreme Court stayed the lower court's decision, but Sanjay was by now worn out by the pretence of respect for legal restraints on power. State transport vehicles were requisitioned illegally to bus in tens of thousands of people from neighbouring states to put on a pro-Indira spectacle in Delhi.[25] The judge in Allahabad was ritually denounced as a clandestine Hindu nationalist.[26] A resolution exalting Indira as 'indispensable for the nation' was placed before the Congress Party. And Sanjay began mastering a manual on press censorship procured from the Philippines.[27] Rumour went out in Delhi that the Prime Minister was readying to jettison the Constitution, but the opposition, submerged in slowly simmering waters, refused to believe the boiling point had been reached.[28]

On 25 June 1975, Indira's advisers, having hastily pored over a copy of the Constitution borrowed that morning from the library in Parliament House, drafted an ordinance declaring a state of internal emergency to maintain the 'security of India', which they said was 'threatened by internal disturbances'. The president of India, Fakhruddin Ali Ahmed, signed the document without hesitation. Electricity supply to newspapers was cut off that night and the police were ordered to sweep up Indira's critics.

Indians woke up the next morning in a dictatorship.

For the next nineteen months, Sanjay terrorised the country. His thinking was always plain. He wanted to construct casinos in the Himalayas. He wanted to 'beautify' Delhi. He wanted to curb population growth. He did not like the sight of slums, so he yelled orders to have them pulled down. Where would the people go? He did not care to know. When an activist complained about the demolition of stalls outside Delhi's grand mosque—its imam had urged congregants to resist Indira—police carried him away in the dead of night, tortured him, then paraded him in chains in the old quarter of the capital.[29]

The bloodiest instance of slum-clearance occurred in Turkman Gate, a mostly Muslim slum. When bulldozers began gathering outside the shanties in the summer of 1976, the residents, anticipating trouble, formed a small committee and drafted appeals to everybody who mattered. One evening, they learnt that Sanjay and his friends were 'conferring' with two women in a nearby hotel. They forced their way into Sanjay's suite and implored him to call off the demolition. Sanjay remained silent. One of his goons barked: 'I give you exactly five seconds to get out of this room.'[30] A massacre unfurled the next day when police opened fire on peaceful protesters. Turkman Gate was razed. Families were packed into vans at gunpoint and disgorged beyond the Yamuna river, out of sight.

As urban India was subjected to Sanjay's prettification programmes, rural India was exposed to a more intimately degrading form of terror. Forced sterilisation was by far the deadliest exercise undertaken by the government during the Emergency. The International Monetary Fund and the World Bank had periodically shared with Delhi their fears about an uncontrolled rise in India's population levels. Democracy, however, was a hurdle: no government could conceivably enact laws limiting the number of children a couple could have without incurring punishment at the ballot box. But with dictatorship in place, they fell behind forced vasectomies. Visiting India in 1976, Robert McNamara, the president of the World Bank, was full of praise for Indira. 'For the first time, I sensed in India,' he said, 'a disciplined, realistic approach to development programmes; and a willingness to find practical solutions to economic problems rather than an attitude of falling back on "socialist ideologies" and didactic debate.' He left India 'feeling that a growth rate of 3 per cent per capita per annum is possible in the next ten years' if India continued down the path inaugurated by the Prime Minister's suspension of the Constitution.[31] Sanjay and Indira, habituated to whisking up noxious xenophobia among Indians by enumerating the West's crimes and plots against India, now basked in the vindication supplied by Western loan sharks.

Sanjay personally oversaw the sterilisation programme. Incentives—radio sets, cash, food—were at first offered to men who volunteered to put themselves under the knife. When bribes failed to draw numbers, Sanjay handed down targets to government officials. The 'find and operate' missions that followed were directed at the most vulnerable and defenceless men in the country. One state reported 600,000 operations in two weeks.[32] In another state, a widower picked up from a bus and forcibly sterilised died of an infection. Officers on sterilisation assignments ransacked whole villages in their search for men. Hordes of policemen descended on crowds at railway stations and bus stops and dragged away adult men to operation tents. Teenagers, middle-aged men, the elderly: anyone with procreative equipment would do.[33] In villages, men abandoned their houses and lived in the fields to evade capture by roving sterilisation squads. The terror was banalised into bureaucratic routine. Teachers at state schools, mandated to offer up men for sterilisation in order to be paid their salaries, produced beggars they found on the street.[34] Headmasters were given authority to detain students until their parents volunteered for sterilisation. Pay, promotions, and bonuses in government departments became contingent on offering oneself up for sterilisation. Soon enough, obtaining even the most rudimentary government services required people to show documents attesting to their sterilised status, giving rise to an enormous demand for fake certificates.

India, forged in the dialectic of Gandhism, now had a homespun version of Kimilsungism. Buses and billboards were plastered with 'stray thoughts of the prime minister' exhorting Indians to work hard and slogans extolling the Great Leader

('Courage and Clarity of Vision, Thy Name Is Indira Gandhi'). Sanjay was breathlessly glorified by India's once-free press, which, adorned with the censor's fetters, functioned as an implement of agitprop. Foreign journalists were expelled. 'In ten years of covering the world from Franco's Spain to Mao's China,' *Newsweek*'s India correspondent wrote, 'I have never encountered such stringent and all-encompassing censorship'. 'In my four years in Moscow,' the *New York Times*'s correspondent added, 'I was never pulled out of an interview by the police as I was here.'[35] Trailed by an entourage of reporters and cameramen, Sanjay, like his Korean compeer Kim Jong-Il, materialised everywhere and dispensed curt instructions to engineers, doctors, bureaucrats, and other professionals on how to do their jobs. 'Impatient' and 'visionary' were among the less orotund adjectives summoned to garland the dropout.

Elderly elected officials who had toiled in the freedom movement abased themselves to tickle Sanjay's ego. The sexagenarian chief minister of Maharashtra, India's most commercially vibrant state, eulogised Sanjay as 'a new star rising in the political firmament of India' whose accomplishments were apparently 'written in letters of gold'.[36]

Opposition figures who had miraculously been spared incarceration had to face the taxman, reinvented by the new regime as an instrument of intimidation. Even Research and Analysis Wing, India's foreign intelligence agency, was co-opted by Congress to dig up dirt on people perceived to be Indira's opponents. Habeas corpus suspended, India's prisons became congested with activists whose families, in many cases, had no clue where they were. 'The Indian citizen,' Indira's solicitor general declared in earnest, 'has absolutely no right to his liberty, even if he is totally innocent.'[37] A great many Indians refused to surrender. One man immolated his body in a Gandhian act of protest.

But a substantial segment of what passed for the nation's intellectual gentry either caved before or collaborated with Sanjay.

Distinguished pundits who should have been the defenders of democracy tripped over themselves to cheer on its chief cremator. Ayub Syed: 'He has electrified the nation with his fearless call for breaking fresh ground.'[38] Russi Karanjia: 'In contrast with the Niagara of nonsense that falls from the lips of our politicians, Sanjay Gandhi is a young man of few, very few words. To him words spell works, action, performance.'[39] Khushwant Singh: 'Despite his receding hairline he is an incredibly handsome young man.' If the religious pluralism of this pro-Sanjay triune—a Muslim, a Parsi, a Sikh—was a testament to the health of Indian secularism, the doggerel flowing from its pens was sufficiently obsequious to make even Corneliu Vadim Tudor, balladeer in Ceausescu's court, blush with embarrassment.

Indira's rule is periodised today as the summit of Indian 'socialism'. This is bizarre. There was no redistribution of wealth during the Emergency—only the usurpation of power. True, the Prime Minister and her son pronounced themselves tribunes of the poor. But the faction that most sedulously supported the tyranny of the pair—and was most lavishly recompensed for its support—was composed almost entirely of India's gilded elite. Big business energetically backed the Gandhis. Naval Tata, India's most eminent industrialist, queued up with his wife to 'pay our respects' to Sanjay when the princeling held court in Bombay.[40] When a travelling American journalist asked a member of the Oberoi family, India's top hoteliers, for her opinion of the Emergency rule, she replied: 'Oh, it's wonderful. We used to have terrible problems with the unions. Now when they give us any troubles, the government just puts them in jail.'[41] The Emergency budget was the most pro-business to date. And it wasn't by accident that, while the government deactivated the articles of the Constitution concerning free expression and liberty, it preserved the provisions protecting property rights. In one of the most unexpectedly courageous speeches in parliament—which functioned as a rubber-stamp—Krishan Kant, a Congress backbencher, dismantled the myth of 'socialist' Indira: 'No privileges of the privileged classes are being touched,' he said on the floor of the house. 'They have been reassured. There is going to be no nationalisation of textile and sugar industries ... On the other hand, the emergency will come down on the workers, on students, the intelligentsia, and the fixed-income groups. I would like to ask my friends if this is really a swing to the left or whether it is not in fact a swing to the right?'[42]

Indians who happened to be socialists were branded enemies of the state and dispatched post-haste to the torture chamber. When the trade unionist George Fernandes—who decades later retired as India's defence minister—made a patriotic 'appeal' from hiding 'to the people in the north to get rid of this dictatorship if they want to preserve the unity of this country, because a situation is bound to arise where people from the south are going to say that we are part of a democratic India, we are not a part of an India that is ruled by a dictator from Kashmir', his brother, Lawrence, was picked up by the police and brutally tortured for weeks.

Socialism, like much else, was a meaningless catchword camouflaging the gangsterisation of Indian politics, initiated by Sanjay, at the very highest levels. Until his takeover, the Prime Minister's closest advisers were led by a cast of generally scrupulous Kashmiris. With Sanjay in command, the upper and middle ranks of Congress became saturated with racketeers and ruffians, mostly from Punjab, with a chilling penchant for 'getting things done'. 'They are the kind of people,' an Indian insider told the journalist J. Anthony Lukas in 1976, 'you always find near the top of an authoritarian regime: cool, pragmatic men uninhibited by many scruples.'[43] One of these henchmen was inducted into the cabinet as defence minister. Others continued to thrive in Indian politics long after their benefactor had left the scene. Zail Singh, a Punjabi politician who distinguished himself by once sprinting to pick up Sanjay's sandals when they slipped from the crown prince's feet, went on to serve as India's president.[44] Kamal Nath, one of Sanjay's conscripts, was in 2018 inaugurated as chief minister of Madhya Pradesh. The late Pranab Mukherjee, brought in from Bengal to the chancellery by Sanjay, retired as president of India in 2017.

The Congress leadership, consumed with the solitary obsession of self-perpetuation, extended Indira's term in office and began seriously toying with the idea of discarding parliamentary democracy and adopting a presidential form of government. Potentially combustible exigencies that could sunder the union in the long run were given only passing attention. In Punjab, Sanjay and Indira patronised an illiterate Sikh preacher called Jarnail Singh Bhindranwale, whose extremism, they believed, would neuter the Akali Dal, an ethno-religious party. Instead, their sponsorship of the obscurantist sant, generating a climate ripe for radicalism, spawned a crisis that destroyed Punjab and devoured India. But concerned above all with keeping power, the pair was incapable of turning down a fix that was quick. Divide and rule, the doctrine imputed to the British by Indian nationalists, was now the animating philosophy of the party that succeeded them.

Sanjay, appointed leader of the youth wing of Congress, was on the threshold of taking over the party—one of the largest political machines in the world—when Indira abruptly revoked the Emergency and announced fresh elections. Her decision to call the vote has posthumously been ascribed to some vestigial commitment to democracy lurking in her Nehru blood. In reality, she was driven to it by the report of a Delhi think tank that assured her easy victory.[45] Re-election would instantly purge the taint of dictatorship attached to her name in the West. She would be celebrated as a democrat abroad and still be able to tyrannise Congress and India. Her intelligence officers endorsed the think tank's message. Sanjay was sceptical, but Indira was sold.[46]

The opposition—socialists, conservatives, capitalists, religious nationalists—scrambled to form a united front against

Congress. Even the most upbeat among them did not really believe that their unwieldy coalition stood a chance. But as Indians delivered their verdict at the ballot booth in 1977, thirty years of uninterrupted rule by the Congress Party came to a crashing end. Indira lost her own seat. Sanjay lost his deposit. Just as Pakistan's Ayub had been misled by his terrified minions into misreading India, so Indira was duped into misestimating the Indian electorate. She had expelled Krishan Kant from Congress for warning her in parliament that 'when you stifle the flow of information to the people in this country, you are blocking the channel of information to yourself'.

One of the blessings of learning history, historians tell us, is that it prevents us from likening every atrocity to the crimes of the Nazis. And yet the magazine *India Today*, surveying the wreckage of the Emergency, was far from being obtuse when it wrote that the torture that inmates endured in the Emergency months was 'of a kind that would make the Nazi interrogators lick their lips in approval'. The only distinction was that the horrors in India were perpetrated by a 'sovereign democratic government which had pledged itself to the dignity of the individual'.[47] Sanjay superintended the sterilisation of 6.2 million people—fifteen times the number of people sterilised by the Nazis.[48] Nor was the *New Yorker* exaggerating when it wrote that Indira was on the brink of 'ushering in an Indian version of Hitler's National Socialist regime, with private ownership of industry, farms, and service enterprises' before her defeat.[49]

It was India's forsaken multitudes—whose suitability for democracy was repeatedly questioned and whose disenfranchisement high-mindedly rationalised away by the country's post-colonial elite—who resuscitated the Republic. But Indira's dictatorship had by then ravaged the conventions by which politics was conducted in India. Self-restraint, constitutionalism, institutional autonomy, deliberative governance: everything that made Indian democracy more than an exercise in balloting was left severely bruised. One of the first major acts of the ideologically kaleidoscopic regime that replaced Indira was to pay the defenestrated Prime Minister the compliment of imitation by dismissing a series of Congress-ruled state governments by invoking emergency provisions in the Constitution. Nehru and Shastri had also used such powers, but reluctantly, acknowledging that they were carrying out a necessary evil. The necessity vanished under Indira.

'Fratricide,' Krishna Menon once wrote, 'is part of our national heritage.' The Indian state made citizens of a people who throughout history had brutalised their own with the same efficiency with which they served foreign rulers for centuries. The Constitution adopted by the Republic placed prohibitions on rulers and conferred privileges on peoples: guarantees of dignity, equality, protection from exploitation in the form of inviolable rights. By repurposing what began as a source of hope into an instrument of oppression, Indira and Sanjay shattered the republican dream and bequeathed a ruinous blueprint. In a plaintive letter to the Prime Minister before the elections, Jai Prakash Narayan, the Gandhian freedom fighter thrown in jail for leading protests against her, had pleaded with Indira:

> Please do not destroy the foundations that the fathers of the nation, including your noble father, had laid down. There is nothing but strife and suffering along the path that you have taken. You inherited a great tradition, noble values, and a working democracy. Do not leave behind a miserable wreck of all that. It would take a long time to put all that together again.[50]

The new government, a ramshackle affair beset by infighting from birth, collapsed long before it could find its feet. Internal democracy had vanished completely from the Congress Party, still one of the most vital institutions in India, when it was returned to office in 1980. You could go to the Kaaba and doubt the omnipotence of Allah, but you could not be a member of Congress and question the paramountcy of the Gandhis. When Sanjay, poised for a sinister comeback, died in a freak plane crash in 1980, Congress reflexively fielded Indira's elder son, Rajiv, as the party's candidate in his brother's seat. And in 1984, when Indira was assassinated by her Sikh bodyguards in retaliation for the military assault she had ordered on their religion's holiest shrine earlier in the year, the party turned spontaneously to Rajiv. The leadership of 750 million people was thrust, without discussion, into the hands of a forty-year-old career commercial airline pilot whose sole claim to the highest political office in the largest democracy in the world was his surname.

2

SURRENDER

Frankenstein stares us in the face ...
P.V. Narasimha Rao[1]

In liberal lore Rajiv Gandhi is the redeemer Prime Minister. He was handsome and young, forty when he took office. Touring Bengal when news of his mother's death reached him, he flew to Delhi and was Prime Minister by the evening. The established convention of appointing a caretaker was discarded without a murmur, let alone any discussion. Indira was gone, leaving India incorrigibly mired in the miasma of her legacy.

Dynastic succession is ordinarily pre-ambulated with effusive puffery designed to warm the subjects to the incoming monarch. Rajiv's public persona was constructed *after* his investiture. Congress's public-relations mavens publicised the new Prime Minister as 'Mr Clean'. His halo, powered by the family name, was cleansed of the family's excesses. His demeanour, they said, was pleasantly different from his brother's and mother's. He was said personally to walk guests to the door and address even his subordinates as 'sir'.[2] This exceedingly courteous personality was hard, for many in Congress, to reconcile with the Rajiv they knew. Who could forget his visit to Andhra Pradesh, in

1982, soon after being installed by his mother as the party's general secretary? The chief minister of the state, Tanguturi Anjaiah, a Dalit—a member of the formerly 'untouchable' community deemed so 'impure' by the scriptures that it is placed outside the hierarchical Hindu caste system—went to receive him at the airport. In this, he was following the custom instituted by Sanjay. But Rajiv, who considered himself 'modern', took great umbrage and exploded with invective. The chief minister had endured a lifetime of vicious abuse at the hands of upper-caste Hindus, many of whom still considered physical contact with him spiritually defiling. But being berated in late life by a man who looked half his age broke him. He began to shed tears. Rajiv called him a 'buffoon' and drove away.[3]

Rajiv was not motivated by any palpable prejudice. India's hatreds were dormant presences in the world in which he grew up. The sophistication of the students at the elite boarding school he attended as a child with Sanjay was measured by their distance from the India they were being trained to lead. After school, Rajiv was sent up to Cambridge, but returned home without a degree and took a job flying domestic routes on the national carrier. Politics was Sanjay's fixation. Draped in designer denims, Gucci shoes, and a Cartier wristwatch, Rajiv was mostly to be found at Delhi's chicest restaurants with his Italian wife, Sonia—a private man, decent and generous by all accounts, living a rich and fulfilling life away from the public eye. But secluded from Indians who were unlike them, and without the vocabulary to comprehend them, Rajiv and the school friends he surrounded himself with upon becoming Prime Minister struggled with India. They thought of themselves as enlightened democrats, but oligarchy was the condition of their supremacy.[4]

Only strongmen, the British had suggested, could bring order to India. Congress internalised that lesson. It functioned as the British did, with this difference: no British viceroy dressed down a native leader of Congress the way Rajiv denigrated the Dalit leader of his own party. Rajiv's behaviour, enraging the Telugu-speaking people of Andhra who felt collectively belittled, resulted in the formation of a powerful sub-national party that swept Congress out of power in the largest state in southern India. Northern India went up in sectarian smoke the day Rajiv was sworn into office as Hindus turned on Sikhs.

Perhaps the only redeeming quality in Indira's political career was her unwavering adherence to the most important component of Congress ideology: secularism. After Sanjay's demise, Indira fell into the habit of touring Hindu temples and consulting swamis. Yet she also personally ordered the reinstatement of a pair of Sikh officers relieved from her protection squad because their faith came to be seen as a disqualifying factor for proximity to the Prime Minister. 'Aren't we secular?', she asked the aides responsible for their transfer.[5] The two Sikhs, returned to their sensitive posting on the Prime Minister's personal instructions, riddled Indira with bullets on the morning of 31 October 1984. They were avenging, they said, her decision to send the army into the Golden Temple, Sikhism's most sacred site.

Jarnail Singh Bhindranwale, the preacher sponsored by Sanjay and Indira in the hope of undercutting the organised Sikh party in Punjab—the Akali Dal—had grown over the years into an untameably lethal beast. The strife in Punjab originated in the demand of the Akalis for a Sikh state within the Indian union. For Delhi to relent would have been to confer legitimacy on religious reconfiguration of territory consolidated under the banner of non-confessional nationalism. It would have reduced non-Sikhs within the Sikh state to second-tier citizens, instituted a religious hierarchy of citizenship within the union, threatened the rights of non-Hindus in other states, encouraged other ethno-religious communities to demand what the Sikhs got, and led ultimately to the Balkanisation of India. So Indira met the Akalis half-way. Using the accepted convention of reorganising India along linguistic lines, she carved out portions of Punjab to create the state of Haryana on the somewhat dubious grounds that most people in the new state were not speakers of Punjabi. Haryana's birth left a Sikh majority in Punjab, but with a substantial non-Sikh minority.[6]

This compromise, rather than pacify the Sikh ethnocrats, emboldened them to clamour openly for secession. Indira and Sanjay had hoped that Bhindranwale would eclipse the Akalis to the advantage of India. Instead, he rebelled against his masters and became a born-again evangelist for Khalistan, a puritanical Sikh state modelled on Pakistan. He incited violence by describing Sikhs in his sermons as an 'historically separate' nation toiling away as 'slaves' of Hindus in India.[7] As history, this was drivel. Sikhism was founded as an egalitarian brotherhood by a great Hindu reformer, its theology borrowed from Hinduism, and for centuries it was regarded, like Buddhism and Jainism, as a highly autonomous branch of Hinduism. But upon being enjoined to 'smash the heads' of Hindus, a community with which the Sikhs had *never* before been in conflict, Bhindranwale's acolytes—mostly unemployed young men—proceeded to gun down a busload of Hindus. Journalists covering the terror were slain, and Sikh officers in Punjab's police department were branded collaborators of the state and shot dead.[8]

The violence ceased to be viewed by Delhi as a simple police matter when support for Bhindranwale's terror in the form of weapons and training began pouring in from across the porous border.[9] Bhindranwale, anticipating a response from the government, moved into the Akal Takht, the seat of temporal authority in Sikhism, and began fortifying the complex. At the end of May 1984, Indira ordered in the military to extract him from the temple. Kuldeep Singh Brar, the officer leading the mission—codenamed 'Operation Blue Star'—was a Sikh who abhorred Bhindranwale for 'converting the House of God into a battlefield'.[10] Tanks rolled into the Golden Temple compound on 4 June. When the firing stopped, several days later, Bhindranwale was dead, as, by some estimates, were 5,000 civilians and 700 army personnel. The building's library, which housed the original scripts of the Sikh holy book, lay in ruins.

Blue Star was a disaster. Hasty in conception and reckless in execution, it canonised a psychopath as a martyr in the minds of once-vacillating Sikhs by the manner in which it dispatched him. Before the assault on the Golden Temple, the Khalistan project appeared destined to disintegrate because an overwhelming majority of Sikhs in Punjab rejected secession and favoured unity with India. At the summit of Bhindranwale's terror, Andrew Major, a scholar of Punjab, emphasised that 'genuine commitment to the creation of a separate Sikh state is still rare within the Punjabi Sikh community'.[11] Khalistan always was the obsession of 'overseas Sikhs', who, fattening themselves in the cosmopolitan havens of the West, financed violent sectarianism in the land they had left behind. It was in Canada that Air India Flight 182 was hijacked and blown up by Sikh terrorists, killing more than 300 passengers from nine countries. It was in Britain that the self-appointed president of the 'Republic of Khalistan', Jagjit Singh Chauhan, headquartered his operations for many years. He flew to Pakistan from London, issued his own currency, passports and stamps, and expressed the gentle hope on the BBC that Sikhs would someday 'behead' the Gandhi family.[12] Untiring advocates of 'multiculturalism' and minority rights in the foreign lands they had inveigled into letting them in, chauvinists such as Singh sought remorselessly to incinerate the historic pluralism of Punjab to engender yet another procrustean state consecrated to preserving the 'purity' of a 'people' defined exclusively by their ethnicity and religion.

Indira, like Benazir Bhutto, was devoured by the ogre she fostered. Unlike Benazir Bhutto, Indira was secular to the marrow. She married outside her faith and forced through an amendment to insert the word 'secular' into the Indian Constitution's preamble. It is possible that Indira might have deployed religion in the future if her hold on power appeared to be in peril (she had also smuggled 'socialist' into the Constitution, and she was self-servingly flexible about what that word implied). Yet her obstinate refusal to allow the men fated to become her killers from being discharged from their jobs because of their faith bespoke an undeniably valiant commitment to secularism. For a generation of Indians shaped by India's Partition in the name of religion, her resolute undoing in her final days of what she perceived to be discrimination on religious grounds raised her up in their hearts and minds when she was gone.*

The tragic irony was that Indira, reviled in life by Hindu supremacists as a villainess, was reduced in death to her religion and then claimed as the faith's bloodied mascot. As Rajiv drove to the presidential palace on the evening of his mother's death to take the oath of office, a vehicle burned every fifty yards on either side of the road. A few hours earlier, a mob had attacked the motorcade of the president of India, Zail Singh, a Sikh, as he rode to the hospital. The police did not intervene. By nightfall, Hindus were dragging Sikh men—easily identifiable by their beard and turban—from buses and trucks and pulling their beards and slapping them about. The government had a firm protocol for containing communal violence: to call in the army. Not only was this procedure not activated, but the police in Delhi also stopped recording or acting on complaints of harassment and threats brought to them by Sikhs. Instead, they went to Sikh-heavy neighbourhoods in the city and disarmed the *Sikhs*. No sooner did they leave than armed mobs of Hindus, led by the city's familiar Congress Party leaders, appeared on the scene and slaughtered Sikhs. Dozens of Sikh women were gang-raped by Hindu men.[13]

The mayhem was too meticulously choreographed to be called anarchy. Congress, whose moral authority after the

* My own father, among the thousands of activists imprisoned and tortured during her dictatorship, flew to Delhi upon hearing the news of her death on the radio and reverently touched her feet as she lay in state.

Emergency rested entirely on its claim to being the bulwark against 'communal forces' in the country, maintained a conspiratorial silence for three days as Delhi burned. It's as though the government and its security organs had granted a licence for a seventy-two-hour purge of civilians. Is it possible that ordinary Hindus harboured such a deep pool of hatred against a minuscule community—whose members accounted for 2 per cent of India's population but made up more than 10 per cent of its armed forces, were over-represented in the police, were the backbone of Indian agriculture, were seen historically by Muslim conquerors as defenders and protectors of Hindus—that they needed three days to drain it?

The defence of 'spontaneous eruption' of rage insults the intelligence of those to whom it is retailed. Violent mobs acquire a momentum of their own, but they do not form impromptu: they coalesce around some tangible idea. And when intent is established—killing a specific group of people, or pulling down a place of worship—the mob must be armed, directed to the target, and supervised. The disorder of a mob, the thing that makes a mob a mob, conceals a great deal of order in India: people who are part of it know the names, addresses, and families of one another. A genuine rabble can easily be dispersed with a minor show of force. In Delhi, the 'mobs' were assisted by the authorities.[14]

What happened in Delhi in the aftermath of Indira's assassination was a pogrom—an organised slaughter abetted by the state in which, by official estimates, 3,000 Sikhs were murdered—the first of its kind in the Republic's history.[15] And more than humans were killed in Delhi. Trust forged over decades between communities was dead too. Why didn't the government intervene? Were the killings, molestations, and plunder tolerated for cold reasons of the state: to telegraph to the Sikhs, as a community, the cost of rebellion against India and to disabuse them of any mistaken faith in the state's willingness to intervene on their behalf against the country's wounded majority? If this was the case, Indian secularism was a sham all along. Or was it something as chillingly banal as the desire on the part of Congress leaders to aggrandise Indira posthumously through violence? When Rajiv finally acknowledged, two weeks later, the blood spilled all around him, he used a clarifying metaphor: when a big tree falls, he said, the earth shakes a little. Reverse the figure of this callous speech, and you grasp the logic of the anti-Sikh rampage: if the earth did not shake, the tree risked being written off as puny.

Abroad, the killings of Sikhs barely registered beyond the Sikh diaspora. Instead of sustained scrutiny, the violence occasioned the dusting off of flyblown stock phrases—of ancient hatreds, of the propensity of Indians to lapse periodically into inexplicable savagery—which culminated invariably in reminders about the need for the civilising presence at the zenith of India of the selfless Gandhi clan. Six months after the worst sectarian bloodshed in decades, the late American journalist Mary McGrory gushed about Rajiv in the *Washington Post*. 'Watching him,' she wrote, 'you had to believe in genes.'[16]

Within India, too, memories became distorted with time. Confronted by the menace of Hindu nationalism, it was possible to imagine the past under Congress as more virtuous than it had actually been. In 2002, as Muslims were being butchered in Gujarat on Modi's watch, the *Indian Express* adduced Rajiv's handling of the anti-Sikh violence in 1984 as a model of accountability for the government of the day. 'Congressmen whose names surfaced or were even popularly mentioned in connection with the killings all paid the price', the *Express*'s then editor, Shekhar Gupta, asserted. 'Political careers of HKL Bhagat, Jagdish Tytler and Sajjan Kumar never recovered from the taint of 1984.' As a matter of fact, two of the three men whose careers Gupta said ended in ignominy were inducted into the government by Rajiv *after* the riots and served for years as ministers; one served as a Congress minister in 2004, twenty years after the anti-Sikh carnage of Delhi.[17] Asked in 2014 if he felt any sorrow for the death of Muslims in 2002, Modi replied: if 'someone else is driving a car and we're sitting behind, even then if a puppy comes under the wheel, will it be painful or not?'[18] The answer outraged liberal commentators in Delhi. Yet hardly anybody seemed to recall that Modi was only echoing the phrase used by Rajiv's government to explain the outbreak of violence against Sikhs: 'even when a baby or a cow is killed in an accident, the anguish of the mob is discernible.'[19]

1984 was the most violent year since Partition, and the eighties was *the* decade of gruesome communal rioting. And yet what happened in Delhi, the seat of the union government, was *sui generis*. Congress's claim to being the guardian of Indian secularism was in tatters. When elections were announced, the RSS, sworn foe of Indira, campaigned for her son, who refused to disavow its support.[20] Riding the wave of sympathy aroused by Indira's assassination, when Rajiv was returned in December 1984 to government with 415 out of 543 seats in parliament—the largest mandate recorded in the Republic's history—he radiated uncertainty rather than confidence. He had no convictions, and what passed for his political philosophy was a collage of banalities. He railed against corruption but became embroiled in a massive corruption scandal. He spoke of the importance of secularism yet crumbled before religious nationalists. Fixated on keeping power, he oscillated between capitulations to fundamentalist followers of Islam and militant votaries of Hindu nationalism.

The surrender began with Rajiv's response to the Supreme Court's decision in 1985 upholding the right of Shah Bano Begum, a Muslim divorcee, to a meagre maintenance from her ex-husband. India's Constitution, drafted in the aftermath of Partition, sought to reassure the Muslims who refused to go to Pakistan by preserving for them a separate civil code. Future generations were passed the task of bringing other religious communities under its purview when India's unity was consolidated. Four decades on, the Supreme Court quickened the secular aspiration of the Indian Constitution by voiding the mullahs' prerogative to determine the fate of Shah Bano by recognising her entitlements as a full citizen of the state. This was an exult-ant moment for all who believed in equality before the law. Rajiv, however, sank into despondency. Muslim 'leaders' were inundat-ing him with threats to pull their support from Congress if he did not intercede on behalf of the 'community'.

The monumentality of what had just occurred might have prompted another leader to test the strength of the panjan-drums who put themselves up as spokespersons of India's Muslims. Rajiv had a bigger parliamentary majority than any Prime Minister before him. But crippled by what one shrewd member of his cabinet called 'a peculiar sense of political inse-curity',[21] Rajiv refused to engage directly with ordinary Muslims and instead huddled with his political advisers to locate a pain-less way to placate the reactionaries who called themselves, with no evidence, the authentic representatives of Muslim citizens.

Congress's defeat in the state elections of Assam in eastern India that year deepened the anxieties of the Prime Minister and his coterie. Convinced that the result was the upshot of the crisis generated by the Shah Bano case, the government drafted and rushed through parliament the Muslim Women's bill, a craven piece of legislation which liberated Muslim husbands—who could take up to four wives and discard them on a whim by chanting 'talaq', or divorce, three times in accordance with the laws of Islam—from the obligations of maintenance post-talaq, and shifted the responsibility for the upkeep of penurious divorced Muslim women to their families and charities. A Muslim minister in Rajiv's government resigned in disgust at the Prime Minister's cowardice.

The only Indians who rejoiced were hidebound Muslim men and Hindu nationalists. Rajiv's prostration preserved the male privileges of the first and lent credence to the claim of the second that Congress secularism as enforced by the state, essen-tially a form of 'appeasement' of Muslims, was effectively anti-

Hindu. Hindu protests in the 1950s, when Congress was resolutely reforming the religion's orthodox traditions, had elicited only contempt from Nehru; Muslim protests in the 1980s, on the other hand, resulted in express legislative redressal of their grievances by Nehru's grandson. The demand for equal treatment of all Indians irrespective of their religion implicit in the Hindu-nationalist agitation against Rajiv's climbdown should have been treated with derision coming from ideologues whose ambition was to establish a nakedly majoritarian state in India.

But Rajiv was too compromised to laugh at them. Having disenfranchised Muslim women in order to propitiate Muslim men, he hastened to mollify aggrieved Hindu nationalists by allowing them to lay the foundations for a future temple inside the Babri mosque by ordering the gates of the building, sealed explicitly to forfend communal flare-ups, to be opened. The mosque became the symbol, in Hindu-nationalist propaganda, of India's millennium-long subjugation by Muslims. After extracting such a colossal concession from a nominally secular Prime Minister, Hindu nationalists, a negligible force in mainstream politics until then, claimed parity with Congress. Muslims, understandably, became livid. So Rajiv atoned at the next available opportunity—not by forcing Hindus out of the mosque but by imposing a pre-emptive roundabout ban on Salman Rushdie's *Satanic Verses* because it was deemed offensive by Muslim zealots even before it had been published. The world's largest democracy became the first country on earth to proscribe the novel.[22]

What remained of Rajiv's prestige was devoured by a major corruption scandal when credible allegations surfaced that he may have been aware of the massive kickbacks received by Indian officials on a defence contract placed by the government in 1986 with Bofors, the Swedish arms manufacturer. It was the first time that a Prime Minister had become personally implicated in a scam. And what made it all the more scandalous was that it involved the defence of the nation. The absence of internal democracy in Congress meant that Rajiv could not be removed. Instead of accountability from the Prime Minister, what India witnessed was the repeated shakeup of the cabinet; an open confrontation with the president, who threatened to dismiss Rajiv's government; and the demotion of Vishwanath Pratap Singh, a minister with a cast-iron reputation for integrity, because he was looking too closely into allegations of graft. Singh, eventually sacked by his paranoid Prime Minister, left Congress and floated his own political front with Arif Mohammed Khan, the young Muslim minister who had resigned from the government in protest of Rajiv's betrayal of Shah Bano.

The Prime Minister's decision, against the backdrop of his dissolving domestic prestige, to threaten Sri Lanka with military action on behalf of that island's Tamil separatists should have revived his fortunes. Indian jets breached Sri Lanka's airspace in 1987, leaving Colombo in no doubt that a full-scale invasion was imminent if it did not agree to a truce with the Tamils. But this show of force produced the opposite result. Dispatched by Rajiv to safeguard the peace accord signed reluctantly by Colombo, Indian troops came under attack from the Tamil rebels. Sri Lanka became India's Vietnam, a bleeding ground that claimed too many lives because the cost of extraction came to be equated with the loss of pride. Thousands of Indian soldiers were wounded and almost 1,200 killed on the island—the largest toll suffered by Indian forces on foreign soil since the Second World War in what was the first total defeat for India in South Asia.[23]

At home, the political terra firma was rapidly yielding to single-issue parties. These regional formations began attracting substantial support with appeals built around sub-identities. In the north, parties consecrated to social justice for marginalised castes acquired momentum. In the south, social justice mixed with linguistic pride. It was this democratic fragmentation, rather than Rajiv's lip-service to the Republic's foundational values, that complicated the BJP's effort to consolidate the electorate under the standard of religious solidarity. But on a pan-Indian level, Hindu nationalists were the principal beneficiaries of Congress's collapse. They carried to voters their pledge to heal the Hindu pride injured by Muslim invasions by constructing a temple to Lord Rama on the site of the Babri mosque in Ayodhya.

When elections were called, in 1989, Rajiv desperately attempted to out-Hindu the Hindu nationalists by launching his campaign from Faizabad, the district headquarters of Ayodhya, with the promise to inaugurate Rama Rajya—the rule, the kingdom, of Rama.[24] What remained of the secular character of India after the slaughter of Sikhs and the cascade of concessions by Congress to competing communal claims was now on the line. Muslims abandoned Rajiv. Hindus who wanted Rama Rajya had more authentic alternatives on offer. Having begun with the biggest parliamentary majority in Indian history, Rajiv led Congress to its second defeat. Hindu nationalists, accounting for two seats in 1984, returned with eighty-five members of parliament.

3

DECADENCE

*Let the whole world hear it loud and clear. India is now wide awake. We
shall prevail!*

Manmohan Singh, July 1991

Consider the view from Delhi in 1991. India was a nation of
843 million people and five million telephone lines.[1] Two billion
dollars separated the country from bankruptcy. The Indian map
had rarely looked so vulnerable to another cartographic revision. If the flames of separatism in Punjab appeared to be abat-
ing, the secessionist strife in Kashmir was just peaking. Hindu
nationalists, a fringe force in Indian politics a mere decade ago,
now occupied the bulk of opposition seats in parliament, poised
to banish permanently the secularism that was the foundational
basis of Indian nationalism. Indians were voting in the tenth
general election, the most violent in the Republic's history. Eight
hundred people had already been killed in political clashes
when, on 21 May, a Tamil suicide bomber from Sri Lanka
assassinated Rajiv Gandhi at a campaign stop in Tamil Nadu,
triggering a fresh burst of bloodshed and renewing questions
about India's ability to survive. Beyond its own imperilled borders, the Soviet Union, India's guardian and lodestar, was lurch-

ing towards disintegration. Moscow had shielded India from international criticism for its repression in Kashmir, maintained a crucial US$ 6 billion trade relationship, and supplied defence equipment in exchange for goods.[2] For a generation of Indians, the USSR's demise upended the certitudes of a lifetime. Visiting India at this time, Ved Mehta felt 'a sense of dread about the economic, political, and religious direction of the country which I don't remember encountering in any of my other visits over the past twenty-five years'.[3]

The barren rhetoric of economic self-reliance and political non-alignment could no longer cloak the Republic's deep decay. Here was a colossus of a country that compelled its enterprising middle-class citizens to make fifty trips to Delhi and wait three years to import a computer. Did you want a telephone connection? That could take anything from six months to three years. Did you wish to buy a car? The waiting period for the Morris Oxford knock-off ran up to twenty-two months. Did you want to manufacture vacuum cleaners? You needed a licence for that. In the mood for Coca-Cola? That Yankee beverage was as contraband in the 'sovereign socialist secular democratic republic' of India as liquor in the Islamic Republic next door.

How did India retreat from the threshold of economic collapse to reform itself and emerge, by the start of the twenty-first century, wealthier and more powerful than at any point in its history? It is now *de rigueur* to credit Manmohan Singh, who became finance minister in 1991, with India's rapid metamorphosis. But in a country where economic isolation was an inviolable ideological axiom, putting Singh's prescriptions into action was a distinctly political challenge. The man who shouldered this responsibility was an unlikely figure. He was seventy and had undergone triple-bypass surgery when he became Prime Minister. A career politician, he had no political constituency of his own. There was hardly a voice that did not lament his rise to the top. And yet if Nehru 'discovered' India, it can reasonably be said that P.V. Narasimha Rao *reinvented* it.

On the evening of 21 May 1991, Rao was packing the extensive library in his Delhi mansion in preparation for something unheard of in Indian politics: retirement. After spending two decades in the capital, he was eager to revive the scholastic life curtailed by his conscription into government. Born in 1921 in Muslim-ruled Hyderabad, Rao was adopted as a child by an affluent Brahmin family. In the Nizam's kingdom, the law, literature, and activism were privileges available to a very small minority. Rao excelled in all of them. He had garnered a reputation as a freedom fighter, barrister, and scholar before he turned thirty. He trained as a guerrilla to fight the Nizam, smuggled bombs and materiel into Hyderabad, founded and edited a literary journal, translated a Marathi novel into Telugu and a Telugu novel into Hindi, and published a clutch of short stories. After Hyderabad was incorporated into the newly independent India, and then appointed capital of the newly created state of Andhra Pradesh, Rao was elected to the provincial legislature. He stumbled through a number of ministries before Indira Gandhi, disregarding caste-based opposition, made him the state's chief minister. Rao pushed through an ambitious land reform act, compelling feudal landlords, many of them his colleagues, to distribute their enormous holdings to landless peasants. He, in turn, gave up most of his own inherited estate. Such reformative zeal was not, however, welcome in a centralised party that answered to one family. When Indira dismissed Rao's government and summoned him to Delhi, he was over fifty but sufficiently pragmatic to grasp the secret of survival in Congress: never display autonomous drive or initiative.[4]

Despite lacking a political base, Rao thrived in the capital because he committed himself, in his own words, to 'masterly inactivity'. His career became a model of fealty to Indira. He supported her during the Emergency and she, appreciative of his erudition and loyalty, rewarded him with safe seats and major portfolios in her cabinet. To his colleagues, Rao remained an enigma, a man who was fluent in twelve languages but, they complained, spoke his mind in none. He sparked in the role of foreign minister. Visiting Havana in 1980, he received instructions from Indira to persuade the leaders of the Non-Aligned Movement to move their next summit from Iraq—then at war with Iran—to India. Rao disarmed the gathering by arguing India's case in Spanish to the Cubans, Persian to the Iranians, Arabic to the Iraqis and the Egyptians, French to a host of African representatives, and Urdu to the Pakistanis.[5]

After Indira's assassination, Rao transferred his loyalty to Rajiv. Minister of home affairs during the anti-Sikh pogrom, he was nowhere to be seen. And by 1991, he was a spent force in Indian politics. Denied a party ticket, he was marginally involved in the general election campaign that year, issuing the occasional statement ridiculing the BJP's foreign policy pronouncements. His declamations were buried in the inside pages of newspapers, if they were printed at all. No one listened to him.

Everything changed on the night of 21 May, when an aide arrived with news from Tamil Nadu: at 10.20 p.m., Rajiv Gandhi was killed in an explosion while campaigning in the town of Sriperumbudur.

With the monarch gone, and no successor in place in a party bereft of democracy, Congress collapsed into a hive of intrigue. An effort to recruit Rajiv's grieving widow, Sonia, was halted only when she emphatically rejected the party's entreaties to lead it. Every plausible successor to Rajiv had an equally powerful adversary within the party. By a process of elimination, Rao, who was not even on the ballot in the general election, emerged as the consensus candidate to 'carry forward' Rajiv's legacy. No one knew, of course, that he had authored an anonymous article castigating Rajiv as an arrogant, insecure force of destruction.[6] To his colleagues Rao was a man without ideological leanings or antagonists or friends. Weighty regional leaders such as Sharad Pawar, N.D. Tiwari, and Arjun Singh, believing Rao would serve only as a stopgap leader and intending fully to displace him after the vote was in, fell behind his candidacy. Their differences only sharpened when Congress, crested by a sympathy wave, was returned as the largest single party in parliament. The placid, inscrutable man suddenly showed his stripes. None of his backers was given a ministerial department of his choice and their supporters were kept out of government altogether.[7]

Before the party could fathom this unanticipated ruthlessness, Rao unleashed the unthinkable upon them. He plucked Manmohan Singh, a career bureaucrat, from the University Grants Commission and appointed him finance minister. Ten days later, acting on Singh's advice, he devalued the rupee by 8.7 per cent against international currencies. In less than forty-eight hours, he devalued it again. He then went on national television and delivered what seems in retrospect the most consequential speech since Nehru's address to the nation at India's birth in 1947. Rao did not aspire to grandiloquence, but the momentousness of the moment was not lost on those who witnessed it. 'Desperate maladies call for drastic remedies,' Rao told his compatriots as he announced an austerity programme, much of it devised by the IMF and Singh. India, he explained, had just recovered from a debilitating balance of payments crisis which had left it without adequate 'foreign exchange to import even such essential commodities as diesel, kerosene, edible oil and fertiliser'. His solution was to cut the 'fat in government expenditure', deregulate industry and emancipate the private sector, pull down the barriers to foreign investment, provide tax concessions to private corporations, slash subsidies to farmers, and curb labour activism.[8]

Rao, his critics grasped, was dismantling Nehruvian India. Congress rose up in opposition. The *Herald*, the party's newspaper, complained that Rao and his finance minister wanted nothing more than to give 'the middle-class Indian crispier cornflakes [and] fizzier aerated drinks'. 'That,' the paper asserted, 'could never have been the vision of the founding fathers of our nation'. Parliament erupted in fury. Left-wing members accused Rao of imposing 'anti-people' policies on the nation. Dozens of senior Congress members beseeched Sonia to take over the party and rescue the country.[9] Rao's response was bold and brazen in equal measure. 'Reversing the policy options is not available to this government any more,' he said frankly. 'It is a one-way street and on all sides I have red lights.' He then gave the rebels a scare by proposing to reintroduce internal elections to Congress. Asia's oldest political party operated under a system of patronage introduced by Indira. Appointments to party posts were doled out in Delhi. Some of the most powerful politicians in India had no mandate at all. Rao, of course, was the most conspicuous beneficiary of this arrangement (he bolstered his position by contesting a by-election in 1993, which he won with a majority of more than half a million votes). But his threat jolted his opponents who, after showing some early signs of defiance, became submissive.

Backbenchers and the cabinet dealt with, Rao began cultivating the BJP. Heading a minority government, he feared a floor-test in parliament. He frequently invited L.K. Advani, the BJP's president, to dinner at his residence. A Hindu refugee from the Pakistani province of Sindh, Advani was the most poisonous figure in Indian politics at this time.[10] In 1990, he led a massive rally in a motorised chariot—modelled on prototypes in the Hindu epics *Ramayana* and *Mahabharata*—from Somnath, where a majestic Hindu temple had repeatedly been ransacked by Muslim invaders, to the ancient town of Ayodhya, where the founder of the Mughal empire had erected a mosque by bringing down a Hindu temple. Hindu nationalists, buoyed by Rajiv's surrender, recast the old building into an emblem of Muslim despotism and Hindu defeat. Protecting the mosque from Hindu nationalists now became *the* measure of the non-confessional state's commitment to secularism.

Even though his decision to court the BJP was driven by pragmatic reasons, Rao extracted assurances from Advani that Babri would not be harmed. A year later, on 6 December 1992, Advani led another march to the mosque. This time, his supporters brought it down. The police did not so much as attempt to stop them as they went about butchering Muslims in Uttar Pradesh, the site of the worst violence that swept through India. The unthinkable had happened—and it had happened on Congress's watch. This was the greatest affront to India's secular core since the foundation of the Republic. Rao, napping as the mosque was being levelled, dismissed all four BJP-run state governments in India when he woke up. He banned Hindu religious organisations, threw Advani in prison, and made a solemn pledge to rebuild Babri. Addressing the nation over the radio, he warned Indians of the 'grave threat' now faced by the 'institutions, principles, and ideals on which the constitutional structure of our Republic has been built'.[11] Indian cities were placed under curfew. Heavily armed paramilitary forces patrolled the streets.

Rao's response may have been proportionate to this *moment* of terror, but it could not wipe clean the stain left by the destruction of Babri. The mood everywhere was sepulchral, full of self-loathing. Yet it was possible to detect relief, even rejoicing. India had, finally, crossed the Rubicon.

For the expanding Hindu middle class—demoralised for decades by Congress's betrayals and being rapidly unshackled by Singh's liberal economic policies from Nehruvian shibboleths about self-restraint—the barbarism in Ayodhya contained a self-empowering, even redemptive, message: an ancient civilisation had purged itself of the shame inflicted by history by razing the monument to its subjugation. The past, so many felt, had been avenged.

The promise of a violent release for the resentments and confusions incubated by Hindus' unresolved feelings about their history is what gave Hindu nationalism its visceral appeal. The anti-colonial nationalism pioneered by Congress, cohering in opposition to the British, had applied a romantic gloss on pre-colonial India: it was Eden vandalised by satanic Europeans.

But had the British really ruptured India's historic continuity? Or was it India's decline, precipitated by centuries of conquest, that had enabled Britain so swiftly to overpower the subcontinent? The conceit of the freedom movement led by Congress was that a fully developed national consciousness existed in the subcontinent before the British arrived, smashed it, and divided the natives. Singling the British out as uniquely disruptive villains proved a convenient way for Republican India's secular intellectuals to bypass awkward questions that ought, in the long-term interests of the country, to have been confronted head on. The airbrushing of the pre-colonial past was intended to deny ammunition to all those who cited the creation of Pakistan to intensify their clamour for a Hindu state.

Historiographers tasked by the secular Congress establishment to clarify India's past, motivated by the desire to do good, caused immeasurable harm by blurring it. They applied recondite techniques and treatments to source material, ladled their prose with jargon, and, lost in disciplinary sport, neglected the needs of lay readers outside the priesthood. Students emerged from exposure to their output without a rudimental apprehension of their difficult past. Medieval India, despite all the evidence of its methodical disfigurement, was depicted in schoolbooks as an idyll where Muslims and Hindus coexisted in harmony and forged an inclusive idea of India which the British came and shattered. This elaborate fable was so wholly internalised by the secular establishment which dispensed it that, as late as 1998, K.R. Narayanan, India's first Dalit president, was able to tell an audience in Turkey that the most 'amazing fact' about his homeland before it was defiled by 'European intrusion' was 'that the interaction between the old civilisation of India—the Hindu civilisation—and the Islamic civilisation was a friendly experience'.[12] Such a thesis was always going to struggle against the overwhelmingly contradictive evidence—from the ruins of Hindu liturgical buildings to the ballads of dispossession passed from generation to generation—arrayed against it. The chronicles of the subcontinent's medieval rulers are full of pornographic descriptions of the horrors with which the place teemed. Here is the Persian historian Vassaf relating with elation the reduction of Cambay in Gujarat by the forces of Alauddin Khilji:

> The Muhammadan forces began to kill and slaughter on the right and on the left unmercifully, through the impure land, for the sake of Islam, and blood flowed in torrents. They plundered gold and silver to an extent greater than can be conceived ... They took captive a great number of handsome and elegant maidens, amounting to 20,000, and children of both sexes, more than the pen can enumerate ... In short, the Muhammadan army brought the country to utter ruin, and destroyed the lives of the inhabitants, and plundered the cities, and captured their offspring, so that many temples were deserted and the idols were broken and trodden under foot, the largest of which was one called Somnat, fixed upon stone, polished like a mirror, of charming shape and admirable workmanship. The Muhammadan soldiers plundered all those jewels and rapidly set themselves to demolish the idol. The surviving infidels were deeply affected with grief, and they engaged to pay a thousand pieces of gold as ransom for the idol, but they were indignantly rejected, and the idol was destroyed, and its limbs, which were anointed with ambergris and perfumed, were cut off. The fragments were conveyed to Delhi, and the entrance of the Jama Masjid was paved with them, that people might remember and talk of this brilliant victory.[13]

The general retort of the 'secular' historian confronted with writings of this vein tended to be that they were an exaggeration meant to impress the rulers—without any meditation on the nature of the rulers who might be flattered by such graphic descriptions of gore staged in their name—or to read into them motives that the text did not support, or to discredit them altogether as British propaganda. Unfortunately for them—and for the national project they were serving—the grand mosques of northern India are decorated with stone tablets in which traces of the pre-existing liturgical monuments that were razed to furnish the building materials for them are still visible. But pick up a history textbook taught at state schools and you will find no explanation of what happened. It was the mission of 'secular' historians and public intellectuals of India to locate mundane causes for carnage in the name of religion. And when those reasons could not be found, they papered over the gruesome deeds of the invaders with nice-nellyisms and emphasised their good traits. A standard history textbook written for Indian schoolchildren by Romila Thapar follows up the admission that the Ghaznavid ruler Mahmud was 'destructive in India'—a phrase that omits so much—with the mitigation that 'in his own country he was responsible for building a beautiful mosque and a large library'.[14] All imperialism is vicious, but that is not the standard adopted by India's secular historians. The Portuguese, the same textbook tells us, 'were intolerant of the existing religions of India and did not hesitate to force people to become Christian'. Indeed, they 'did all that they could to make more converts'.[15] On the other hand, Islamic invaders, in a sentence that catches the breath if only because of its contrast with the candid assessment of the Portuguese, 'did not produce any fundamental change in Indian society but they did help to enrich Indian culture'.[16] Babur, the founder of the Mughal empire whose campaigns made Portuguese pacification look like a picnic, 'enjoyed playing polo'.[17] Imperialism, in other words, was destructive only when Europeans did it. When Asians did it, it was a cultural exchange programme.

Such well-intentioned sanitisation of the past was never, in the long run, going to be able to withstand the eventual awakening of people to their history or sustain an inclusive nationalism. The encounter between 'the strictest and most extreme form of monotheism' and 'the richest and most varied polytheism', Octavio Paz wrote in his luminous study of India inflicted a 'deep wound' on the psyche of its people.[18] The secular establishment squandered a rare opening in the early decades of the Republic to heal that wound by supplying Indians a forthright accounting of their history. Had India been honest about its past—about the atrocities that were perpetrated and the heritage that was ravaged—it might have desiccated the appeal of Hindu supremacism. It might have reconciled Indians to their harrowing past, provoked a mature detachment from it, and denied Hindu nationalists the opportunity to weaponise history. To come to terms with the past, to move on from it, we must first acknowledge and accept it. A thousand years of Indian history were obfuscated. The reasons were lofty; the consequences of the well-meaning distortions, alas, baleful. Secularists endangered the extraordinary religio-cultural synthesis India arrived at by airbrushing its unbeautiful genesis. No Indian individual or community bears any responsibility for what happened in the pre-colonial era. By downplaying and denying what happened, secularists unwittingly implied otherwise.

Rao embodied the conflict between private knowledge of the past and public ideals of the Republic. Unlike other Congressmen of his generation, his personality was forged in opposition not to the British but to the Nizam of Hyderabad. The overthrow of the sovereignty of his native state's Telugu-speaking Indians, who have a continuous history of more than 2,000 years, predated British rule of the subcontinent by painfully long centuries. It was only with the arrival of the British—and only in those territories ceded to them in the late eighteenth century by the Asaf Jah dynasty which had taken possession of much of the Telugu country—that an intellectual revival of sorts began to occur. The coastal east of the state (Seemandhra) and the jagged south (Rayalaseema) went to the British. Telangana, the arid inland Rao called home, remained under the Nizams as part of Hyderabad. The former modernised; the latter stagnated. Telugu, which had fallen into catastrophic decline, was rescued and revitalised in the British-held areas by English civil servants such as Charles Phillip Brown.[19] A literary ferment erupted in coastal Andhra between the late nineteenth and early twentieth centuries. The possession once again by the natives of the means with which to assess the past gave rise to some of the Telugu language's most extraordinary poets, novelists, and playwrights—Gurajada Apparao, Dharmavaram Ramakrishnacharyulu, Vedam Sastri.

The contrast with Telangana could not have been starker.

By the time of India's Independence in August 1947, Hyderabad's Muslim overlord was the world's richest man and his subjects numbered among its poorest people. Rao's fiction contains poignant descriptions of the terror visited upon them by the Nizam's mujahideen—villages torched, men hacked apart, women molested—as they sought to subsume Hyderabad into Pakistan. Rao witnessed the carnage and would have known the people who became its casualties.

Babri's demolition haunted Rao for the rest of his life. Yet the acute emotional distress that leaps from his fictional writings set in Muslim-ruled Hyderabad makes it impossible to shake off the sense that his mystifying conduct in the run-up to that fateful day—neglecting the gathering storm, deceiving himself with the assurances given to him by Advani, going to sleep as Advani alighted at Ayodhya—was in some measure animated by a sub-liminal yearning for closure. But the trouble with those who search for personal consolation in bloody retributions against the past is that they do not bring history to a terminus: they endow it with an insoluble fury. Someday, the victims of Rao's derelic-tion of his high office's sacred duty to safeguard *all* Indians may seek a similarly sanguinary resolution for the wounds inflicted on them by the Hindus who stormed Ayodhya to correct the past. And another day the victims of the victims … History cannot be revenged. The best we can do is strive to emancipate ourselves from its punishing torments by being honest about it.

Rao weathered the fallout from Babri's destruction and con-tinued to lead a minority government for five years. Indian elites, hypnotised by Singh's pitch to turn India into 'a major economic power in the world', quickly moved on. The opening up of the economy is also what saved Rao from becoming a toxic figure overseas: it was clearly seen to be counterproductive to censure a man who was granting access to so many consumers. Foreigners overwhelmingly cheered him on. After berating Indians for 'clinging to the past' by electing Rao, the *Economist* showered him with praise. In Berlin, industrialists hailed him as 'a corporate chief executive'. German chancellor Helmut Kohl considered him a refreshing departure from Rajiv.[20] In America, the *Christian Science Monitor* congratulated him for 'negating Nehru'.[21] In Britain, the *Financial Times* nominated him alongside China's Deng Xiaoping as its Man of the Year.[22] Rao, lauded by the traffickers of the post-Cold War economic consensus, grew increasingly impatient with the unchanging obsessions of fellow developing countries. When Zimbabwe and Malaysia delivered blistering attacks against the West at a summit, Rao pointedly asked the gathering: 'Have you come across any conference where all the speeches are identical?'[23]

He even agreed to meet the influential Jewish leader Isi Liebler, who came to India in 1991 to lobby for Israel. Such a meeting would have been inconceivable even for a Congress premier with a firm majority. Rao took the meeting despite his shaky position. An historic vote to overturn the Zionism-equals-racism resolution, which India had backed, was about to come up at the United Nations, and Liebler appealed to Rao to vote for it. He argued passionately for full diplomatic relations between Delhi and West Jerusalem and complained that India had treated Israel as a 'pariah'. Rao assured his guest that India did not equate Zionism with racism but refused to make a commitment.[24] When details of the conversation were leaked to the press, India's longstanding Arab friends reacted angrily. Rao remained unperturbed. When the resolution to revoke 3379 was tabled at the UN, India voted with the majority for revocation. As talk of upgrading relations with Israel gathered momentum,

Rao quickly moved to mollify Arab sentiment by inviting Yasser Arafat on a state visit to India in January 1992. The Palestinian leader was lavishly feted in Delhi for his 'efforts to promote peace and international friendship'. At the end of his tour, Arafat blessed Rao's plans to befriend Israel.

Rao aggressively renewed India's lapsed relations with East Asian states, particularly Singapore and Japan, with his 'look east' policy. He travelled to Singapore and Seoul, Tokyo and Beijing, Kuala Lumpur and Bangkok, and Tehran, Paris, Bonn, and London. The only two major capitals he omitted from his hectic early itinerary were Moscow and Washington.[25] He ignored the former and, in 1994, made a groundbreaking visit to the latter—the first by an Indian head of government in a decade. Bill Clinton's decision to sell F-16 fighter jets to Pakistan, coupled with his administration's ceaseless rebukes of Delhi over its conduct in Kashmir, provoked a furore in India. Rao was subjected to severe pressure to cancel the trip. There was intense clamour, too, to assert India's independence by staging a nuclear test. Rao ignored the cacophony and got on a plane.[26] The Americans received him as something of a revolutionary. The *Wall Street Journal* praised him effusively for repudiating Nehru's 'xenophobia' and embracing free markets.[27] Morgan Stanley released a report prophesying that Rao's economic reforms were destined to move India towards 'tigerisation'. A group of major American businesses—including AT&T, GE, Ford, and Coca-Cola—formed an autonomous body called the 'India Interest Group' to lobby for Delhi in Washington. Bowing to the markets, Clinton assured Rao that the US would no longer air its concerns about human rights in public. Rao, in turn, vouched that 'there will be no turning back' from the liberalisation of the economy.[28]

By the close of 1995, India was pulling in more foreign investment than it had managed in the previous four decades combined. Two-way trade with the US leaped to US$ 7.3 billion. There were 422 American companies with investments in

India. CEOs of major companies streamed in and out of the country. George Soros showed up to invest a billion dollars. Coca-Cola was back after twenty years. General Electric poured in US$ 200 million.[29] 'Foreign exchange coffers are filled as never before. Industry is booming as never before. Most of all, there is a palpable hope in the air,' one commentator wrote.[30]

Babri had fallen by the wayside.

Rao's India was now a different country. The middle class became more conspicuously consumptive than ever. Indians now drank 2,880 million bottles of fizzy drinks and flew ten million times each year. The credit card industry, which had a negligible presence in India before the reforms, expanded into a US$ 64 million business by 1996. Mastercard alone grew by 106 per cent in India—the highest growth ever registered by the company in Asia.[31] The creed of this emerging 'New India' was captured in the advertising jingles on TV and slogans on the billboards of big cities: 'I. Me. Mine.' 'It's My Life.' 'Keep Up or Be Left Out.' 'Wear Your Attitude.' 'Zamana Badal Gaya Hai: *The Times Have Changed*.' The *Economic Times*, an early supporter of Rao's reforms, saw its circulation surpass 500,000 from less than a meagre 100,000 just four years prior, making it the second-largest financial newspaper in the world.[32] 'One of the psychological legacies of the Nehruvian socialistic era was that the more affluent sections of the society were branded as being rather vulgar and spending money to live well was considered an even greater sin,' Aroon Purie, the proprietor of *India Today* magazine, wrote. 'Today, that stigma seems to have vanished for many.'

But even as New India erupted in self-congratulation, it had to contend with the odd spectacle of seeing its architect run from his accomplishments. As elections approached, a different India was screaming for attention. Rural poverty in the reform years remained largely static. The benefits that accrued to a small group of Indians did not percolate downwards. Ninety-seven per cent of Indians in the countryside lived without access to sanitation.[33] The parvenus perusing *India Today* could now exhibit their wealth without remorse. But most Indians felt crushed by rising food prices. A disproportionate burden of the deficit reduction programme was borne by the poor. Since the government's tax concessions to the corporate sector made it impossible to increase revenues, it resorted to cutting public investment and social expenditure.[34] At the same time, a dozen or more of the country's top fifty private corporations—the cathedrals of New India—succeeded in avoiding taxes altogether.[35]

As economic liberalisation intensified between 1993 and 1995, Rao's party was defenestrated from power in traditional Congress strongholds throughout the country. In Rao's home state, it was reduced to twenty-six seats in the 294-seat legislature. Campaigning for re-election in 1996, Rao dropped all references to economic reforms. The *New York Times* reported that he 'feared provoking a backlash among poor Indians who have had to pay more for rice, sugar and fuel' by appearing in their midst. Party leaders pleaded with Rao to stay away from their constituencies. He cut a desperate figure on the campaign, sitting alone in his aircraft and gazing out of the window. In the elections that followed, Congress suffered the worst defeat in its history.

Five years after Babri, Hindu nationalists stitched together a governing coalition. For the first time, India had a BJP Prime Minister.

Nehru had erected the Indian Republic on four pillars: democracy, secularism, socialism, and non-alignment in foreign affairs. Rao took a hammer to what remained of them four decades later. He implemented Singh's economic policies by subverting democracy: critical reforms were made as executive decisions, prices were hiked when parliament went into recess, and parliamentary opposition was overcome by exploiting legal technicalities and blackmailing recalcitrant MPs with the intelligence agencies' files on them.[36] The Indian state's commitment to secularism also collapsed under Rao's rule. It did not occur when Advani's Hindu hordes tore down Babri. It happened when the government failed to honour its pledge to rebuild the mosque. India's secularism thereafter looked increasingly like a myth, a promissory note to be cherished but never cashed. This was the upshot of Rao's reluctance to pulverise Hindu warriors with the fullest might of the state when they declared war on India at Ayodhya.

Rao was the first Indian leader who made foreign industrialists feel as if they were in the presence of a 'chief executive', not a politician—an early incarnation of praise which, sanctified by years of repetition at Davos, became the highest aspiration of third-world 'modernisers'. But in applauding him and Singh for supposedly correcting the failures of Nehru, the beneficiaries of New India at home and abroad overlooked the seeds of discontent planted by the pair. Those seeds soon after Rao left office. Across India's most impoverished regions, untouched by material development, armed Maoists intensified their guerrilla warfare against the state. Rao's own ancestral estate was seized by Maoists in the nineties and distributed among the poor.

Rao led India out of one of the worst economic crises in its history, opened it up to the world, tore down the licence–permit–quota raj, dismantled old orthodoxies, and pursued unthinkable new friendships. In doing so, he corrupted India's democracy and crippled its commitment to secularism. He left behind an India that was wealthier (but more unequal), confident (but less empathetic), and integrated into the world economy (but closed off to its poorer citizens). He is now reviled in his own party, forgotten by the world, and neglected in India. He remains the only departed Prime Minister to be denied a memorial in the country's capital. It is under him that India made the most total break from its foundational beliefs. His embrace of capitalism, quickening the rise of Hindu nationalism, demonstrated to all those aspiring to succeed him that you could vandalise the values of the Republic and still be vaunted— so long as you pleased the markets.

Sonia Gandhi finally took over Congress in 1998 and Rao, deemed insufficiently deferential to the family when he was in office, was swiftly ostracised. Credit for his achievements was given to Singh and to Rajiv, and Rao's name was gradually effaced from Congress's history. Rao spent his final years fighting corruption charges dating back to his time in office. He became the first former Prime Minister to be convicted in a criminal court on the charge of suborning MPs not to vote against his minority government. The decision was overturned on appeal, but it was an ignominious twilight. When he died, erstwhile colleagues in Congress, indulging the Gandhi family's vindictiveness, refused to allow his wake to take place in Delhi. His body was flown back to Hyderabad, where it lay in state in an empty hall. His funeral was poorly guarded and thinly attended by the party hierarchs.

'I am the only Congress Prime Minister not of the family to complete a full term, and I am still paying for it,' he had told a visiting journalist months before his death in 2004.[37] After he was gone, stray dogs, it is said, tore at the remains of his partially cremated body.[38]

4

DISSOLUTION

India is all set to regain its due place in the comity of nations, as a plural, secular, and liberal democracy.

Manmohan Singh, 2007

In 2004, Manmohan Singh was sworn in as the thirteenth Prime Minister of India. Congress had unexpectedly returned to power at the head of a coalition that year after almost a decade in the opposition. Singh, nowhere to be seen during the campaign, crawled out of restful oblivion for the second time in his life to take centre stage in government. Sonia Gandhi viewed her Italian birth as a disabling factor for the top job. Her judgement was unsupported by facts: scattered before her were the remains of the nativists who had sought to mobilise voters against her origins. Indians had long ago accepted her as one of their own. When John Fisher Burns, the doyen of American foreign correspondents, travelled through the country in the late 1990s, he found ordinary citizens bristling at the mere mention of Sonia's heritage. 'If you call her a foreigner,' a veteran of India's freedom struggle warned Burns, 'I will not talk to you, not another word.' 'At rally after rally, in state after state,' Burns recorded, 'ordinary Indians said her origins were irrelevant, and often then portrayed the issue as a matter so insulting that it should not have been raised.'[1] The 'nationalists' arrayed against her were 'Indian' by accident of birth. She was Indian by choice.

Sonia's insecurities about her identity intensified, ironically, in the moment of her triumphal vindication. She became overcome by fear that her ascension to the premiership might resurrect the xenophobes fixated on her descent, generate consequences she may not be able to contain, and potentially jeopardise the inheritance of her children, Rahul and Priyanka. So she turned to Singh, a trusted family retainer with a lustrous pedigree—Oxbridge, Planning Commission, Reserve Bank, Finance Ministry—to serve as a placeholder. This act of self-preservation, enabling Sonia to minimise her exposure while retaining maximal authority, was given the gloss of sacrifice and high moral purpose. Singh's installation in the highest political office was certainly a tokenistic affirmation of Indian secularism; for some in Congress, it also expiated the party's sins in Punjab and Delhi. But most of all, it was a measure of the family's disdain for the conventions of the Republic. As a minister in Singh's cabinet explained to the press, Sonia 'is the queen. She is appointing a regent to run some of the government's business.'[2]

Politically, Singh was the least qualified candidate for the job. He had never won an election to any office—not councillor, not ward member, not dogcatcher—in his entire life. The one election he contested, in 1999, was for one of the safest Congress boroughs in Delhi. The establishment, from major newspapers and corporate titans to famous columnists and film personalities, loudly endorsed him. Singh made history by losing the seat.[3] But accustomed to being inserted by his powerful patrons into the heart of government without ever winning a vote, the thought of contesting a parliamentary election seemed to him surplus to the requirements for holding India's highest political office. He became the first Prime Minister of the Republic to govern for two full terms from the upper house. Delegated the job of steering the economy by Sonia, he had no contact—no avenue for contact—with ordinary people. A lifelong theoretician, he was suddenly placed in a position where he could implement his theories without having to account for their social ramifications. Nobody could dispute the theoretical soundness of the logic underlying his deference for the market: that to finance social welfare, India had to generate wealth. But what he engendered in practice was a lavish social welfare scheme for the rich financed by the public.

The nexus between politics and business under Singh deepened to the extent that it destroyed governmental oversight. India's burgeoning cast of billionaires raided state banks for loans. When they failed to repay what they borrowed, they were granted additional lines of credit.[4] The thought of seizing and nationalising their assets was anathema to the man who had launched the fetish for privatisation. The government used half of a US$ 4 billion loan package from the World Bank in 2009 to capitalise state banks depleted by the defaulters.[5]

While the *soi-disant* wealth creators were being rewarded with more cash for their failures, the countryside lit up with the funeral pyres of farmers ruined by Singh's neglect. Their dire state was captured by a survey conducted by the government in the last years of Singh's rule. It showed that the average monthly income of agricultural households in India was 6,426 rupees, while the average expenditure was 6,223 rupees: 203 rupees was all that families could put away.[6] Unable to access credit, left to the mercy of usurious private lenders, 16,000 farmers killed themselves every year for all but two years that Singh was in office;[7] many addressed their suicide notes directly to the Prime Minister.[8]

Singh was unfazed. He had form. Two years into his term, as foreign dignitaries, including German Chancellor Angela Merkel and former US treasury secretary Henry Paulson, descended on Delhi to attend yet another conference on India's 'rise', thousands of tribal peasants and landless famers from fifteen Indian states marched to the capital to register their peaceful protest and demand land rights. The rally's organiser, a Gandhian activist called P.V. Rajagopal, described it as an unprecedented event. 'Non-violent direct action has never been tried so effectively,' he said. 'These people are living, walking, and sleeping on highways since we set out.' But as soon as they arrived in Delhi, having walked over 600 kilometres to get there, the Congress government had them herded into a roofless enclosure and posted armed guards to keep them there.[9] The heat in Delhi can bake human flesh; the protesters were not even given water.

The severest bruises of Singh's reforms were borne by the historically marginalised and trod-upon layers of Indian society. Dalits and tribals—aboriginals whose existence in India predates its oldest civilisations—constitute only one-fourth of India's population; but as the economist Amit Bhaduri has shown, they account for 40 per cent of those whom modernisation has 'dispossessed of land, livelihood, and habitat'.[10] Democratic protest was not a tool they could wield in Singh's India without inviting a homicidal backlash from a state increasingly beholden to private interests. In 2008, when tribals in central India passed a resolution in a free vote against the government's decision to hand their land over to a private company for the setting up of a power plant, the authorities ignored them. When they then staged a peaceful mass rally, with some 10,000 participating in a procession, the police opened fire.[11] The government traduced troublesome tribals as Maoist sympathisers, a charge that instantly negated the need for due process. The Maoist insurgency is real enough, and it is true also that it often preys on the poor it claims to be rescuing.

Which raises the question: why is it that the poor in the most marginalised regions of India keep migrating into the arms of the Maoists? Is it because they cannot resist the sirenic appeal of Mao Zedong's revolutionary exegesis of the historical contradictions of dialectical materialism? Or might it be because India has so remorselessly molested them? Singh evidently did not ponder such questions, or the implications of his actions, when he called Maoism the greatest internal threat to the Indian state. A year after he became Prime Minister, Congress constituted a militia called Salwa Judum—'purification hunt'—to strike down tribals suspected of harbouring Maoist sympathies in one of the most destitute parts of central India. Two of India's top corporations had paid billions to extract the mineral wealth buried under the homes of the inconvenient aboriginals, whom the state's official literature portrayed as sub-human. They were not 'cleanly in their habits', resembled 'cattle' when they drank water from streams, practised 'free sex', led a 'savage life', and refused to 'mingle with the modern civilisation'.[12]

Singh's administration took modern civilisation to them. Armed with police licences, weapons, and total impunity, members of the Judum, tribals themselves, were enjoined to enforce order. They torched entire villages and corralled villagers at gunpoint into concentration camps, where the captive women, men, and children became material for abuse of every variety. Police forces raped the 'savage' women they were sent to liberate from the spell of Maoism.[13] Children were conscripted as soldiers into the Judum.[14] Men were slaughtered.

When this civilised alternative to Maoism failed to win converts among the tribals and instead intensified reprisals by the Maoists, Singh's government retaliated by launching, in November 2009, Operation Green Hunt. Some of the most sophisticated weapons were transported to one of the most wretched regions on the planet. The prospect of innumerable collateral deaths of aboriginals did nothing to deter the government, which contemplated using air power against its own citizens.[15] Maoism was the one bugbear that dissolved differences among middle-class Indians. If you questioned the government's actions, you were a fifth columnist, an enemy of democracy.

As Green Hunt got underway in India, Barack Obama hosted a sumptuous state dinner, his first, for Singh, where the

US president paid rich tribute to the 'enduring bonds shared by the US and India', 'the world's largest democracies … speaking out and standing up for the rights and dignity to which all human beings are entitled'. Witnessing the two leaders together, the *New Yorker* was moved to praise Singh, 'a seminal figure of India's transformation from socialism … to managed capitalism and rising power status', as 'one of those … admirable figures that India's independence movement and democracy have managed to produce regularly'.[16] Reality could not easily ruffle a fantasy bomb-proofed by such self-cherishing certitudes. To the people exposed to Green Hunt, Singh was not the soft-spoken economist feted in the councils of the world. He was the sub-continental Pinochet.

The Prime Minister's stock rose in Washington in part because he could be leaned upon. A year before Obama toasted Singh, terrorists from Pakistan had besieged Mumbai for four days. Acting on instructions relayed in real time by their handlers in the military-intelligence camorra of Pakistan, they brought India to its knees. A hundred and seventy people were slaughtered. Mumbai's Chabad House was specifically targeted. For the first time in India's immemorial history, Jews were killed for being Jews.

Singh cut an abysmal figure. He placed a call to his counterpart in Islamabad and demanded that Pakistan send the chief of its intelligence agency to India. Pakistan agreed, and then reneged on the agreement. Singh's ultimatum had yielded nothing but sniggers.[17] The man who was willing to use the might of the Indian Air Force against his own impoverished compatriots shrugged and moved on. He had no contingency plan. A grateful Washington—worried all along that escalation by India might further deteriorate its own faltering war of choice in Afghanistan by diverting the attention of its perfidious ally, Pakistan, away from its western front—sprang into action. It spun Singh's capitulation, catastrophic in the long term, as an heroic act of statesmanship. But by amplifying the self-exculpating lie that the choice before India was inaction or nuclear war,

Singh effectively conveyed to Pakistan's military overlords that they could get away with murder—and invited yet more bloodshed by their henchmen. And by failing to appear tough against Pakistan, he created an opening for Hindu nationalists at home to paint 'secularists' as weak on national security and accelerated the dissolution of what remained of the secular state.

Those who profited from Singh's abjectness, in the long run, were Muslim extremists in Pakistan and Hindu supremacists in India. But if his actions were anything to go by, what mattered most to Singh was a pat on the back from Washington: he chose to spend the first anniversary of the worst terrorist atrocity on Indian soil in the twenty-first century not with the victims of Mumbai but among his admirers in the White House. The Americans, for all their florid proclamations of friendship, neither halted their sale of weapons to Pakistan nor granted India extensive access to David Headley, the Pakistani-American double-agent in their custody whose knowledge was instrumental to piecing together the planning behind Mumbai. Nobody could blame them: they were serving their own interests—so, to India's misfortune, was India's Prime Minister.

Singh's star began to fade after the Congress-led coalition, bleached of the communists who had objected to Singh's pro-American lurch, won a second term in 2009 as a result largely of the disarray in the ranks of the opposition and the welfare schemes steered by Sonia Gandhi. It did not take long for the scams—and the mutually profitable relationship between politics, finance, and journalism—to come to light. Phone calls between Niira Radia, a political lobbyist on the payroll of India's billionaires, and some of the country's most distinguished journalists, intercepted by the tax office, were aired on television networks in 2010. Men and women who would go on to reinvent themselves as the resistance under Modi were heard energetically pimping themselves to the rich. They were willing to convey Radia's employers' choice of politicians for key ministries to the Congress Party's leadership—or make the case for them in their columns. 'What kind of story do you want?', Vir Sanghvi, the former editor of *Hindustan Times*, was heard asking Radia. 'Because this will go as Counterpoint [the title of Sanghvi's column], so it will be, like, most-most read, but it can't seem too slanted, yet it is an ideal opportunity to get all the points across.'[18]

Corruption, of course, has a hoary history in India. As early as 1964, the ministry of home affairs reported that corruption had 'increased to such an extent that people have started losing faith in the integrity of public administration'.[19] In the decades thereafter, graft become a quotidian fact of life: in an ordinary citizen's interaction with the agents of the state, there were few transactions unaccompanied by the demand for a bribe. India's command economy served as a catalyst for malfeasance in the state's high offices. It spawned a culture of patronage in which senior politicians and bureaucrats showered favoured individuals with lucrative business permits and licences. But the scams of the time seemed almost trivial in comparison to the scandals that began erupting on Singh's watch in 2011, the twentieth anniversary of his original market reforms. One senior Congress leader, Suresh Kalmadi, was placed in judicial custody at Delhi's Tihar prison on charges of pocketing millions in the run-up to the Commonwealth Games in 2010. Billed as the coming-out party for 'superpower' India, the games cost ten times the estimate and were a national embarrassment. Another inmate at Tihar was Singh's communications minister, Andimuthu Raja—the man promoted by Radia—who stood accused of defrauding the national treasury of US$40 billion by selling bandwidth spectrum at grossly undervalued rates. Raja was subsequently found not guilty, and the integrity of the comptroller general whose audit implicated him is now in question.[20] But what remains beyond doubt is the pernicious inroads made by big business into the highest offices of the state.

As always with Congress, corruption flourished alongside the heavy moral rhetoric of the party's proprietors. The cult of the dynasty was perpetuated with the same ruthlessness with which its interests were protected. According to an analysis carried out in 2009, some 450 government projects, schemes, and institutions worth hundreds of billions of rupees carried the names of members of the Gandhi family. From breakfast programmes for the poor to the national nursery scheme for children, from drinking-water projects in rural India to food-security missions, from public housing to roads, buildings, universities, airports, national parks, sanctuaries, sports stadiums, sporting championships, museums, and even neighbourhoods—almost everything of any value in India bore the name of one family. You could go for a stroll in Mumbai's 'Sanjay Gandhi National Park' and drink milk bottled by the 'Indira Gandhi Calf-Rearing Scheme'.[21]

'Our economy may increasingly be dynamic, but our moral universe seems to be shrinking,' Sonia bemoaned at the 'Indira Gandhi Conference' in 2010.[22] Two years after her high-minded speech on the ravages of corruption, Ashok Khemka, a senior civil servant with a hard-earned reputation for integrity, was banished by the government to some barren district days after ordering a probe into the land dealings of Sonia's son-in-law, Robert Vadra. Khemka—who found the whole affair 'demoralising [and] dehumanising'—had failed to grasp that, in the universe run by Congress, certain areas were no-go.[23] And five years before Khemka became persona non grata, India's premier investigative agency, the CBI, had allowed Ottavio Quattrocchi—an Italian businessman long wanted in relation to the Bofors scam that had brought down Rajiv years ago—to escape extradition from Argentina, before dropping the case altogether.[24]

Despite retaining the worst habits of her in-laws' family, Sonia was also a figure of deep Nehruvian convictions and Indira-like political savvy. It is because of her that the government enacted landmark legislation enshrining rights to information, work, and education. And it is she, the conscience of Congress, who held the coalition together. Her authority meant that, in spite of her decision to remain outside the cabinet, her constant supervision was indispensable to the survival of the government.

In 2011, she briefly marooned herself in secrecy to receive treatment for an undisclosed ailment at a cancer institute in New York. This was the moment when the growing anger against corruption erupted into a massive protest in Delhi. It was an urban explosion, lit by the frustrations of the middle class, and covered extensively by the media that catered to it and functioned as its bullhorn. Calling the movement India's own 'Arab Spring' was a measure of the vanity of its organisers: their predicament was very far removed from the plight of the Tunisians under Ben Ali or, for that matter, the suffering of Indian tribals under Manmohan Singh.

The figure who gave the movement wings was a seventy-four-year-old former soldier called Kisan Baburao 'Anna' Hazare. The old man went on a hunger strike for ten days and threatened to starve himself to death if an anti-corruption bill drafted by his team was not voted post-haste into law by parliament. The law would create an anti-corruption agency, Jan Lokpal—a supra-constitutional super-committee of eleven citizens vested with sweeping powers over the executive, legislature, and judiciary. India's expanding middle class, exhausted by the slow-moving democratic politics of the country at large that threatened to retard its own rapid economic progress under Singh, passionately backed it. Their grievance had merit. Yet questions abounded about the wisdom of Hazare's demand. Hazare and his associates—who branded themselves 'Team Anna'—were easily exasperated by scrutiny, however. Invited by the government to talk, their side of the negotiation amounted to a reiteration of their original demand: if you don't pass our plan into law, Anna will kill himself. How about we ask a parliamentary standing committee to examine it, proposed the government. Hazare will die if you do, replied Team Anna. In desperation, the government made a counter offer: we'll try to pass the bill, but how about we make some changes: keep parliament, which is the elected sovereign of India, outside the scope of Jan Lokpal? Anna will die, came the reply.

Unanswerable to parliament, above the Constitution, beyond the traditional checks and balances of democracy, and its incorruptibility apparently assured because its functionaries were to be drawn primarily from a pool of distinguished prize winners, Jan Lokpal as devised by Team Anna was a crystallisation of the emergent Indian middle class's yearning for a benign dictatorship. Coming on the heels of what then looked like pro-democratic revolutions in the Arab world, the assault on democracy in Delhi seemed strange. But there was an internal rationale to this clamour for authoritarianism. The Indian middle class experienced democracy primarily as an impediment to its progress. Democracy spared them the ignominy endured by people in nearby dictatorships and gave them bragging rights in other third-world countries. But it did not enhance their standard of living. They worked hard, eschewed politics, and retreated into a private world of their own. Recession of the government in the 1990s was the cause of their emergence as a globally potent consumer class in the twenty-first century. Now they had money, influence, and power. They mattered. And this agitation was the first major national platform that brought them together. Its purpose, unsurprisingly, was to insulate governance from the commotions of democracy. What it demanded of the state was disciplined expediency—no matter the cost.

The politician who typified the style of efficient governance followers of Hazare yearned for was Narendra Modi. Many of the movement's architects eventually migrated to Modi's camp. It didn't trouble them that he had presided over a pogrom of Muslims in his state only a decade before. Hazare himself, it turned out, was quite a fan of Modi's. And Modi, laying the groundwork for the top job, wrote an open letter to Hazare, telling him that 'a prayer … came quiet [sic] naturally' when he learnt of the old man's fast, and revealing that 'my respect for you is decades old'—dating back to Modi's days as an RSS propagandist.[25] Hazare, cast by the media as an heir to Gandhi, was a crotchety reactionary who, as a self-anointed social reformer in his village, had a record of tying up with barbed wire and administering public floggings to men who flouted his rules against the consumption of alcohol.[26]

Faced with an uprising by the children of his revolution, Singh was flummoxed. The man who had dealt so brutally with tribal populations approached his bourgeois blackmailers in Delhi with a cap in hand. It was too late. The beneficiaries of his reforms had already begun ditching him. The robber barons spawned by Singh, seeing Modi as a more dogged champion of their interests, regrouped in Gujarat.

The free rein Singh allowed capital is today credited with lifting millions of people out of poverty. A more accurate description would be that millions of people moved out of dire poverty and into barely tolerable destitution. Viewed in isolation this is an achievement that justifies every plaudit that has been hurled at Singh. Seen in conjunction with the wealth accumulated during Singh's premiership by the top one per cent—who now own more than half of the national wealth—it is an indictment of his trickle-down economics. So much was generated at the top: India became a trillion-dollar economy in 2007, added 42,000 new members to its ranks of dollar millionaires in 2009, and was home to eight of the world's richest people in 2010.[27] Yet so little seeped down: more than 400 million Indians lived below the international poverty line in 2010, and 46 per cent of all children were malnourished in 2011.[28] In one of his last public speeches, P.V. Narasimha Rao, the man who had plucked Singh out of bureaucratic obscurity, offered a public atonement by bewailing his successors' rush to sell national assets and warned Indians that 'trickle-down economics—the practice of cutting taxes for the rich, hoping it would benefit the poor—does not work'.[29]

Unable to eradicate poverty, Singh's regime attempted to redefine poverty. In 2012, Singh's planning commissioner, Montek

Singh Ahluwalia, pegged the poverty line at 32 rupees per day: anyone earning more than that was not poor. Asked if *he* could survive on 32 rupees a day, Ahluwalia was candid enough to admit he could not.[30]

Embattled and desperate to look tougher than Modi, but unable to arraign the criminal masterminds behind Mumbai, Singh's government executed in 2013 a Kashmiri man who had been on death row for nearly a decade. Singh's cabinet, joined by a callous middle class whose self-restraint vanished in the 1990s, celebrated the pre-dawn legal murder of a defenceless man, whose family was not extended the courtesy of being notified in advance. All the repressed rage of the Prime Minister was directed at a broken inmate cut off from his wife and children for years.[31] That execution will always be a stain on India. It pleased Pakistan, too, because it drove Kashmir further away from India. For three decades, Kashmiri bodies have been the canvas for India's impotent indignation at Pakistan. Singh, snuffing out the life of an Indian Muslim because he could not squeeze the true source of terror, reminded Kashmiris yet again that this was their reward for choosing secular India over Islamic Pakistan in 1947.

In his first speech to parliament in 1991, when he presented his austerity budget, Singh had affirmed that he would 'not in any way renege on our nation's firm and irrevocable commitment to the pursuit of equity and social justice. I promise that in dealing with the people of India I shall be soft hearted.'[32] Two decades on, it fell to the Supreme Court to upbraid him for pushing the poor 'to the wall' and unleashing violence in the countryside with 'predatory forms of capitalism, supported by the State'.[33]

Not since the British barrister Cyril Radcliffe was flown to Delhi from London in 1947 to redraw the subcontinent's map had India's fate been thrust into the hands of a man so totally isolated from its people. And there was something of a reprise of 1947 in the way Singh's stewardship was portrayed during his first term. Those who profited from his reforms praised him—as the British once praised the officials who oversaw the dissolution of the Indian empire—as wise, thoughtful, visionary, compassionate. An army of intellectuals rose up to defend him and vilify his critics; the victims of his reforms were airbrushed out of the picture almost entirely.

Singh's reign was an epoch of such discombobulating paradox that it could induce vertigo in anyone attempting to make sense of it. All around you was evidence of epic social upheaval: families wrenched apart, millions migrating from the decaying countryside into expanding slums in the cities, thousands of indebted farmers killing themselves every year, massacres of peaceful protesters demanding land, the torching of villages by government-sanctioned militias, the mass corralling of defenceless tribal populations into pens for refusing to cede their land to mining barons, extra-judicial killings, and rape, plunder, torture, mutilation, and murder of the poor. But open the newspapers or switch on the television, and you saw a nation enjoying the best of times: stories of cricketers being auctioned for millions of dollars, blonde cheerleaders imported from the West shaking their hips at gaudy Indian Premier League events, Western politicians and investors streaming in and out of India, Hollywood celebrities dancing at opulent Indian weddings, Bollywood parties, billionaires' beach soirees, dollar millionaires proliferating, Indian billionaires competing for top spots on the Forbes index of the global rich. It was an age of audacious gaslighting by the powers-that-be and their minions among the opinion-formers. India, under its first unelected and unaccountable technocrat Prime Minister, degenerated into what the Princeton economist Atul Kohli called a 'two-track democracy', where 'common people are only needed at the time of elections, and then it is best that they all go home, forget politics, and let the "rational" elite quietly run a pro-business show'.[34] 'Growth', accruing to the few, was the principal metric by which the government's performance—and the nation's worth—were judged:

whether or not its proceeds percolated down to the many was an afterthought at best.

In his second term, abandoned by his flock of fickle worshippers, Singh took to amplifying his sycophancy—lavishing praise on Rahul Gandhi, pleading with him to join the cabinet, telling the press about the books recommended to him by the backbencher. But Congress sidelined Singh just as briskly as it had drafted him into service. Against Modi went up the latest scion of the Nehru-Gandhi dynasty.

In his last press conference—his third in the decade that he was Prime Minister—Singh attempted to make a case for himself. It was not going to be possible. So he mumbled inaudibly: 'History will judge me kindly.' Substantial portions of the countryside were by then firmly in the grip of Maoist insurgents. Rural India remained a hellishly violent place. Urban India was a theatre of hideous inequality. India's relationship with the US, so highly prized by Singh, had suddenly deteriorated over a diplomatic spat. In the east, the Chinese continued freely to encroach on Indian territory. To the west, the malign men who had directed the assault on Mumbai were openly inciting terror against India. At home, Hindu nationalists stood poised to seize the reins.

The once glittering citadels of Congress power in the capital looked drained of colour and life in the summer of 2014. They were like the deserted palaces of Shah Reza Pehlavi just before the Ayatollah Khomeini glided into Tehran.

PART TWO

INDIA UNDER NARENDRA MODI

5

CULT

Like all the moral pygmies, I praised in vain,
The ever greatest clown—The Leader, born-again.
And bending halfway down, I kissed his ass ...
May long you live, Beloved Nicholas!

Adrian Paunescu[1]

There wasn't a shadow of resistance as Narendra Modi stormed Delhi in the summer of 2014. After six decades of faltering secularism, India yielded spectacularly to the Hindu nationalist insurgency. Congress was wiped out. The BJP had an absolute majority in parliament for the first time. Modi's triumph shattered a thirty-year-long spell of rule by coalition: the last time a lone party was hoisted into power was in 1984, when most Indians alive in 2014 hadn't attained voting age. Modi's achievement was of an epoch-making magnitude. It heralded, in the words of a former adviser to Singh, the birth of a 'second republic'.[2] He meant that the India founded in 1947 by Congress was dead, and now Modi, who had drained his youth propagandising for the RSS, would wield the largest democratic mandate in more than a generation to recast the Republic in the mould of his ideology. Who was going to restrain him?

Modi appeared invincible even before he entered office, the most powerful Indian politician since Indira Gandhi.

At a meeting of Congress weeks before the vote, a senior leader of the party, a Cambridge-educated Brahmin and stand-ard-bearer of Indian secularism, had declared with a touch of hubris: 'Narendra Modi will never become the Prime Minister. But if he wants to serve tea here, we will find a place for him.'[3] Modi was the hand grenade hurled by all those who had been sneered at, stamped upon, marginalised, subjected to cultural condescension and objectified for anthropological amusement by the preening cast of English-speaking elites fostered by India's venal secular establishment. The mood in Delhi was euphoric as he took the oath of office. People victimised by Old India saw him as one of their own: for some, an agent of their hopes; for others, an embodiment of their rage.

Modi was born in 1950 to a lower-caste family of Hindu Gujaratis. His mother cleaned dishes. His father hawked tea at the local railway station. It was in the training camps of the RSS—which introduced volunteers to the vast pantheon of vil-lains who had plundered and emasculated India down the ages, and exhorted them to shed their Hindu impotence—that Modi's political and spiritual awakening occurred. The effect on his young mind was so overpowering that, by his early twenties, having attempted nothing else in life, Modi adopted the RSS as his family, abandoned his wife and mother, and wandered through India as a catechist of the Hindu nationalist cause.

His glacial progression up the ranks of the RSS paralleled the gradual collapse of the edifice bequeathed by Nehru. By 2001, he had spent close to a decade in Delhi. His impressive titles and heavy responsibilities—general secretary of the party, the link between the BJP and the RSS, responsible for campaigns in a clutch of northern states—were only partly a reflection of his outstanding skills as an organiser. The principal reason for keep-ing him in Delhi was to keep him *out* of Gujarat. The BJP's hold on that state, a reliable bastion of middle-class Hindu nationalism, began slipping in the 1990s under the strain of internal factionalism. Modi, pitting one side against the other, was seen to be aggravating the schisms. So he was brought to the capital and distracted with other duties.[4] In 2001, a massive earthquake in Gujarat opened up the path for his return. He borrowed a plane from an industrialist and landed on the scene of devastation before the state's chief minister, Keshubhai Patel, could make it. It was a finely calibrated move. Modi did not appear insubordinate; Patel looked incompetent, which he was.[5]

In early October, Prime Minister Atal Bihari Vajpayee summoned Modi to his residence and offered him Patel's job. Modi—according to his version of events—turned down the offer. 'That is not my work. I've been away from Gujarat for six long years,' he claims to have protested to Vajpayee. In reality, Modi had spent the preceding months traducing his rival.[6] L.K. Advani, the deputy prime minister who represented Gujarat's capital in parliament, supported Modi. The RSS wanted him in Gujarat. Days later, he was sworn in as the state's chief minister. It was his first job in elective politics. He was not expected to last long. Then, four months after his arrival, a train carrying Hindu pilgrims from the site of the demolished Babri mosque to Gujarat was set on fire. Fifty-eight charred bodies of Hindu passengers were recovered.

Before the cause of the arson could be ascertained, Modi called it the work of Islamist terrorists. A pogrom of Muslims— one of the worst episodes of communal bloodletting—ensued. In one mixed neighbourhood, a mob of 5,000 Hindus meticulously worked its way through a slum: ninety-seven Muslims were hacked to death and a mosque was blown up with liquefied petroleum gas before they called it a day. Across the road from the scene of carnage stood a reserve police quarters. No one lifted a finger.[7] And nobody was immune from the terror. When a former member of parliament, Ehsan Jafri, was found to be sheltering 250 members of his community, he was dragged out of his house by a mob of Hindus and sliced open with swords and torched alive. Jafri had spent the day making desperate calls to Modi's office. The deputy prime minister, the most extreme face of Hindu nationalism before Modi appeared on the scene, reached out to his protégé on Jafri's behalf. No help was sent. Sixty-nine people seeking refuge inside Jafri's house were killed over seven hours.[8]

The lives of at least a thousand Muslims, by a conservative estimate, were taken on Modi's watch in 2002. Vajpayee, at the head of a coalition of nearly two dozen parties, came under intense pressure to sack him. The RSS, overjoyed by Modi's refusal to express contrition, overruled the Prime Minister. (Vajpayee is posthumously remembered as a 'moderate' by Indian liberals. Their minds have already expunged the inconvenient memory of his first major public address after the worst anti-Muslim violence in decades, in which, instead of rebuking Modi, he lashed out at the victims, telling a crowd in Goa that Muslims 'are not interested in living in peace'.)[9] A special investigative team constituted by the Supreme Court did not find adequate evidence of Modi's complicity in the violence. But of incompetence there could be no question: Modi failed in every respect. Was he remorseful? Yes, he told a foreign reporter: he wished he had managed the media better.[10]

The riots made Modi a reviled figure outside Gujarat: liberal Indians likened him to Hitler, the United States denied him a visa, and Britain and the European Union boycotted him. They galvanised the opposition and drew phalanxes of anti-BJP activists to Gujarat. Modi survived. 'Skilfully wading his way through the onslaught of a massive slander campaign,' he 'dealt a convincing and crushing defeat to the principal opposition party, the magnitude of which stunned friends and foes alike.' So says his official profile published by the Gujarat government after the state elections following the bloodshed that returned him to power.[11] Effaced from that effusive panegyric is the labour of the thousands of RSS volunteers, party workers, and veteran leaders who toiled for Modi. The austere martinets of the RSS could not have anticipated, when they deployed the sinews of Hindutva in service of Modi, that their notoriously collectivist movement was incubating the most potent personality cult since Indira Gandhi.

'Popular and progressive', 'tech-savvy and a true democrat in every sense of the word', Modi was venerated by the government's copywriters as a 'youthful and energetic leader with innovative thoughts', 'able and visionary', a 'deft negotiator' engaged 'effectively, substantially, significantly, transparently and convincingly' in improving the lives of Gujaratis, and receiving, in return, 'the love and affection' of 'people from villages and cities … belonging to every faith and religion and every economic strata of the society'. These claims were the product not so much of a leap of the imagination as a flight of fancy. Support for Modi was concentrated in two constituencies: religious fanatics itching for the overthrow of the secular state, and free-marketeers hankering for a powerful pro-business leader.

Modi, in many ways, personified the stock provincial yokel India's metropolitan elites both feared and belittled. They were accustomed to crushing people like him. But Modi's faith made him unassailable. He was not intimidated by those who looked down on him. He knew they were hollow poseurs. In 2003, when leaders of the Confederation of Indian Industry, the preeminent lobbying arm of the nation's proliferating plutocrats, invited him to Delhi and subjected him to hours of invective for his handling of the violence in Gujarat, Modi was unfazed. He dismissed them as a pack of 'pseudo-secularists', went back to his state, and blessed the formation of a rival pro-Modi body of Gujarati industrialists. The CII scrambled to deliver an 'unconditional apology' to Modi for 'hurting' his feelings. Modi did not apologise for his beliefs. He exposed the moral vacuity of those who had denounced them. And having chastened the super-rich, he proceeded to forge a symbiotic relationship with them. Big business thereafter received a bespoke service from the chief minister of Gujarat: permissions were expedited, lands cleared, bureaucratic hurdles eliminated, and taxes waived. Modi was recompensed for his favours with lavish praise from captains of what the press adoringly called 'India Inc.', as the beneficiaries of economic liberalisation—a measure advanced partly as an *antidote* to religious extremism—lined up to deodorise the reputation of the most unbending *trafficker* of religious extremism.

The interests of big business and bigotry fused and became indistinguishable in the 'decisive' personality of Modi. It was at a meeting organised by the Gujarat Chamber of Commerce and Industry that Modi tested his most sinister sectarian dog-whistle in the run-up to the 2007 state elections. Responding to the outcry generated in India by the extra-judicial execution of a Muslim man in police custody in Gujarat, Modi asked his wealthy hosts: 'If AK-57 [sic] rifles are found at the residence of a person ... you tell me what I should do: should I not kill them?' The audience shrieked: 'Kill them! Kill them!'[12] This was the New India, where possession of big cars, higher incomes, modern gadgets did not bury latent murderous impulses; it disinterred them.

Newspapers joined in the act, assailing readers in earnest tones with fables about Modi's childhood. One story in the *Times of India* revealed how, as a boy, Modi swam in waters infested with crocodiles and even brought home a baby crocodile. Another published, without a hint of scepticism or irony, Modi's claim that he could 'digest any kind of poison'.[13] The RSS, alarmed by the personalisation of power, stayed away from the 2007 election. This suited Modi well. He had no opponents left in Gujarat. The one man who challenged him was Haren Pandya. A charismatic Brahmin with a storied RSS pedigree, Pandya dissented from the chief minister in 2002 as Gujarat burned, and deposed before a fact-finding mission. Modi's office ordered the state's intelligence director to keep an eye on the renegade. Pandya was shot dead one morning in 2003.[14] A group of Muslims was later picked up, charged with Pandya's murder, and thrown in jail. Nearly a decade later, the High Court of Gujarat acquitted all of them.[15] But the question of who killed Pandya remains unresolved to this day. Modi's Gujarat, like Putin's Russia, was a place where circumstances fell into the habit of becoming mysterious when it came to the departure of the leader's enemies.

Amit Shah, Modi's closest confidant and dreaded enforcer, was in 2010 charged with involvement in an extortion racket and prohibited from entering Gujarat.[16] As Modi's home minister, responsible for the state's security, Shah was taped instructing the police repeatedly to stalk a woman with whom his boss—'Sahib'—had apparently become besotted.[17] Shah was appointed manager of Modi's prime ministerial campaign, before being inaugurated as the national president of the BJP and then promoted in 2019 to the job of home minister. The Supreme Court justice who exonerated Shah was made governor of Kerala on retirement—the first time in India's history that a retired chief justice was offered a sinecure of such constitutional significance.[18]

None of this seemed to trouble the tycoons being toasted in Delhi and Davos. They chanted the virtues of democracy abroad while abetting its subversion at home. Their embrace of Gujarat's chief minister tightened after Modi's victory in 2007. Barred from entering the United States, Modi hired an American PR firm, APCO Worldwide, to deterge his image.[19] The number of investors, diplomats, politicians, and public intellectuals making the pilgrimage to Gandhinagar, the capital of Gujarat where Modi held a biannual business summit, multiplied over the next five years. By 2012, Gujarat received almost a trillion dollars in investment pledges. Only a fraction of this figure trickled into the state, but the legend of Modi was now firmly in place, burnished by the boundless adulation heaped on him by business leaders. In actuality, Gujarat differed little from the rest of India. It was, as a joint study by the World Bank and the Massachusetts Institute of Technology put it, 'a state with very high economic growth but relatively low mobility'.[20] People in Andhra Pradesh, Maharashtra, and Kerala enjoyed a superior standard of life from birth to death than their Gujarati counterparts. If you were a non-Hindu, if you happened to be a Muslim, Gujarat was a pit of horror and humiliation.

Yet in the minds of many Indians, Gujarat came to be imagined as a subcontinental Shangri La, a land of plenty where roads had no potholes, people enjoyed uninterrupted supply of electricity and clean water, and the government attentively served its citizens. The internet became replete with doctored photos that passed off sparkling foreign ports and roads as Gujarati. Whenever scepticism was expressed about the claims made for Gujarat, Modi complained that Gujaratis were being belittled and insulted. Nobody asked why anyone was obliged to respect the people of a state that sustained in power a man of Modi's record with repeated plebiscitary ratification. Instead, men of influence prayed impatiently for the day when the rest of India would come to resemble Gujarat. If only 'India had just five Narendra Modis', proclaimed the editorial pages of the *Financial Express*, the house journal of India Inc., in 2008, 'we would be a great country'.[21]

Billionaires fell over themselves the following year to pronounce Modi the saviour of India. 'I have to say that today there is no state like Gujarat,' Ratan Tata declared in Gandhinagar. 'Under Mr Modi's leadership, Gujarat is head and shoulders above any state.' India's most respected industrialist spoke from personal experience: Modi had cleared lands for Tata's car-manufacturing plant in three days.[22] Anil Ambani, the billionaire businessman based in Mumbai, invited Indians to 'imagine what will happen to the country if [Modi] gets the opportunity to lead it', and offered this wholesome endorsement: 'A person like him should be the next leader of the country.'[23] Three years later, Anil was surpassed by his estranged older brother, Mukesh, who gushed: 'Gujarat is shining like a lamp of gold and the credit goes to the visionary, effective and passionate leadership provided by Narendra Modi. We have a leader here with vision and determination to translate this vision into reality.'[24] Anil caught up with Mukesh the following year when he extolled Modi as the 'king of kings' and beckoned his friends to give a standing ovation to him.[25] Parallels for such pageants of obsequious praise by oligarchs cannot be located even in Putin's Russia or Erdogan's Turkey. One has to search diligently in Turkmenistan and Uzbekistan to find close competitors.

By 2013, the final obstacle to his ambitions inside the BJP was his mentor, L.K. Advani. Modi ruthlessly put the old man out of his misery. And as he made the transition from provincial to national leadership in 2013, his effectiveness in detoxifying his brand confirmed him as the most consummate political salesman of his age. The myth that Modi had shed his Hindu-supremacist beliefs became so pervasive that even sceptics were taken in. Ashutosh Varshney of Brown University, 'hearing Narendra Modi's campaign speeches quite regularly', proclaimed weeks before the general elections in 2014 that 'Hindu nationalism has been absent from his speeches'.[26] This verdict was unsupported by facts—but fatalism had by then overtaken the votaries of secularism who, unable to stop Modi, were training themselves to see him as somebody he was not.

The beliefs of the RSS—to establish a Hindu state, to revenge the trauma of Islamic invasions and Partition on the bodies of Indian Muslims, to demote minorities to the status of second-class citizens—were never incidental to Modi's politics. They are what animated Modi's politics. He gave up his family for them. He wandered around India for three decades, living out of a suitcase, in their service. An interview he gave to Ashis Nandy, the distinguished social theorist and trained clinical psychologist, during his peripatetic phase reveals how thoroughly he is defined by them. 'Modi,'

Nandy later wrote, 'met virtually all the criteria that psychiatrists, psycho-analysts and psychologists had set up after years of empirical work on the authoritarian personality. He had the same mix of puritanical rigidity, narrowing of emotional life, massive use of the ego defence of projection, denial and

fear of his own passions combined with fantasies of violence—all set within the matrix of clear paranoid and obses-
sive personality traits. I still remember the cool, measured
tone in which he elaborated a theory of cosmic conspiracy
against India that painted every Muslim as a suspected traitor
and a potential terrorist.' Nandy emerged from the interview
'shaken': he 'had met a textbook case of a fascist and a prospective killer, perhaps even a future mass murderer.'[27]

Modi's bloated coterie of supporters, who pitched him as the
saviour of India, appeared untroubled by any of this. If Modi
'doesn't come to power', the Columbia professor Jagdish
Bhagwati told the *Financial Times*, 'I am not optimistic about
[India]'. What about Modi's reputation as an authoritarian?
Well, said Bhagwati, 'if people don't exercise authority, nothing
gets done. You need someone who is providing a vision of some-
where where you can go'. Modi's authoritarianism was not
denied: it was recast as an asset.[28] Gurcharan Das, a private sector executive who reinvented himself in the post-liberalisation
years as a public intellectual, called on voters to concentrate on
Modi's 'economic agenda'. He acknowledged matter-of-factly
the risk inherent in electing Modi to high office, but followed it
up with the warning that *not* voting for Modi would entail an
even 'greater risk', before castigating all 'those who place secularism' above economic growth as 'wrong and elitist'.[29]

The phrase 'useful idiots', suggesting unwitting dupes, doesn't
do justice to these cheerleaders. Das and Bhagwati numbered
among the wilful enablers of the Hindu nationalist project:
well-heeled intellectuals aware of the sectarian poison coursing
through Modi's veins but willing nonetheless to make, as Das
candidly admitted, 'a trade-off in values'. The mention of
2002, already fading from memory, provoked furious eye-rolling.
The final humiliation for the survivors of the Gujarat violence,
dispossessed and displaced as a result of Modi's incompetence
(if not complicity), was the lionisation of Modi as the competent
and compassionate choice. The blood of Muslims spilled with

impunity under Modi only a decade before was shrugged off as though it were ancient history by ideologues who never tired of complaining about the crimes committed by Muslim marauders centuries ago.

On the campaign, Modi conjured up a picture of a corruption-free India and a Congress-free India—the two had become interchangeable in voters' minds—and promised 'good days': twenty million jobs every year, repatriation of trillions of rupees stashed illegally in the vaults of Swiss banks to be distributed equally among Indians, dozens of Singapore-like 'smart cities', a sparkling clean Ganges, a muscular foreign policy. His campaign became a capsule of the India he promised to bring into existence. His chief strategist, Amit Shah, used religion to mobilise voters.[30] Modi himself made dog-whistles about 'pink revolution', a reference to the rising export of beef under Congress.[31] But the mode of transmitting incitement was high-tech: in villages without electricity or running water his team entranced voters by beaming his speeches live with 3D holographic projectors imported at astronomical cost from London. The total money spent on the election was US$5 billion, the second most expensive election in the world. When the votes were counted that summer, Modi and his party surpassed the most bullish predictions. The BJP won 282 seats in the 543-seat lower house of parliament. Congress scraped forty-four seats: an irrelevance in parliament.

Before Modi's rise, supporters of Hindu nationalism in the media, civil service, academia, and the professions, bereft of historical icons identifiable with their cause, cut rather forlorn figures. Their plight was doubly hopeless because the characters venerated in the swamp of Hindutva were, with exceedingly rare exceptions, men who had collaborated with the British, eulogised Hitler, peddled race myths borrowed from the Nazis, rationalised the Holocaust of the Jews in Europe, baited Muslims and Christians at home, and done nothing negligible towards the liberation of India. The national creed fostered by

Congress did not in any case have room for non-Congress (and, later, non-Nehru–Gandhi) heroes.

Modi has sought to correct this imbalance since coming to power. He has showered posthumous honours on a raft of individuals overlooked, for good reason, by Congress. As the first Hindu nationalist to receive an absolute majority in parliament, he has decided to erect himself as the towering totem of the Hindu *rashtra* he has set about constructing on the ruins of the secular state. His ambition is to lodge himself in the national consciousness as a personage on a par with Nehru and even Gandhi, the twin emblems of secular nationalism. It was not by accident that Gandhi vanished in 2017 from the calendars published by the governmental commission that oversees the production of hand-spun cloth and Modi, posing beatifically beside the *charkha*, Gandhi's spinning wheel, appeared in his place as the new father of the nation.[32]

It was this very need to supplant Gandhi—in whose honour Desmond Tutu and Shirin Ebadi, Nobel Peace Prize winners both, successfully lobbied the United Nations in 2007 to declare 2 October as the International Day of Non-Violence—that prompted Modi to press for a similar global day for yoga. The Prime Minister, having long promoted himself as a devoted practitioner of yoga, recognised that such a day, in addition to being a minor soft-power coup for India, would provide a platform for him to cast himself as a sagely figure on the international stage. Since 2015, when the UN, yielding to intense lobbying by India's diplomatic missions across the world, set aside 21 June as the International Yoga Day, Modi has set himself up as the global mascot of yoga. The late-Oscar Wilde paunch undulating under the Prime Minister's flamboyant 'Modi jackets'—Hindu nationalism's sartorial rejoinder to the muted Nehru jacket—has always been difficult to reconcile with Modi's boasts about his pre-dawn workout routine. But nobody can deny the tremendous energy exerted by the government machinery in generating slick photo-ops for the Prime Minister every year on 21 June, when he, draped in white, performs a series of unchallenging asanas.

Modi's zealous itch to upstage Nehru, whose birth anniversary is celebrated in India as Children's Day, led him to usurp Teachers' Day—commemorated on 5 September in remembrance of Sarvepalli Radhakrishnan, the formidably educated second president of India—and use it as an occasion to subject young students to prime ministerial prelections via satellite link. What kind of a teacher is Modi? The answer can be detected in the directive delivered by the government to schools across India: 'Attendance is compulsory,' it warned pupils, 'and strict action will be taken against absentees.'[33] The bearded, bespectacled demagogue, who once labelled the crowded refugee camps sheltering the Muslims driven out from their homes by his own murderous acolytes as 'child producing centres',[34] has thus infiltrated the minds of millions of young people in the garb of an avuncular counsellor. In 2018, he published *Exam Warriors*, 'an inspiring book for the youth' marketed by Penguin Random House as 'a friend not only in acing exams but also in facing life'.[35]

One of the troubles with this new avatar of Modi's is that nobody has the slightest acquaintance with his higher educational record. A university degree is of course not a necessary condition of statesmanship. Lincoln, Washington, Truman did not graduate; Jim Callaghan and John Major were school-leavers. Unlike the many leaders who never saw the inside of a university, however, Modi goes to great lengths to conceal the truth. The prime minister claims to have a distance-learning bachelor's degree in political science from Delhi University. But the certificate he released after immense pressure was brought to bear on his office is riddled with discrepancies. Delhi University, rather than clarify facts, rushed to protect him.[36] The information commissioner who directed the university to make the disclosures was sacked from his job.[37] Modi's degrees are immaterial to his job-performance, even if his party, which derided Sonia Gandhi as a graduate of a 'language shop' in Cambridge, has a different standard for opposition politicians. Yet the fact that he has not been forthcoming on this subject, has attempted to dodge it, bespeaks his deep need for validation ever since he became Prime Minister. He wants the very people he despises not only to kneel before his power but also to acknowledge him as a man of intellectual gravitas: a strongman and a savant. When Barack Obama visited India in 2015, Modi instructed his officials to publish a book of his dialogue with the American president—the Hindu-nationalist counterpart to the volumes of Nehru's correspondence with foreign leaders.[38]

The Prime Minister has held meticulously choreographed public meetings with members of the Indian diaspora in almost every foreign capital he has visited since taking office. He even stole time from official business during a visit to London in the summer of 2018 to be interviewed by an ingratiating former copywriter in front of a handpicked group of worshippers. The audience at all such meetings is made up mostly of Hindus who, having long ago discarded their Indian passports, search for redemption from their diminished status as immigrant minorities in the shade of Modi's strongman leadership. These rallies in the first world—London's Wembley Stadium, New York's Madison Square Gardens—are adduced as proof at home of the Prime Minister's wild popularity abroad.

India, notoriously xenolatrous, has long had a habit of being swayed by the seal of first-world approval. Modi, despite being a nativist, yearns for acceptance in the West. This explains why, while most Indian journalists have been treated with contempt by the Prime Minister and his supporters—anybody insufficiently deferential to their leader is branded a 'presstitute'—the two men to whom Modi has granted the deepest access to date, Andy Marino and Lance Price, are both foreigners. Marino, a little-known British author with a doctorate in English literature, produced a 'political biography' of Modi in 2014 after engaging in what he called 'voluminous' conversations with its subject.[39] The objectiveness of Marino's output can be judged from the fact that functionaries of the BJP delivered copies of it to foreign reporters. Amy Kazmin of the *Financial Times* described the book as a 'grown-up version of *Bal Narendra* ... a comic book recently published to demonstrate how the BJP leader was displaying innate leadership skills even as a young boy'.[40] Released just before the elections, the book did not find a foreign publisher and could not succeed in sanitising Modi.

So there followed a second attempt.

Lance Price's interest in Modi was puzzling—not only to political mavens in India but also to journalists in England. *The Modi Effect*, Price's 2015 pamphlet, assures readers that the Indian Prime Minister has cast off his ideological gear and portrays him as an inspired paladin committed to governing as an inclusive technocrat. The work was clearly intended for a foreign audience. But what had drawn its author, an erstwhile New Labour apparatchik who co-ordinated Tony Blair's successful general election campaign in 2001, to the Indian Prime Minister—and how did he succeed in gaining admission to the impenetrably secretive inner world of Modi? Price, claiming he had been following the Indian elections from Europe, skirted such questions in interviews with Indian media. Then, several months after the book's publication, Francis Elliott, the political editor of the *Times*, reported that Price was 'paid an undisclosed sum' for his effort. 'Price has admitted he had never heard of Mr Modi,' Elliott wrote, 'until he was approached by one of the Indian Prime Minister's associates.' The pathetic defence offered by Price's publisher, Hodder & Stoughton, to the *Times*'s expose—'No one, including Narendra Modi, had any right of approval over the book'—far from exonerating the book's author only confirmed the thoroughness of the book's subject: *The Modi Effect*'s genesis appears so expertly to have been managed that approval of its final content was in all likelihood regarded as surplus to requirements.[41]

At home, following the precedent established by Indira Gandhi, Modi has deployed the state broadcaster to expand his reach. All India Radio hosts a monthly address by Modi in which the Prime Minister passes himself off as a profound philosopher and a gentle friend. The broadcast is translated and aired in multiple languages.[42] Outside the studio, an organised digital army of volunteers and keyboard warriors on the ruling party's payroll savages the Prime Minister's critics and pushes lies about his accomplishments.[43] It is not easy to discern the truth in Modi's India. Even the official spokeswoman of the BJP was caught spreading the lie that India's national anthem had been 'adjudged' by UNESCO as the 'best anthem in the world'. In 2015, the government's Press Information Bureau published a doctored photo of Modi surveying post-flood damage in Tamil Nadu. Two years later, a report of the ministry of home affairs carried an arresting photo above the caption: 'floodlighting along the border.' Illuminating India's borders is a supremely strenuous job: how did Modi do it in three years? On closer examination, the picture turned out to be of an island-border between Spain and Morocco. But the lie could not be recalled. It had already made its way into millions of WhatsApp accounts.

WhatsApp, the free smartphone messaging application owned by Facebook, is now the principal medium of political propaganda in India—and the innumerable groups on it are clogged with countless memes, composed almost entirely of lies, glorifying the Prime Minister and demonising minorities.[44] One meme, for instance, shows Barack Obama and his aides riveted to a television screen in the White House playing Modi's speech. 'Congratulations to all of us,' the text of another viral meme, under a picture of Modi at his desk, reads: 'Our PM Narendra D. Modi is now declared as the BEST PM OF THE WORLD by Unesco. Kindly share this. Very proud to be an Indian.' It made its way into my own phone, sent by a friendly acquaintance who supports Modi. Since then I have seen numerous such memes and videos which claim to expose the Muslim roots of the Nehru dynasty. There was a time when it was possible to say, *So what if the Nehrus are Muslim?* In the age of Modi, such lies function as a means to make secularists part from their own faith. To argue that the Nehrus are Hindu is to meet the Hindu bigot halfway. And to wrestle in the morass of Hindutva is to surrender, without even knowing it, to its terms of combat, which hold membership of the majority faith as the non-negotiable criterion for high office in India.

Unlike most Indian political parties, the BJP has traditionally been a democratic institution. There is nepotism, but the party is not owned by a dynasty. In theory, anyone, so long as she or he subscribed to the sectarian ideology of the party, could rise to the very top of the organisation. Modi's most spectacular achievement has been the Congressisation of the BJP. Obeisance to him has become the norm in a party that, for all its repugnance, hoisted the son of a lower-caste tea-seller from provincial India into the country's highest political office.

The cabinet functions as a sycophantic court. Leaders across the country have been reduced to fawning courtiers. The late Sushma Swaraj, the minister for foreign affairs until May 2019, declaimed in parliament in 2017 that Modi, unlike that self-serving Nehru, had 'brought respect to the whole of India' with his jamborees in foreign capitals.[45] Swaraj, once viewed as a future Prime Minister, was being modest compared to her cabinet colleague (and, between 2017 and 2022, India's vice-president) Venkiah Naidu who, in March 2016, moved a resolution exalting Modi as 'god's gift for India' and 'the messiah of the poor' whose greatness was recognised with a place on *Time* magazine's list of the world's most influential leaders and a wax statue at 'London's Madame Tussauds'.[46] Naidu's encomium, illustrating yet again the extent to which Hindu nativists crave Western approval, was a mere echo of Shivraj Singh Chouhan, the chief minister of Madhya Pradesh, who, a few weeks before Naidu's resolution, told a crowd: 'Wherever in the world he goes, people chant "Modi! Modi!" He is god's divine gift to India.'

Neither, however, could compete with Kiren Rijiju, a cherubic minister from eastern India, who hailed the 'Modi Era' as the glorious consummation of a 500-year-old prophecy. 'French prophet Nostradamus wrote that from 2014 to 2026, a man will lead India, whom initially, people will hate but after that people will love him so much that he will be engaged in changing the country's plight and direction,' Rijiju wrote in a Facebook post on 17 March 2016. 'This was predicted in the year 1555. A middle aged superpower administrator will bring golden age not only in India but on the entire world. Under his leadership India will not only just become the Global Master, but many countries will also come into the shelter of India.'[47]

The BJP has acquiesced in Modi's project to manufacture a post-secular heritage centred upon himself. In 2015, the party installed thousands of 'selfie booths' in Delhi. People could wander into them and have their picture taken next to a life-like smiling face of Modi created using, the party boasted, 'augmented reality'. (Modi seldom smiles in pictures unless he is posing with an important foreigner.) The booths didn't catch on.[48] But the Prime Minister more than made up for it: according to the government's own figures, Modi has spent nearly half a billion pounds of public money on publicity since taking office. The expense has been justified on the grounds that it was incurred to raise awareness of government programmes, but nobody has yet discovered a scheme, small or large, that was rolled out without first being glazed with the Prime Minister's face.

In the summer of 2018, a lavishly produced thirty-minute biopic of the Prime Minister's childhood, *Chalo Jeete Hain*, was broadcast on television. The film gives Modi's early years a saintly gloss: the future premier is shown as an enlightened child, a modern avatar of Siddhartha, consumed with an altruistic concern for others, relentlessly probing his family, friends, strangers, teachers with the same question: *Who do you live for?* So transparently propagandistic is the film that any viewer with a dispassionate vein in his body will need a high dose of antiemetic to survive it. But then, so absolute has Modi's grip on the

BJP grown since he entered the Prime Minister's office that, in the days leading up to the film's premiere, ministers and leaders were wrestling with each other to praise, and to be seen praising, it. To Poonam Mahajan, a member of parliament and a former leader of the BJP's youth wing, *Chalo Jeete Hain* was a 'must watch' film on the 'story of a young Narendra Modi ji who is now selflessly heading the country to new peaks of success'.[49] Suresh Prabhu, the minister for Commerce and Industry during Modi's first term, attested on Twitter to being blown away by the 'childhood of our beloved leader … It is a fantastic film already screened for all MPs … Motivational, inspirational! Triumph of struggle!'[50] Devendra Fadnavis, who until November 2019 was the chief minister of Maharashtra, India's richest state, said watching the film helped him fathom 'how this amazing, humble, visionary personality might've taken shape'.[51] The president of India, the vice-president, and the speaker of parliament—occupants of three of the Republic's highest constitutional offices—and Amit Shah and Mukesh Ambani, among others, attended special screenings of the film over several nights.

That the slavish paeans to Modi are not as lapidary as those woven by generations of Congressmen for the Nehru–Gandhis should not eclipse the more disturbing fact that it has taken Modi only a few years to accomplish what it took Indira nearly a decade to achieve.

For their part, Western leaders, desperate to make up for all those years of high-minded repudiation of Modi, grasped early on the utility of flattery when dealing with him. Britain's David Cameron put an honour guard on for Modi even though Modi is not a head of state. France's François Hollande organised a boat ride on the Seine. And, at a state dinner in Delhi for the American president in 2015, Obama tickled Modi's vanity by retelling the folktales about his 'friend', who 'once survived an attack by a crocodile' and now 'only needed three hours' sleep'.[52] Modi's plump face condensed into an effulgent ball of delighted satisfaction. He was being canonised in real time.

6

CHAOS

Former times had chastised them with whips, but this chastised them with scorpions.

Elizabeth Gaskell, *Mary Barton*

Narendra Modi appeared on television at 8 p.m. on 8 November 2016 and announced that all 500- and 1,000-rupee notes would cease to be legal tender at midnight. The two denominations accounted for 86 per cent of all the currency in circulation. Four hours later, more than seventeen trillion rupees' worth of money—in a country where more than 90 per cent of all transactions are conducted in cash—was rendered worthless. Modi justified his action as a bitter but necessary remedy for the malady of 'black money', and assured Indians that they could exchange the voided notes for new currency until 30 December. Pre-emptively inoculating the measure from criticism, he added a national-security codicil: it would invalidate the vast amounts of counterfeit currency allegedly channelled into the Indian economy by the sponsors of terrorism in Pakistan.

No Pakistani could have engineered the wave of distress that instantly washed over India. Demonetisation, unlike any war or calamity in recent times, exposed people in every corner of India to inexpressible hardship. The only precedent for such all-encompassing agony in India's republican history was Sanjay Gandhi's 'mass sterilisation' campaign. But even then, the terror was largely concentrated in parts of northern India. Modi's madness engulfed the whole country.

Farmers in rural India were left without buyers for their agricultural produce. Patients had no cash with which to pay for medicine. People who moved from the decaying countryside to make a living in India's burgeoning cities—as servants, cooks, cleaners, chauffeurs, construction workers—could not feed themselves or send money to families they had left behind because they did not have bank accounts and could not 'whiten' their 'black' earnings. The bank account-holding urban middle classes were only marginally better off: there was one commercial bank for every 12,500 Indians.[1]

The queues that formed outside India's banks evoked the lines outside the supermarkets in Ceausescu's Romania. Dozens of people died in the long, tense wait to redeem their money. And those who made it to the end discovered that the banks, like the shops in communist Bucharest, were understocked. It hadn't occurred to the man acclaimed as a genius by economic commentators in 2014 to print sufficient quantities of lower-denomination notes in advance. Strained spirits collapsed when it was estimated that it would take up to six months for the presses of the Reserve Bank of India, working non-stop and at full capacity, to replace the abruptly withdrawn notes. The redesigned 2,000-rupee notes that were made available did not fit the existing cash dispensers, and the shortage of low-value notes meant that those in possession of the new currency could not put them to use.[2]

The bodies began piling up.

- On 8 November, a businessman in Uttar Pradesh died of a heart attack shortly after listening to Modi's speech.[3]
- On 9 November, a forty-year-old woman whose life's savings amounted to two thousand rupees died outside a shuttered bank in Captainganj.[4]

- On 10 November, a baby with life-threatening complications in Rajasthan died within hours of its birth because ambulances refused to accept 1,000-rupee notes to transport it to the hospital. The bereaved father, who squandered four hours locating 100-rupee notes, now feared losing his wife to trauma. 'She keeps asking where our son is,' he told the *Indian Express*, 'and I keep telling her he is still at the district hospital undergoing treatment.'[5]
- On 11 November, an elderly man called Karavayya died alone in Srikakulam in Andhra Pradesh. His children, toiling as migrant workers in Hyderabad, could not be with their father in his final days because their savings had suddenly become worthless.[6]
- On 12 November, a forty-five-year-old farmer in the state of Chhattisgarh, overcome by the dread of losing his savings, hanged himself.[7]
- On 13 November, a cashier at the State Bank of India, stressed to breaking point by the surging queues of incensed customers, died of a heart attack.[8]
- On 14 November, an eighteen-month-old girl called Komali died because her parents did not have the legal currency to pay for her prescription. The family's neighbours on the Coromandel coast pooled all their small-denomination notes for Komali's treatment, but there wasn't enough left after the tests to buy medicine. 'Many were willing to help,' Komali's mother told the *Times of India*. 'But none of them had the new currency.'[9]
- On 21 November, a three-year-old girl called Ankita died in a village in Uttar Pradesh as her father queued up to withdraw 2,500 rupees in low-denomination notes from the local bank to pay for her treatment.[10]

Modi, exhibiting the same indifference he displayed when Muslims were butchered in Gujarat in 2002, refused to acknowledge the deaths or give an explanation to parliament. Instead, he rallied believers with a series of indignant speeches

in which he portrayed himself as the true victim of the unspool-
ing horror. Shedding tears, he told the faithful in Goa: 'I know
what kind of powers I have taken on. I am aware they will not
let me live.'[11] Who did he mean by 'they'? Every person who
perished in the chaos inaugurated by demonetisation was a
member of the most trampled-upon layer of Indian society.
The Prime Minister brushed aside their suffering as teething
problems, cast himself as their ally while being the architect of
their misery, blamed the turmoil precipitated by his own fool-
hardy decision on some sinister fifth column lurking within
society, and asserted that stability would be restored in fifty
days' time.

Two years later, the Reserve Bank of India was emphatic:
Modi's note ban was not just a failure. It was the ne plus ultra
of failures. In the annals of disastrous ideas, demonetisation
was the undisputed emperor. It took an entire department of
the central bank, 'working in two shifts under strenuous conditions',[12] almost two years to verify the returned pieces of
annulled notes. At the end of the count, 99.3 per cent of all the
abolished currency—amounting to just over a hundred and
sixty billion pounds[13]—had been turned in. One per cent of
Indians own 53 per cent of the nation's wealth, and illegal
assets are rarely hoarded in the form of cash. So, was the tiny
portion of unreturned notes 'black money', or was it cash
owned by the poor, a vast majority of whom had no bank
accounts or even much knowledge of the banking system and,
therefore, would not have been able to bank it or convert it into
legal tender? And what proportion of Indians owned the cash
that was returned?

These are questions to which the government may never find
definitive answers. What is clear is that Indians in possession of
large sums of cash, whatever its origin, found ingenious ways to
alchemise it. The government allowed up to four thousand
rupees of the abolished currency to be swapped without the
need for paperwork, generating a vast network of 'money

mules' who, for a fee, redeemed large quantities at the rate of one small stack a trip.

The return of the notes meant that Modi's promise of a windfall for the central bank never materialised. It is obliged to pay the bearers of the new promissory notes the value printed on them: collectively, almost the same amount as all the currency that was extinguished. The central bank not only gained nothing from demonetisation. It squandered money on the printing of new notes.

Trust in the banking system has severely been impaired by demonetisation. People have come to regard banks as impersonal, incomprehensible, inaccessible extensions of a capricious state. The popularity of cash, tangible, rose after demonetisation.[14]

As much of the banned currency was being turned in, the original ambitions of the prime minister's policy—eliminating 'black money', flushing out counterfeit currency, and combating terrorism—fell by the wayside. Modi and his acolytes assiduously extemporised fresh alibis. Demonetisation, ceasing to be the antidote for all the ills cited at its rollout, was touted as a trigger for the creation of a 'cashless' economy. Like Chairman Mao exhorting the Chinese to make the Great Leap Forward, Modi took to urging his compatriots to 'go digital'. Without a hint of irony, an ingratiating member of his cabinet called the entire exercise India's own 'cultural revolution'. The upshot of this endeavour to make Indians eschew cash? According to the Reserve Bank, household savings in cash grew, post-demonetisation, to nearly 3 per cent of the national income—the highest in a decade.[15]

Modi' shock-therapy immobilised India's economy in the intervening period. Farmers, operating in a sector maximally reliant on cash, were deprived of seeds and fertiliser as acute shortages of cash choked the demand for existing produce: potatoes, onions, tomatoes stagnated in markets despite a significant drop in prices. Unquantifiable amounts of food rotted away. Six months into demonetisation, growth in manufacturing and transport plummeted, and construction, a major source of employment, posted negative growth.[16] Modi, campaigning for the premiership, had promised to create a hundred million new jobs. A million and a half jobs were *lost* in the first few months after demonetisation. Modi once castigated Manmohan Singh for allegedly slowing down growth at a time when India's was still the fastest growing major economy in the world. In 2017, India ceded that position to China as its output shrank in the first quarter of the year.[17]

More than a hundred Indians, by conservative estimates, lost their lives in the maelstrom provoked by demonetisation.[18] There were those who rationalised away the torment of Indians as, in the phrase deployed by the American economist Jagdish Bhagwati in defence of demonetisation, a 'transition cost'.[19] A few dozen deaths in the journey to a digital economy (even though digitising India's economy was not the original reason for demonetisation) can seem like a reasonable price—if you don't have to pay it. It was possible, therefore, for some to eulogise Modi, despite all the disruption he caused, as a courageous moderniser and argue that the benefits of his action, imperceptible in the present, would accrue to future generations of Indians.

Of course, we can all imagine a prospective scenario in which Modi is retrospectively vindicated. But the defence of the long run is the last refuge, as Eliot's *Felix Holt* says, of those who have abdicated their duty to the 'people who live now and will not be living when the long-run comes'. The futurists neglect, too, the fact that the present which Modi set on fire was already the future of a generation of elderly Indians who, having endured hardships in the preceding decades, had earned the right to a dignified later life.

The last time a monetary decision produced so much tumult in India was in the fourteenth century, when Muhammad bin Tughlaq, the Sultan of Delhi, suddenly replaced gold dinars with copper and brass coins. But when his subjects minted counterfeit coins and devalued the currency, Tughlaq recognised his mistake and hastened to make amends. Tughlaq's name has since become synonymous with stupidity; placed next to Modi, he appears Solomonic.

The Prime Minister has never acknowledged his mistake. In the beginning he put on public spectacles of self-pity and proclaimed the note ban a wild success because respondents to a survey conducted exclusively on his personal smartphone app said so, while the chief of the RSS's labour wing blamed the angry ferment precipitated by demonetisation as the handiwork of 'those who eat beef'.[20] The toast of Davos, reduced to a punchline, attempted to incite mass resentments by claiming to be doing battle with 'those who come from Harvard' on behalf of 'the villagers and labourers working in the field'.[21]

Modi's improvised defences of demonetisation progressively ceased to bear any relation at all to reality. Campaigning in central India in November 2018, he claimed that the note ban had worked as he had intended—a 'proper treatment' for the pestilence of corruption (the slogan about a cashless digital economy had quietly been retired)—and had made it possible for him to channel more money into the 'right schemes for the common man'.[22] He was contradicted the same afternoon by the contents of a report by the agriculture ministry, which detailed the ruin that demonetisation had brought to the lives of 'millions of farmers [who] were unable to get enough cash to buy seeds and fertilisers for their winter crops. Even bigger landlords faced a problem such as paying daily wages to the farmers and purchasing agriculture needs for growing crops'.[23] The Prime Minister was shown to be peddling fables. Within a week, the ministry performed a volte-face, attributing the previously revealed findings to a 'mistake in compilation of data' and filing a revised note that said the exact opposite: demonetisation boosted the sale of seeds and fertilisers and hugely benefited the farmers.

What aggravates the woefulness of all of this, even if we ascribe the purest intentions to Modi, is that none of it need have happened. As the occupant of an office that qualifies him as one of the most powerful men in the world, Modi was in a position to summon any number of experts on the planet to advise him. Deliberation, tempering ruinous impulses by subjecting them to dispassionate scrutiny, is one of the major strengths of democracy. But rewarded throughout his career for functioning like a despot, Modi saw discussion as beneath him. The years of extravagant praise from many corners had obliterated even the residues of humility in him. He bypassed parliament, kept his already enfeebled cabinet in the dark, and delegated the minutiae of a policy with such monumental implications to a Gujarati civil servant with a doctorate in yoga and a record of personal fidelity to Modi.[24]

The 'transformation' Modi was credited with superintending in Gujarat, where he expedited land clearances and permissions for big businesses, bred in him the belief that all that was needed to effect *parivartan*, or change, in India was his species of 'strong' leadership. And he put that belief into action when he moved to Delhi. There is a depressing inevitability to the actions of a man who, fetishised as an audacious decisionmaker when he was chief minister, decided to shatter the earth when he became Prime Minister. Demonetisation, flouting democratic safeguards, reduced a country of 1.3 billion people into a hapless laboratory for the reckless fantasies of a deranged strongman whose self-conceit was bomb-proofed by the adulation of a tiny elite who profited from his actions.

Modi's idealism, lethal to the poor, has always been modulated with realism. Perhaps it is just a coincidence that the largest receipts of cash in Gujarat were registered by a bank whose board numbered Amit Shah, Modi's menacing cup-bearer, among its members.[25] The BJP's income between 2016 and 2017 grew by 81 per cent.[26] Months after demonetisation, Modi removed limits on corporate donations to political parties with statutory modifications so brazen that many dictatorships would not consider them. Congress's increasingly desperate pleas for donations from the general public, however, suggest that India Inc.'s generosity is flowing only in one direction. And it is not by accident that those who most energetically pimped demonetisation when it was first announced happened also to be members of India's post-reform aristocracy.

But the consensus they sought to amplify cracked even as economic growth accelerated. Erstwhile cheerleaders of demonetisation have either suppressed their voices or reassessed their views. In 2017, Jagdish Bhagwati, the most ardent apostle of Modism in international academia, offered the qualification that 'if demonetisation is to be judged narrowly on the basis of the triple rationale originally advanced ... it would at best be unclear if it could be accounted a success'.[27] A year later, Aravind Subramanian, the government's chief economic adviser when demonetisation was launched, decried the policy as a 'massive draconian monetary shock'.[28]

The caution that governed dissent against the Prime Minister was a measure of the distance India had travelled from the very recent past when abhorrence of Modi was a common feature of our public life. So many Indians, revolted by Modi's past, seemed resolute in their opposition to him. The betrayals of Congress made it possible gradually to accept him as a necessary evil. But as the American writer Matthew Scully once asked, when you start with a necessary evil, and the necessity either fades away or is never met, what is left?

7

TERROR

If we do not know how to work properly and run an economy, at least we know how to fight properly.

Slobodan Milosevic

On 28 September 2015, Mohammad Akhlaq, a fifty-year-old farm worker, was dragged out of his house in the town of Dadri, an hour's drive from Delhi, by a crowd of young Hindu men apparently incensed by a rumour that he had slaughtered a calf. They killed Akhlaq by striking him repeatedly with bricks, beat his son to within an inch of his life, assaulted his elderly mother, and attempted to molest his young daughter.[1] Akhlaq's forebears had settled in the village just before the subcontinent's Partition, rejecting, like millions of their co-religionists, the snare of Islamic Pakistan for equal citizenship of a secular state. Seven decades on, the state had a new master, and the young men who burst into Akhlaq's house were enforcing *his* idea of what India ought to be. The new establishment did not mourn the dead man. It supplied alibis for his executioners.

Mahesh Sharma, a local member of parliament and Modi's culture minister at the time, described the savagery as an 'accident'. To the chief minister of the neighbouring state of Haryana, another Hindu nationalist, it all amounted to a 'simple misunderstanding'. Top-tier leaders of the BJP issued posthumous condemnations of Akhlaq for wounding the feelings of Hindus by eating beef. Hindus should not be expected to 'remain silent' when a cow is killed, a parliamentarian in saffron robes told the press. He was 'ready to kill and be killed' for the cow.[2] 'When we hurt people's sentiments,' another leader explained, 'such clashes take place.' If the family consumed beef, the local legislator announced, 'they are also responsible' for what happened to them. The village should be left alone, demanded a party bigwig. 'Fear has been generated with people being threatened with arrests,' he complained, but Hindus were in no mood to 'tolerate harassment' by the authorities.[3] They were in control now. Their Great Leader, lost in deliberate isolation, uttered not a word.

The threat of a mass agitation by Hindu supremacists terrified the local administration—run by a secular party—which dispatched the police to seize the meat in the Akhlaq family's refrigerator and send it away to a lab for tests to determine if it was beef. It was not. But the family could no longer live there. Akhlaq's young son had to undergo two operations on his brain to survive. Journalists who covered his plight were pelted with stones by relatives of the men charged with his father's killing. Akhlaq's oldest son served in the Indian Air Force. His boss, the chief of India's air force, had the family evacuated to an air base. For decades they had coexisted happily with people of other faiths. On Eid, they sent packed meals to Hindu neighbours. They could not fathom why this had happened. 'We were completely taken by surprise,' Akhlaq's brother told the BBC. 'Although it is true that we are the only Muslim family here, we have been living here for four generations and had never faced any issues before.'[4] The village that turned on them in the dead of night had until that moment been their extended family.

Communal prejudice has always existed in India. The room for giving homicidal expression to it has expanded exponentially under Modi. Ninety per cent of all the atrocities committed in the name of religion in the past decade have occurred under his reign.[5] The mood music for the terror has been composed and played by card carriers of Hindu nationalism. The Akhlaqs were not victims of an outburst of rage. They were exhibits in an organised campaign to entrench Hindu supremacy. Modi, who has a long history of singing from the hymn sheet of majoritarian bigotry, has rarely halted to even acknowledge the murders of minorities. Rarer still are instances where he has condemned them. Not once, in fact, has he memorialised, by name, Muslims slain by his fellow travellers. This is not by accident. Barbarity against Muslims is not a digression from his beliefs: it is an affirmation of them. The killers are fulfilling the potential for extreme violence Ashis Nandy once detected in Modi.[6] Their achievements can only be a source of pride, not shame, for the Prime Minister: they are advancing a cause he spent a lifetime championing.

Unable to induce Modi to so much as feign outrage at the slaughter of Muslims, the media advanced an elaborate fiction. 'Modi breaks silence on Dadri lynching'. A variation of that headline appeared on the front page of virtually every major Indian newspaper on 9 October 2015. The problem: he did no such thing. Modi's speech to an election rally in Bihar the previous day—the source of those headlines—did not in fact carry a solitary reference to Akhlaq or Dadri. Instead of the execration of Akhlaq's killers suggested by the newspapers and talking heads on television, Modi's speech contained the blandest of warnings against religious violence—a cursory 'appeal' to Indians to reject 'hate speech' by 'politicians [who] are making irresponsible statements' about the cow 'for political interests'. There are Holocaust deniers who have managed more emphatic denunciations of anti-Semitism.

Far from condemning what happened to Akhlaq, Modi in fact sought to profit from it. Immediately after that much publicised speech which the press painted as his finest hour, he proceeded to milk the cow for political mileage. The devil, he thundered at another rally, had penetrated the soul of a rival secular politician—a member of the same lower caste as the beloved Hindu deity Lord Krishna, protector of cows in religious lore—who had vehemently decried Akhlaq's killing and suggested that many Hindus also ate beef. Modi pounced on that remark, insufficiently deferential to the cow, and traduced his rival as a traitor to his caste's tradition of reverence for cows. 'I come from the land of Gujarat,' he reminded the crowd after whipping it into a religious frenzy, 'where people worship cows.'[7]

The cow is sacred to Hindus. Sectarian strife centred upon it is a recurring motif of recent Indian history. Hindus worship it. Muslims dine on its flesh. Some Dalits scratch a living from selling its hide. The framers of the Indian Constitution were subjected to intense pressure to prohibit its slaughter. They resisted, but then reluctantly, in language that omitted any allusion to religion, inserted a directive—a toothless piece of guidance appended to the Constitution—asking future governments to introduce measures to protect certain breeds of cow. As of 2024, there are only six states out of twenty-eight—accounting roughly for a sixteenth of the union's landmass—where cow slaughter is not in some form proscribed.[8] Buffaloes and bulls, on the other hand, are allowed to be slaughtered: and so many of them are killed annually that the land of the holy cow has been the world's top exporter of beef for many years.

Muslims are the principal, though not the only, stakeholders in the beef trade. In his election rallies, Modi seized on this fact to accuse Congress of incentivising traders of beef—of presiding over a 'pink revolution'—and barked: 'Do you want to support people who want to bring about a pink revolution?'[9] After his victory, in states ruled by his party, the life of a cow has become measurably more valuable than the life of humans of the offending faith. Laws have been amended to enshrine severe punishments for the slaughter of cows. Two years after Modi vacated Gujarat for Delhi, the home minister of his native state boasted that his government had 'equalled the killing of a cow or cow progeny with the killing of a human being'.[10] (This is the state, lest we forget, where Muslims still await justice for the massacres of 2002.) In Modi's India, Muslims accused of harming cows are presumed guilty. The lucky ones are hauled away to prisons. The rest become quarry for hunters licensed by the regime. The Prime Minister, diligently dispensing his deepest condolences via Twitter to victims of tragedies in distant countries, maintains a sociopathic silence on the mounting horrors right under his nose.

The killings multiplied after Modi's speech in Bihar. On the very day the press praised the Prime Minister for breaking his silence, a mob of enraged Hindus in Jammu, sniffing around for culprits after coming upon carcasses of cows in their neighbourhood, flung petrol bombs at the first Muslims they encountered.[11] A few months on, the bodies of a twelve-year-old Muslim boy and a thirty-five-year-old Muslim man—their eyes covered with a cloth, hands tied behind their backs—were found hanging from a tree in Jharkhand. The father of the boy, a cattle trader, witnessed the lynching and heard his son's yelps for help. Paralysed by fear, he remained hidden behind some bushes.[12] The following year, a family of Dalits in Modi's Gujarat was skinning the carcass of a cow—the source of livelihood for many 'outcastes' for centuries—they had purchased. As they were going about their business, upper-caste Hindus appeared on the scene bearing sticks and pipes. Four members of the family were bundled into a car, driven to a nearby town, stripped naked, and paraded through the streets as the cow protectors administered lashes.[13]

The dissolution of caste is a theoretical tenet of Hindu nationalism. In practice, however, Dalits have always been treated as chattel by the movement's upper-caste followers. Democracy enabled Dalits to mobilise and make gains. Their successes, such as they were, bred intense resentments among caste Hindus. And those resentments have found the ideal atmosphere for release under Modi.[14] The violence against Dalits—promising converts for Muslim and Christian missionaries—has at least prompted a display of distress by the Prime Minister.

Muslim suffering has elicited nothing of the kind.

Around the third anniversary of Modi's election, a fifty-five-year-old Muslim dairy farmer in Rajasthan called Pehlu Khan was chased along a motorway by a lynch mob of young Hindus wielding rods. He was beaten and kicked so brutally that he died three days later. The police immediately performed a raft of arrests—not of his killers but of alleged cow smugglers.[15] The half dozen men named by Khan as his attackers just before his death were allowed to walk free in less than six months.[16] Snuff films of Khan's lynching, shot by the hundreds of spectators who relished it live, continue to circulate among Hindu nationalists to this day.

There is a tragic irony to the designation of the cow as the mascot of murderous religious nationalism. Indian zoolatry, often ridiculed in the West, is in fact a measure of the sophistication, not the benightedness, of its cultural traditions. It is anchored in Indian civilisation's profound emotional investment in the non-human world, its reverence for nature, its compassion for living beings. It is these beliefs that account for the historic prevalence of vegetarianism in India and the abhorrence for the taking of life, *any* life. Early European travellers to India were astonished to find a society with a highly developed ethic of non-violence towards animals. Voltaire, Thoreau, Emerson were among the Western thinkers who regarded this aspect of India as the instantiation of humanity at its most virtuous.[17]

And more than a millennium before them, the great Chinese emperor Wu, of the southern Liang dynasty, moved by the example of India, wrote and circulated essays about the exploitation of animals, gave up meat, and exhorted his subjects to cultivate benevolence for other living creatures. Wu was haunted by the life of the Indian emperor Ashoka, who, after ravaging the republic of Kalinga in 261 BCE, had asked in horror:

Is it valour to kill innocent children and women? … One has lost her husband, someone else a father, someone a child, someone an unborn infant … What's this debris of corpses?

Tormented by the memory of Kalinga, Ashoka converted to Buddhism, abjured violence, became a vegetarian, and abolished the slave trade. His royal edicts, the first of their kind, extended the state's protections to animals. Wu and Ashoka did not—could not—actualise their ambition to eliminate the suffering of all living creatures. But by their example they ennobled the idea of mercy towards animals—not as a rejection of human supremacy, but as its highest affirmation. When Muhammad Akbar, the mightiest emperor to rule India since Ashoka, declared plaintively in the sixteenth century that carnivores should 'have satisfied their hunger with my flesh, sparing other living beings', he was voicing an ancient human longing to which India had given the most eloquent expression.[18]

Modi, a vegetarian like Ashoka and Akbar, is a different kind of vegetarian. Before he held high or low political office—in those days of ennui in Delhi when the most exciting event in his calendar was the occasional invitation to appear on television, when he baited minorities, circulated damaging gossip about his political rivals, and scolded journalists concerned about the fate of Indian secularism as peddlers of 'footpath politics', when his clothes were actually cheap and his glasses not designer, when he did not have the means to pass himself off as a philosopher of the human condition—in those days, Modi opined sneeringly to a Muslim journalist: 'people who eat meat have a *different* temperament.'[19]

The self-righteousness that sometimes consumes herbivores mixes in Modi with a sinister contempt for carnivores. And in this there is something of John Oswald about him. A Scottish mercenary dispatched in 1782 by the British to subdue Indians, Oswald defected from his side, lived among Hindu ascetics, took up a diet of vegetables, and wrote one of the first tracts ever in English on the toll of mankind's abuse of animals. The year in which his pamphlet decrying meat-eaters for their 'callous insensibility' was published, Oswald was devising, as a member of the Jacobin Club in France, effective methods for staging wholesale massacres of human beings. His idealistic longing for the liberation of animals generated in him a sadistic craving for human blood. Thomas Paine, alarmed by the young Jacobin's impatience to impale the enemies of the revolution with pikes, chided him: 'Oswald, you have lived so long without tasting flesh, that you now have a most voracious appetite for blood.'[20] Modi's Hindu revolution is devoid of such moderating authority. And with no Paines to temper its Oswalds, with an Oswaldian figure at its head, the Hindu affection for the cow, emanating from a canon of compassion, has dissolved into pure terror against human beings.

As the fantasies of instant prosperity purveyed by Modi unravelled under the burden of his own incompetence, the euphoria of 2014 degenerated into full-blown sectarian hysteria. Voters under the age of thirty—the largest demographic group in India—were mesmerised by Modi's promise of twenty million jobs every year. After coming into office, Modi stamped on their prospects with his shock therapy of demonetisation. According to a 2018 study by the independent Centre for Sustainable Employment, unemployment has been 'the highest seen in India in at least the last 20 years'.[21] An entire generation has missed the tide that may have carried them to a stable, contented future.

Into this crucible of foiled aspirations, Modi tossed a tonsured fireball called Ajay Bisht. The head abbot of a militant monastery, Bisht—who goes by his born-again name, Yogi Adityanath—is an unadulterated bigot. He was one of the first politicians to demand the prosecution of the Akhlaq family. In 2002, he founded a private militia that recruited from the human debris of India's transition from 'socialism' to capitalism—men left behind in the Republic's rush to remake itself—and grew over a decade into an army of more than a quarter million foot soldiers. Bisht enjoined them to claim ten Muslim scalps for every Hindu killed. And if a Muslim should 'take one Hindu girl', he roared at a rally, 'we will take a hundred Muslim girls'.[22] In 2007, he spent nearly two weeks in jail for defying a ban on public gatherings to deliver a speech dripping with sectarian malice. His worldly possessions included a revolver, a rifle, and two luxury cars.[23] And among the litany of criminal cases filed against him over the years were attempted murder, trespassing on burial sites, criminal intimidation, and rioting.[24] This is the character whom Modi installed, in the summer of 2017, as the chief minister of Uttar Pradesh. The largest state in the union, home to more than 200 million people, suddenly found itself placed at the feet of a feral priest enrobed in saffron. Yogi's first order of business was cracking down on Muslim-owned businesses such as abattoirs. 'Humans are important,' he explained a year into his appointment, appalled by the coverage being lavished on the lynchings of Muslims, but 'cows are also important.'[25] Once written off as a fringe figure, Yogi is now a cynosure of the BJP.

The hunting of defenceless minorities has become so normalised under Modi that often there is no spark for violence. The victimisation of Muslims lay simply in the thrill of being vicious. Consider the events over the course of a single month in 2017. On 9 June, a mob of 'educated' Hindus in Delhi nearly lynched a young reporter when they discovered that he was a Muslim from Kashmir. He was so badly bruised that he couldn't move for days.[26] On 19 June, more than a dozen Muslims in central and southern India were arrested and charged with sedition—one of the gravest offences on India's statute books—following complaints from their Hindu neighbours that they had been celebrating Pakistan's win against India in the cricket world cup the previous night.[27] On 22 June, Hindu passengers on a train picked on a group of Muslims, shrieked 'anti-national'—the favourite phrase of Hindu supremacists—into their faces, pulled their beards, and then

stabbed to death Junaid, a sixteen-year-old Muslim boy returning home after shopping for Eid in Delhi.[28] The Great Leader,
touring the United States, took no notice. On the day that
Junaid was knifed, Modi tweeted a snippet from his speech to
expatriate admirers in the United States: 'India is a youthful
nation with youthful dreams and aspirations. It is our constant
endeavour to turn these aspirations into achievements.'[29] Not a
word about the youthful dreams snuffed out by the mob in that
stream of banalities.

The arid hate of Modi's India has desiccated what is perhaps
the most potent remedy for the curse of religious schism:
romantic love that transcends the bounds of religion. Interfaith couples have been exposed to the furies of Hindu men
yelling 'Love Jihad'—a phrase that captures all the psychological dysmorphia of its believers, who say that Muslim men are
buying flashy clothes with cash channelled to them by Islamic
governments, seducing impressionable Hindu women, and
then converting them to Islam. It is an old bugbear, forged in
envy and spite, that has become monstrously invigorated in
Modi's New India. In 2018, a Bangalore-based sales manager
doxxed inter-religious couples, posting on Facebook what he
called 'a list of girls who have become victims of love jihad'.[30]
Muslim men spotted with Hindu women have been brutally
mauled. Muslim–Hindu weddings have been disrupted and
attacked by Hindu gangs and leaders of the ruling party.[31] In
2017, when a groom in Yogi's state was pulled from a court
building where he was to be married and horrifically beaten
the police attempted to intervene.[32] The following year, when a
woman in his bailiwick suspected of having a relationship with
a Muslim man was 'rescued' by Hindu men and handed over
to the authorities, the police filmed themselves physically
assaulting her for choosing a 'mullah' over Hindu men.[33] The
video of the assault joined the library of murder reels whose
most chilling entry was made by a man in Rajasthan, in 2017,
who had his nephew shoot the entire episode. It shows its star,

Shambhulal Regar, sliding up to a Muslim labourer going about his work and plunging a pickaxe in his back. The Muslim man, unaware he is being filmed, falls to the ground, faintly mouthing the words 'I am dead', at which point Regar addresses the camera: 'Jihadis—this is what will happen to you if you spread love jihad in our country.' He then showers his victim with kerosene, throws a match on him, and walks away as flames consume the body.

When Regar was arrested, more than 500 people from across the country donated 300,000 rupees to a fund launched in his name.[34] The government's rush to freeze the bank account could scarcely conceal its complicity in inflaming the bigotry that created an enabling climate for Regar's work. Earlier in the year, the BJP-run government of Rajasthan had instructed schools in the state to take their pupils to a 'spiritual fair' where they could be taught about the evil of 'love jihad'.[35]

The hideousness of a society stigmatising Muslim men as agents of terror and slaughtering them, the full extent of the depletion of empathy in the age of Modi, was revealed only weeks after Regar's video was posted when the crumpled body of a child—an eight-year-old girl—from a Muslim nomadic family was found in Jammu. Asifa Bano was grazing horses when a pair of Hindu men lured her into the woods. There, according to police reports, they drugged her, then carried her to a temple. Locked inside the temple for three days, she was starved, beaten, repeatedly raped, before being strangled to death. Her bloodied body, draped in the purple dress flecked with yellow roses she wore when she was abducted, was then discarded in a nearby forest. The men accused of the crime were entitled to presumption of innocence, the keystone of any civilised criminal justice system; what followed was akin to a smearing of a dead child, who was cast posthumously as an agent of Muslim separatists in neighbouring Kashmir. Lawyers physically blocked the entrance of a courthouse to stop the authorities from filing charges. There was no discernible outrage at the fact that a Hindu place of worship had been dese-crated—or that an eight-year-old child had been raped and murdered. What troubled BJP leaders was that the officers investigating the crime were Muslim.[36] The Hindu capacity for depraved savagery in Modi's India is exceeded only by the Hindu capacity for diabolical self-pity.

Unless cushioned by wealth or political connections, criticis-ing Modi is an extremely hazardous undertaking. For a man who boasts about the size of his chest, he is, unsurprisingly, very thin-skinned. Since his election, teachers have lost their jobs, students have landed in prison, a police officer was suspended, and a rickshaw driver had criminal charges slapped against him—all for saying unflattering things about the Prime Minis-ter.[37] Even well-heeled agnostics are mercilessly bullied into submission by Modi's digital mobs. The people operating the pro-Modi Twitter and Facebook accounts are not freelancers but members of an organised online army. According to a repentant former propagandist for Modi, interviewed by the journalist Swati Charturvedi, the shady 'social media unit' of the BJP administers 'a never-ending drip-feed of hate and big-otry against the minorities, the Gandhi family, journalists on the hit list, liberals, anyone perceived as anti-Modi'.[38] Even a man as wildly popular as the film star Aamir Khan could not evade the wrath of the 'social media unit'. In 2016, Khan shared his (Hindu) wife's apprehensions about rising 'intolerance' in Modi's India. No sooner had he made the remark than a fero-cious online campaign was launched against an e-commerce giant that had hired Khan to advertise its brand.[39] The com-pany was coerced into severing ties with him. Khan, proved right, never revisited the subject. The message for other celebri-ties was as unmistakable as it was chilling.

For all the noise they made about the dangers of Hindu nationalism, affluent Hindus seldom radiated fear of saffron-clad supremacists. They saw their own faith as a form of indem-nity against the savagery of men who slaughtered Muslims and

Christians. This secret sense of imagined security fostered a smug complacency that blinded them to the danger staring them in the face. Unlike Muslims who deviate from Muslim fundamentalists, the editor Vir Sanghvi wrote in the *Hindustan Times* in 2007, Hindus who 'condemn the worst excesses' of Hindu nationalists 'face no real danger'.[40] Gauri Lankesh, a Hindu journalist who did just that, was shot dead in an ambush outside her house in 2017, almost ten years to the date after Sanghvi's assertion about the innocuousness of Hindu nationalists appeared in print.

The decade in between was the decade in which Modi became the undisputed leader of the Hindu-nationalist cause. If his election to the premiership energised Hindu supremacists, his silence as Prime Minister emboldened them. Lankesh, the scion of a distinguished family, edited a tabloid in the Kannada language that hardly anybody outside the state of Karnataka read. She struggled to make ends meet and paid the bills by writing occasionally for English newspapers.[41] But not for her the preening platitudes about the relative harmlessness of extremists who happened to be her co-religionists: in her work and her life, she was an unrelenting critic of Hindu supremacism and Modi's project to recast India as a Hindu nation. Seemingly well-to-do and 'progressive', she was the archetypal 'presstitute' despised by Modi's myrmidons. Her killing, and the shock it induced, was an exhilarating spectacle for them. 'A bitch died a dog's death and now all the puppies are wailing in the same tune,' a businessman in Gujarat tweeted after she was pronounced dead. Another Twitter user rejoiced: 'So, Commy Gauri Lankesh has been murdered mercilessly … Amen.' Such ravings would probably not matter—were it not for the fact that the accounts that published them were among those followed by the Prime Minister.[42]

This was not an aberration.

Possibly the most tech-savvy politician on earth, Modi follows dozens of accounts on social media that routinely dispense threats of rape against journalists and incite violence against Muslims and ideological dissenters.[43] Modi did not disavow the handles that greeted Lankesh's death with glee by pressing the Unfollow button on Twitter. Nor did he condemn Lankesh's murder, which, according to investigators, was in all likelihood the work of a Hindu terrorist organisation that had assassinated two other left-leaning intellectuals the previous year.[44]

Railing against Modi's silence is perhaps beside the point because the assumptions of Indians outraged by it may already have become obsolete. Modi may have elected to seal his lips because opening them may only expose his inability to contain and control with speech the monster he catalysed and condoned with silence. In December 2018, in Uttar Pradesh, a senior police officer was run to ground and killed by an armed mob of cow protectors he had tried to pacify. The passions supplicated and legitimised by Modi to seize the state have begun, under Yogi, to devour the enforcers of the state's will. All the confusion of a country that deferred the task of dealing sincerely with its wounded past is ripe for exploitation by Yogi. All the grievances piled up over decades of misrule by Congress for which Modi did not, could not, find a productive release are waiting to be converted into an even more explosive anger by his protégé. We may yet look back on Modi as a moderate.

8

VANITY

Great causes and little men go ill together.
Jawaharlal Nehru

'[T]he world,' Narendra Modi said six months into his term, 'is looking at India with renewed respect.'[1] For once, it was not bluster. Modi galvanised stagnant foreign relations from the moment he was elected. He promised a 'neighbourhood first' foreign policy. And his decision to invite the leaders of India's adjoining states, including Pakistan, to his inauguration in Delhi semaphored the magnitude of his ambition. His speedy conclusion in the summer of 2015 of an historic land swap with Bangladesh was a refreshingly energetic departure from the languid old days when difficult issues were clumsily shelved away. Modi's decisiveness, even his critics had to concede in the early months of his premiership, was the jolt India needed after Manmohan Singh had reduced the country to a nonentity in its own backyard. But the cost of turning to a strongman to revive India's flagging image and fortunes soon became apparent.

Foreign policy fell prey to the Prime Minister's vanity, and national interest became indistinguishable from narcissism. Since becoming Prime Minister, Narendra Modi has travelled to more than eighty countries, and he has used every tour to stage extravagant public events with the diaspora. The cost to the exchequer of the prime minister's event management in his first four years in office: 280 million dollars.[2] The upshot of his exertions on the global stage: an historic run from India by overseas institutional investors (who withdrew more than US$5 billion in October 2018 alone);[3] the slowest growth in foreign direct investment in five years (3 per cent between 2017 and 2018);[4] a country despised by its once-dear neighbours; a virtual war with Pakistan; eruption of serious conflict with China; alienation of old friends; uncertain new partnerships.

Determined to concentrate power in his own office, Modi has dismantled the already feeble structures of debate, deliberation, and accountability on which India's notoriously makeshift foreign policy has always rested. India's foreign minister during Modi's first term in office, the late Sushma Swaraj, was demoted to the role of a minor bureaucrat: there was never a more enervated occupant of the office. The platform on which Swaraj was most visible—when she was not bidding Modi farewell or receiving him at the airport—was Twitter, where she personally responded to expatriate Indians' pleas for repatriation or expedited passport clearances from citizens at home. Modi, meanwhile, functioned as the *de facto* foreign minister. Never before has India's engagement with the world been informed so totally by the caprices of one man. Momentous decisions that will affect India long after Modi is gone have been made with barely any debate. Visiting Paris in 2015, Modi placed an order for three dozen fighter aircraft that superseded an existing arrangement for no apparent reason other than that he was pleased with French hospitality: his own defence minister learnt about the decision from news reports.[5] Travelling to Beijing the same year, he announced the rollout of electronic visas for Chinese tourists to India: his foreign secretary at the time, sitting in the audience, had no advance knowledge of what was coming.[6] Even Nehru, who retained the foreign ministry for the entirety of his premiership, subjected his actions to parliamentary scrutiny.

The content of republican India's foreign policy was supplied by an idealistic resolution passed by the Congress Party in 1938 that committed India to an internationalism centred on disarmament, peaceful coexistence, and the abolition of imperialism. India's behaviour in the aftermath of Independence, while largely consonant with that resolution, was filtered through Nehruvian imperatives: an admixture of utopianism and self-interest. It was a worldview made untenable by its own inconsistency. India, constrained by the lofty ideals it espoused, opened itself to accusations of hypocrisy whenever it breached them in order to advance its own interests. The result: India was able neither to realise those ideals nor properly to protect its interests. Nehru's impatience with Western imperialism was braided together with a self-wounding tolerance of Chinese revanchism. When Portugal's Salazar dictatorship refused to vacate its Indian possessions in Goa, Nehru, ignoring America's pleas to remain true to his own sermons on non-violence to the Western world, liberated the territory by force. But on the eastern front he remained serene despite accumulating advice from colleagues on the rising cost of inaction. Not only did he neglect warnings about China: he even recommended Mao's pariah state for a permanent seat on the UN Security Council that had first been proffered to India.[7] But this perforated idealism, always hazardous in the foreign arena, cracked when communist China, restless to assert itself as the predominant power in Asia, invaded India in 1962. The Non-Aligned Movement, co-founded and led by India, was of no assistance.

After Nehru, Delhi was driven by a cold national interest flavoured with the third-worldism of its secular elites. India was a democracy that rejected the overtures of the United States and secured the protection of the Soviet Union during the Cold War, deplored nuclear proliferation while pursuing its own nuclear programme, extracted military assistance from Israel even as it publicly censured the Jewish state, and maintained its standing in the Arab world even after it enhanced its relations with Israel. It did all this with the aid of an exceedingly resourceful diplomatic corps roughly the size of Singapore's.

India's global ambitions over the past quarter century have grown with its wealth. But where once its foreign relations were governed by a realistic appraisal of India's interests in the world as it existed, they are now an expression primarily of uncontainable vanities—the vanities of a Hindu supremacist boosted by the vanities of a solipsistic elite clamouring for 'superpower' status for a country that, for all its new riches and hard military strength, is still home to the largest number of the world's poorest people.

Modi, addled by this vain agitation for the recognition and respect that his supporters believe is their due, conducted himself with smaller states in ways that no self-respecting nation could abide. His 'neighbourhood-first' policy, floated with so much promise, is now in the same league of disasters as the 'zero problems with neighbours' policy advanced by Recep Tayyip Erdogan, another strongman in thrall to his own atavistic fantasy of exhuming the Ottoman Empire.

Nepal, bound to India by an umbilical relationship, was the unlikeliest place for its unravelling. The treaty of friendship signed by the two nations in 1950 eliminated virtually every barrier between them. Goods moved freely, people travelled without documents, bought property, acquired citizenship, and married across the border. For many Indians, Nepal might as well have been another state of the country. It was an attitude destined to provoke resentment in Kathmandu, which gradually began warming to China. Yet, despite deepening differences, so close to indestructible was the affection between the two countries that only an extraordinarily sustained effort could destroy it.

It took Modi just over a year to do it. He managed to arouse what once seemed almost impossible to achieve: a near-universal resentment for India in Nepal. It was the summer of 2015 and Nepal had just endured one of the worst earthquakes in its known existence. The constituent assembly convened against

the backdrop of this devastation to give the battered country—
functioning without a Constitution after its monarchy was abolished in 2008 following years of civil war—a new charter of
governance. It was a poignant occasion that would have justified
the dispatch of a high-level delegation from India to offer solidarity. Modi, instead, dispatched his foreign secretary (now
foreign minister) with instructions, reportedly, to delay the
promulgation of the new Constitution. According to Ameet
Dhakal, one of Nepal's most distinguished journalists who was
privy to the discussions, Modi's emissary 'didn't have a message;
he only had a threat', and his 'stiff body language and the harsh
tone matched the arrogance of British Viceroy Lord Curzon'.
The Nepalis were outraged that the 'largest democracy in the
world, and Nepal's steadfast friend' was demanding that Nepal
'call off her momentous day'.[8] The apparent reason for the
showdown was that the Constitution—an evolving document—
had not granted adequate representation to ethnic Indian
minorities in the Nepalese plains. The irony of a nakedly
majoritarian strongman arguing for the rights of a minority in
a foreign land was not lost on the Nepalis. But even the real
reasons for Modi's intervention in the affairs of Nepal were
wretched. Bihar, the Indian state that shares a long border with
Nepal, was about to hold an election—and, by squeezing
Nepal, Modi was hoping to win the votes of Biharis with relatives among the ethnic minorities across the border. When
Nepal ignored Modi and voted for the Constitution, not even a
dry note of congratulation went from the prime minister's
office. Nepali representatives' ratification of the Constitution's
conversion of the formerly Hindu kingdom into a secular
Republic, affirmed by rejecting the entreaties of Hindu nationalists across the border, evidently dismayed Modi.

As the sole self-proclaimed Hindu state in the world, Nepal
has long been a lodestar for Hindu nationalists. Its constitutional embrace of secularism was a serious blow. But Modi
didn't merely stop at being sullen. His government demanded a

series of amendments to the Constitution. When Kathmandu did not relent, there followed a lengthy and criminal blockade of Nepal. Oil containers and trucks carrying medicine piled up at the open border. Dozens of Nepalese citizens were killed in political unrest and, according to UNICEF, more than three million children were placed at risk of death or disease.[9] Post-earthquake reconstruction came to a halt. Marooned by Modi and faced with drastic shortages of food, medicine, and fuel, Nepalis made desperate appeals to the world for emergency assistance and diplomatic intercession. A deep revulsion for India crystallised in Nepali minds and hearts. Nepali politicians resolved thereafter to diversify their friendships and dependences. China immediately stepped in to exploit the rage against India with an assistance package of US$ 146 million.[10] And for the first time, Kathmandu and Beijing held joint military exercises. As Modi drove India's soul-sibling into the arms of Beijing, the lesson absorbed by other small states in the region from Modi's mess: never embrace India too tightly. Modi annihilated the influence and goodwill India had built up over decades to win a few extra votes and, more egregiously, to make Nepal a reliquary of his hideous genre of nationalism.

The fiasco in Nepal might have humbled a less conceited figure. But it did nothing to wrinkle Modi's self-conception as a geostrategic genius. And so on Christmas day of 2015, fresh from stamping on India's relationship with Nepal, he tweeted: 'Looking forward to meeting PM Nawaz Sharif in Lahore today afternoon, where I will drop by on my way back to Delhi.' Modi was seized by the belief that all that India's most intractable foreign relationship needed was his personal touch. He treated the challenge that had consumed generations of Indians as though it were another application to open a factory in Gujarat. By turning up in Pakistan with barely any notice— a few hours after announcing his trip on Twitter—Modi immediately undermined the opposition and his parliamentary colleagues on an issue so vital to India's national security that it had always remained above partisan politics. More Pakistanis in power than Indians knew about Modi's travel plans. His decision was all the more contemptible considering his own record, in opposition, of tormenting any politician who dared to make an overture to Pakistan. After supping with Pakistan's Prime Minister at his inauguration, Modi assiduously cultivated the image of a tough guy and encouraged the intensification of Indian hostility towards Pakistan. He instructed India's armed forces to respond forcefully to Pakistani provocations on the *de facto* border between the two nations in Kashmir. He abruptly cancelled talks between Indian and Pakistani diplomats after Pakistan's high commissioner to Delhi held a meeting with Kashmiri separatists. There was certainly no demonstrable change in Pakistan's behaviour to justify Modi's volte-face. The men behind the Mumbai massacre still remained at liberty. Hafiz Saeed, a terrorist carrying a US$ 10 million US State Department bounty on his head for his role in the atrocity, continued openly to incite violence against India. Dawood Ibrahim, the man behind the worst terrorist assault in India's history, was still living in palatial splendour in Karachi's Clifton neighbourhood.

Modi's visit to Pakistan was the first by an Indian Prime Minister in more than a decade. When Nixon went to China, it was said that only a man of his standing among America's hawkish conservatives could have risked making that momentous voyage. Modi's acolytes began making similar arguments for Modi. An Indian Prime Minister belonging to a Hindu-supremacist party, they said, had fostered peace simply by 'dropping by' the Islamic Republic for a couple of hours on his way back from Afghanistan. If anything, the opposite was true. Nixon's journey to China was preceded by arduous preparation. Modi's visit to Pakistan was not a daring deed of statesmanship: it was an unhinged display of hubris. His personal diplomacy, in any case, was a non-starter because Nawaz Sharif, his Pakistani counterpart at the time, was never the real decision-maker in the Islamic

Republic. That job has always been held by the military and intelligence chiefs, and they legitimate their unchecked power and endless plunder of Pakistan's resources by magnifying the 'threat' from India. Unrehearsed efforts at détente by Delhi have always elicited deadly reprisals from them. The last time Sharif hosted an Indian Prime Minister in Lahore, in 1999, his army, unbeknown to him, launched a war against India. Sharif was deposed from office and exiled to Saudi Arabia, and Pakistan was placed under military dictatorship for a decade.

The animosity between Pakistan and India was always anchored in irreconcilable national ideologies. One regarded itself as the authentic home of the subcontinent's Muslims; the other, until Modi came along, saw itself, at least in theory, as the paragon of a pluralistic secular nationalism that transcended religion. Each nullified the other: rejection of its Indian past is the condition of Pakistani patriotism, and Indian secularism is a repudiation of Pakistan's schismatic nationalism. The two could exist in peace only if they existed in isolation from each other. This explains why the most substantial stretches of tranquillity between the two nations broke out when they spurned each other. Like a divorced couple, the states of India and Pakistan, especially Pakistan, needed time apart to evolve identities independent of the other. Alas, to the detriment of their peoples, they have been in each other's faces ever since the British departed the subcontinent. And like every Indian Prime Minister before him—and like every well-intentioned commentator who advocates 'sustained dialogue' with and champions engaging 'moderates' in Pakistan—Modi never grasped that, far from nurturing peace, India endangers genuinely peaceable democratic politicians in Pakistan merely by befriending them.

As Modi departed Lahore, I wrote in the *Observer* of London that his '"diplomacy" will do nothing to advance peace. Instead, it will embolden elements within Pakistan's military–intelligence complex to act in ways that will be adversarial to Pakistan's democracy—and India's security'. Within days of Modi's return to India, men from Jaish-e-Muhammad, an asset of Pakistan's military–intelligence, staged a major attack on an Indian airbase on the border with Pakistan. A joint investigation instituted to catalogue the facts dissolved into the usual recriminations when Islamabad, under duress from its uniformed men, accused India of executing a false flag attack 'to malign Pakistan'.[11] Far from jumpstarting a peace process, Modi aggravated the already dire enmity between the two nations.

When the next terrorist attack occurred—this time at an army base in Uri in September 2016—he did something else that was unprecedented: he shamelessly used the military to bolster his own cult. Delhi has periodically ordered the Indian Army to stage covert attacks against terror camps within territory in Pakistan's hands. The secrecy that governed these missions, allowing Pakistani authorities to save face, averted escalation between the nuclear-armed states. Modi, stamping on this tradition, breathlessly publicised the 'surgical strike' he claimed to have authorised inside Pakistan-held territory. Anyone caught questioning the wisdom of boasting about it all was thrown to Modi's digital hounds.

The man who had so brazenly undermined India's non-partisan political traditions by visiting Pakistan, and was exploiting the Indian military's valour, was deified as a patriot and those who refused to worship him were demonised as 'anti-national'. Having kept the Indian parliament and his own cabinet in the dark as he hugged the Pakistani Prime Minister, Modi fostered an atmosphere in India in which any relationship with Pakistanis became tantamount to treason. A major Bollywood producer was bullied into donating a substantial sum of cash to an army fund for the crime of casting a Pakistani actor in a film shot at a time when Modi himself had materialised in Pakistan. The army refused to accept the money, but the producer was forced into recording an abject apology in which he pledged never to 'engage with talent from the neighbouring country'.[12]

The principal association of Indian film producers placed a blanket ban on Pakistani actors and technicians from working in India.

A self-confident and secular India would never countenance the segregationist nationalism around which so many Pakistanis rally. It would also never persecute Pakistanis, who are our flesh and blood, for self-identifying as Pakistani. But Modi, who seeks to convert India into a Hindu facsimile of Pakistan, has done the opposite: he has paid the ideology of Pakistan the compliment of imitation while victimising ordinary Pakistanis who should have been welcomed by India.

After opening up India to renewed attacks from Pakistan, Modi proceeded to wreck other existing security partnerships. The Indian Army has routinely conducted clandestine counter-insurgency operations against militant posts inside Myanmar with the acquiescence of the country's rulers. Modi vandalised this hugely advantageous arrangement to advertise a raid conducted on his watch in June 2015. Preoccupied with his insatiable craving for personal aggrandisement, he forgot to contemplate the effect the decision might have on the delicate partnership India had laboriously cultivated with the establishment in Naypyidaw. The generals in Myanmar, outraged at being cast as impotent guardians of their own nation's borders in Modi's self-promotional stunt, were left fuming.[13]

Having demolished India's standing in South Asia, Modi cemented an alliance of sorts in the Middle East with Israel. His visit to the Jewish state, the first by an Indian Prime Minister, was historic. But there were squalid ideological reasons that made it special for so many Hindu nationalists. India, after all, was once considered, in the words of Bernard Weinraub, 'the loneliest post in the world' for Israeli diplomats.[14] Having voted against the creation of Israel at the UN in 1947, India desisted from establishing full diplomatic relations with West Jerusalem until 1992. For decades, Israel's presence in India was limited to an immigration office in Mumbai. In between, India voted with

VANITY

the majority to pass UN resolution 3379, condemning Zionism as a form of racism, became one of the first non-Arab states to recognise Palestine's declaration of independence in 1988, and was generally among the more vocal non-Arab voices against Israel. But by the twenty-first century, India had become Israel's closest eastern partner and its largest arms market. Since 2001, the diasporas of the two countries have emerged as energetic allies against a shared enemy: Islamic extremism. A survey by the Israeli foreign ministry in 2009 found India to be the most pro-Israel country in the world, well above the US. Once a bastion of pro-Palestinian sentiment, India appeared at the bottom in a worldwide poll in 2011 of countries sympathetic to Palestinian statehood.[15]

What precipitated this dramatic shift?

Israel had all along been a quiet friend to Delhi, volunteering clandestine support as India sought to repel attacks by China (in 1962) and Pakistan (in 1965). Israeli officials knew also that India, which had no traditions of anti-Semitism, had arrived at its Israel policy through a combination of post-colonial hauteur, realpolitik—particularly its desire to placate Arab Muslim opinion in its contest against Pakistan—and an ethical commitment to the Palestinian cause. Partly for these reasons, India's anti-Israel sloganeering rarely provoked any anxiety in West Jerusalem.

A triad of reasons account for the revision of India's attitude towards Israel. The first is the belated realisation that no amount of deference to Arab sentiment could alter Muslim opinion in the Middle East in India's favour: when it came to Kashmir, Shia and Sunni united in supporting Pakistan's position.[16] The second was the collapse of the old world order: the demise of the Soviet Union meant that India had to forge new partnerships. The third cause of the intensification of Indo–Israeli ties is less well known: the rise of Hindutva in India. As the liberal Israeli newspaper *Haaretz* once phrased it, 'Relations between Israel and India tend to grow stronger when ... India experiences a rightward shift in anti-Muslim public opinion or in leadership.'[17] For

Hindu supremacists, Israel has always been something of a polestar: a nation to be revered for its ability to defeat, and survive among, hostile Muslims. In 2009, Mumbai's anti-terror squad arrested, among others, an officer in the Indian Army, Prasad Purohit, for masterminding a terrorist attack on Pakistani citizens and plotting to overthrow the secular Indian state. In his confession, Purohit admitted to making plans to approach Israel for help.[18] The saffron obsession with Israel was always enmeshed with a yearning for the termination of India's support for Palestine. The Congress Party's pro-Palestine stance—largely meaningless after 1992, when India established a full diplomatic relationship with Israel—was impugned by the BJP as a sop to Indian Muslims. In truth, Indian Muslims have made noticeable efforts to build bridges with Israel. In 2007, for instance, Maulana Jamil Ilyasi, the leader of 500,000 imams of India, travelled to Israel to interact with 'Jewish sisters and brothers'.[19]

But the irony of Modi steering India closer to Israel has been lost on the pro-Modi Likudniks in Israel. The founding luminaries of Hindutva were enamoured of Hitler. A key ally of the RSS, speaking for 'sensible Hindus of India' in 1939, 'welcomed' with 'jubilant hope' 'Germany's solemn idea of the revival of the Aryan culture, the glorification of the swastika, her patronage of Vedic learning, and the ardent championship of Indo-Germanic civilisation'.[20] Social studies textbooks published in Gujarat when Modi was the state's chief minister contained such chapters as 'Hitler the Supremo' and 'Internal Achievements of Nazism', and students were taught that 'Hitler lent dignity and prestige to the German government. He adopted the policy of opposition towards the Jewish people and advocated the supremacy of the German race.'[21]

Is the capacious imagination of Theodor Herzl, who envisioned a socialist 'New Society' for *all* inhabitants of Palestine, disgraced or upheld when Modi—forged in an ideology that lionises the tormentors of Herzl's people—mouths platitudes about democracy with Netanyahu, an ethno-religious bigot whose anti-democratic politics are awash in the venom of Dr Geyer, the villain of Herzl's foundational text on Zionism?

Modi's success in Israel occurred against the backdrop of a dangerous escalation with China next door that has not received the kind of attention it merits. If Pakistan's neurotic nationalism makes it the most complex and urgent security challenge for India, China's view of India as an obstacle in its path to a permanently predominant position in Asia makes it Delhi's gravest long-term threat. Beijing recognises India as the only power in Asia with the potential to stymie China's expansion. At the same time, with a GDP five times the size of India's, China is outwardly contemptuous of comparisons with India. Yet both nations are haunted by the same question: can the twenty-first century accommodate the aspirations of India *and* China? It is difficult to conceive of it now—when China entrances the world with its glitzy buildings and much of India still sports a slovenly look—but there was a time when China esteemed India as a fount of spiritual and intellectual enlightenment. The great Buddhist monk Faxian, travelling to India in the fourth century, hailed it as the true 'Middle Kingdom' and described his own motherland as being merely India's 'border land'.[22] A host of Chinese scholars, trained at Indian universities and seminaries, returned with ideas that reshaped their native land. The Tang emperor Taizong, spellbound by the Buddhist scriptures hauled back from India by the monk Xuanzang, became a patron of the Indian religion and adopted its tenets throughout his realm. As Singapore's founder Lee Kuan Yew once averred, India exerted the same civilisational influence in Asia as Rome and Greece did in Europe.[23]

But then India, repeatedly ravaged by a variety of imperialisms, fell grievously behind. Post-colonial histories now club the two countries together. In truth—even though Britain relied on Indian muscle to inaugurate China's century of humiliation, and a handful of Indian families made massive fortunes in the trade of opium—India, physically separated from China by the buffer zone of Tibet, remained largely ignorant of China for much of the past millennium. Once the communists expelled their rivals and established a firm grip over China, Churchill was among those who wrote to Nehru—'the light of Asia'—with the hope that India should defend the 'freedom and dignity of the individual' against 'the Communist Party drill book'.[24] India's self-abnegating generosity, rather than eliciting gratitude, only inflamed Chinese resentments. Mao, smarting at Nehru's paternalistic pretensions to leadership of the post-colonial world, radiated the arriviste's disdain for his regime's most illustrious advocate on the international stage. Impatient to reclaim China's position after a century of dishonour, Mao could not abide an Asia with multiple centres of power. And Delhi's decision to grant asylum, in defiance of Beijing's feelings, to the Dalai Lama following Tibet's decimation by Han supremacists confirmed it as a potential contender. Certainly, India seldom troubled China more than when it dissented from Beijing in order to uphold its own liberal democratic values. When Beijing demanded that the growing number of Tibetan refugees in India be banned from staging protests against China, the foreign office in Delhi told the mandarins across the Himalayas that there was 'by law and Constitution complete freedom of expression of opinion in parliament and the press and elsewhere in India'.[25]

China initiated a surprise multi-pronged attack against India in 1962, occupying a substantial portion of contested territory on the Tibetan plateau. Nehru's comrades in the Non-Aligned Movement were of little use. Egypt's Nasser was rebuffed by China and Yugoslavia's Tito was denigrated as 'a lickspittle of US imperialism' for appearing to side with India. It was Washington that rushed military aid to India. But just as American jumbo jets, flown to bolster India's retaliation, began landing in West Bengal, Beijing announced a unilateral cease-fire. The war ended quickly, but India, thoroughly worsted, never recovered from the experience. Delhi took great pains thereafter to maintain the fiction that it was on excellent terms with Beijing. Routine provocations by China—incursions into Indian territory, sponsorship of anti-India insurgencies, and clandestine nuclear assistance and lavish subventions to Pakistan—did nothing to temper the tributes flowing eastward from Delhi.

In 2003, Atal Bihari Vajpayee, the first Hindu-nationalist Prime Minister at the head of a coalition government, incinerated India's last card against Beijing when he recognised Tibet, which India accepted as an autonomous region of China, as an *integral* 'part of the territory of the People's Republic of China'.[26] Since Mao's violent annexation of Tibet in 1950—when monasteries were razed, monks executed, thousands of non-violent protesters massacred, and many thousands more detained, starved, tortured, uprooted, and carted away to communes to toil in conditions so severe that some resorted to cannibalism to survive—China has relentlessly disfigured that hypnotically beautiful country. It has mined and expropriated Tibet's mineral wealth, dammed and diverted waters from its bountiful rivers, herded innumerable Tibetans into what it calls 'New Socialist Villages', suppressed the expression of Tibetan identity, annihilated whole ways of native life, and repopulated Tibet with Han Chinese settlers. There is no colonialism on earth more absolute than China's in Tibet, and there is no people in the world more poorly equipped to resist it than the Tibetans. The Buddhists under occupation there now protest by immolating their own bodies, and more than 3,000 of them flee every year to India, where authorities detain anyone of Tibetan appearance to appease visiting Chinese leaders.

Tibetans, however, aren't the only victims of Tibet's tragedy. The third-largest reservoir of freshwater on earth, Tibet is the source of some of Asia's most vital rivers: Yangtze, Mekong, Yarlung Tsangpo. The survival of more than 750 million people in nations downstream—India, Pakistan, Bangladesh, Burma,

Laos, Cambodia—depends on waters originating in Chinese-controlled territory. By aggressively damming transboundary rivers and curtailing their flow, China has not only jeopardised Tibet's fragile ecology: it has also gained political leverage over the downstream nations. The rapidly proliferating megadams within China's ever-expanding borders—more than 26,000, or half the world's total—are taps that Beijing can turn on and off at will. Unlike India, which has signed generous water-sharing treaties with Pakistan and Bangladesh, China has repeatedly rebuffed efforts aimed at equitable resource allocation. In 1997, it rejected a United Nations convention that prescribed a framework for water sharing. When Vladimir Putin threatens to cut off oil supplies to Europe, it at least spurs talk among his clients of alternative sources of energy. But for China's weak and impoverished neighbours, there are no alternatives to water. They are at Beijing's mercy.

Vajpayee's surrender on Tibet was the single most ignoble concession to China by Delhi. It yielded no tangible benefits for India. And under Manmohan Singh, China, deploying a combination of aid and ammunition, tightened its noose of influence around India—beginning in Pakistan in the north-west, running through Nepal and Myanmar in the east, and ending in Sri Lanka in the south. Nothing more depressingly conveys India's psychological dread of China than Singh's decision in 2007 to downgrade, on China's demand, Japan's participation in exercises with the United States designed to boost India's defence preparedness against … China.[27]

Modi's election held the promise of disrupting this disastrous trend. Unlike his abject predecessor, Modi cut an imposing figure on the world stage. He refreshed relations that had fallen into catastrophic neglect. He loudly courted defence partnerships with fellow democracies. He moved India closer to Washington. He even echoed America's denunciation of Chinese aggression in the South China Sea. And his 'Act East' policy, discarding the caution of past governments, confidently projected Delhi as a democratic rival to Beijing. China's communist overlords, long accustomed to treating India shabbily, appeared in the beginning to be unsettled by Modi. And Modi translated his muscular attitude into action in 2017 when Chinese troops materialised in Doklam—a piece of territory that is the subject of a dispute between Bhutan and China—to pave over an existing road. The road would have granted China easy access to a small strip of land (at its narrowest only 23 kilometres) which connects India to its easternmost states. The amputation of this corridor by China in the event of war would instantly sever Delhi from 45 million Indian citizens, while converting the territory they inhabit—roughly the size of Britain—into a bargaining counter which Beijing, already in illegal possession of vast tracts of Indian land, might exploit to extract concessions elsewhere.

Modi ordered in Indian troops to halt the Chinese construction work in Doklam and restore status quo ante. For two months, the Chinese Communist Party and the People's Liberation Army inundated India with lurid threats, and there were moments during the edgy stand-off when the two nuclear-armed adversaries appeared poised for another all-out war. Some felt Modi overreacted; others believed he had no choice. Wherever one stood on his handling of Doklam, the high-altitude drama served to clarify the fragility of Indian assumptions about another important relationship that underlay Modi's decision to confront China.

India has been moving closer to the United States since the end of the Cold War. The cordial rediscovery, after decades of mutual hostility, was lubricated by the economics of globalisation. But the courtship of India by the US in the post-9/11 years—when Washington, seized by a zeal for spreading democracy, began viewing India as a 'democratic counterweight' to China in the long run—infected India's financial and political elites with deleterious delusions. Years of isolation had made them dangerously susceptible to flattery. Goaded by the US, they began to envisage an external role for India that the country's internal realities did not justify. A burgeoning cast of 'strategic experts' began exhorting India, where most people do not have access to clean water or toilets, to act like a *global power*. The world, to quote from a book on Indian foreign policy, is apparently 'looking to India to shape the emerging international order'.[28] Anybody who has actually travelled in the world and interacted with people outside of the self-venerating circles of academia and think tanks will find that statement ludicrous. But well-heeled Indians became so besotted with the vision of high status crafted in Washington that, in 2003, the Indian government contemplated sending soldiers to Iraq as part of Bush's coalition.

The rhetoric of 'values' was, of course, vacuous gloss. If Washington was animated by values alone, it would not have stocked the arsenal of Pakistan—founded on values antithetical to India's—with weapons, or indulged Islamabad's nuclear programme in violation of its own laws. Nor would it have subordinated its avowed principles to business interests in the 1990s to legitimise China's communist regime. The American accommodation of totalitarians who had so recently butchered pro-democracy activists on Tiananmen Square was marketed by Washington as an innovative way of influencing China—by partnering with it and giving it a prominent position inside, rather than keeping it outside, global institutions. It is because principles came last that, far from moulding China's behaviour, it is Washington that incrementally surrendered to Beijing. A good way to measure any country's grand claims to standing up to China is to look at its treatment of Tibetans. It has been customary for American presidents to invite the Dalai Lama to Washington. Obama did away even with this minor gesture of solidarity with the Tibetans for fear of offending Beijing. Even the brief private audience he eventually granted Tibet's beleaguered spiritual leader was accompanied with ritualistic humiliation intended to propitiate China: the Dalai Lama was made to exit the White House through the back doors, surrounded by bags of trash.[29]

Emboldened by such meek displays of deference, Chinese goons roughed up British civilians on British soil in the run up to the 2008 Olympics for exercising their right to protest.[30] Rather than complain, the British Prime Minister at the time, like the leaders of every other major democracy, showed up to pay court to China's rulers at the Beijing Olympics stadium. Western authors now self-censor for the tawdry privilege of being published in China; Hollywood modifies its films to placate the CCP; and governments that never tire of puffing their chests at the Middle East's tinpot tyrannies routinely abase themselves before Beijing.

Against this backdrop, Delhi's diminishing hesitation in signing up to Washington's policy of containing China speaks of the increasingly powerful hold of the fantasy of a democratic alliance on the psyche of India's governing elite. There was some anxiety in Washington and even Delhi that Modi, shunned by successive US administrations after the Gujarat pogrom, might upend the emergent partnership. When he did not, it was explained away as a measure of his maturity: he was setting aside personal rancour for the larger national interest.

Modi was motivated by baser reasons.

His trumpeting of the fact that he was on a first-name basis with Barack Obama, followed by gasconades to fawning reporters that 'Barack and I tell jokes to each other', bespoke a deep need, after enduring that humiliating entry ban, for validation and legitimacy from the US president. The Americans met the need by kneading his enormous ego. Obama accepted Modi's invitation to be his guest at India's Republic Day parade in January 2015—the first time an American president attended the event in Delhi.

Anyone who felt that India's pro-American tilt under Modi was driven primarily by anything other than the Prime Minister's vanity need only have studied him around Obama. He was showing Obama off to Indians, showing himself off in the company of Obama to the world, an outcast breathlessly announcing his arrival. He greeted Obama wearing a £10,000 Savile Row suit with his own name monogrammed in golden pinstripes. Introducing Obama to his radio audience, he became properly sycophantic. 'Some people wonder, what does "Barack" mean?', he said. 'I was searching for the meaning of Barack. ... Barack means, one who is blessed. I believe, along with a name, his family gave him a big gift.'[31] And at the Republic Day procession, lost in statesmanly banter with his important 'friend', he did not rise to acknowledge the sacrifice of a martyred Indian soldier's widow who had just collected a medal from the president of India and paused fleetingly to greet the Prime Minister. This is the man, lest we forget, who accuses his opponents of displaying insufficient deference for the armed forces.

Obama's own homage, of course, came with a price. Modi amply rewarded the US president by reviving a logistics agreement with Washington that had been frozen by the Congress-led government. All the agreement does, its proponents said, is formalise existing military-to-military arrangements between Delhi and Washington. The terms of the deal enable each side's military to access the other's facilities—including bases—to retool and refuel. America's assets, theoretically accessible to India, were of no use to Delhi; but India's assets were immensely valuable to America as it was 'pivoting' to Asia. At minimum, the deal should have been debated. But Modi, eager to please, bypassed democratic deliberation. Anybody who questioned his haste in pushing the deal through was besmirched as a relic of the Cold War, a carryover from the days of schizoid anti-Americanism.

A partnership with Washington is indispensable to India's security and economy. But the pace at which Modi is reorienting India risks turning it into a frontline state in someone else's strategy to contain China, an exalted foot soldier, a tritagonist in its own backwaters. The intensification of relations with

Washington has done little to enhance India's security. At the 2016 BRICS summit, held in Goa, China managed successfully to shield Pakistan from censure. Even Russia, not long ago India's all-weather foreign partner, seemed indifferent to Delhi's concerns. Moscow even proceeded to stage a joint military exercise with Pakistan in defiance of India's objections—unthinkable only a few years ago.[32]

Modi, maintaining a continuity with India's traditions of autonomy in other areas, put too much store by the idea of a democratic alliance against communist China. 'There is no bond that is stronger than a bond between two democracies,' the Prime Minister once asserted. History is replete with the tragic consequences of the miscalculations of those who mortgage their security to others to bask in the mythic virtues of ideological consanguinity. Indians who had clamoured for closer ties with the US were left complaining that Donald Trump did not extend Delhi any support during its stand-off with China at Doklam. Nehru, it is fair to say, got much more from Washington in 1962 without giving an inch to American demands than Modi did in 2018 after having offered up India's bases to America.

India's geography makes it vulnerable to conflict on both sides of its border. Modi, by attempting to expel China from territory claimed by Bhutan—a foreign state—created a precedent that China could have cited to squeeze Delhi: all Beijing needed was an invitation from its clients in Pakistan to do to India in disputed areas of Kashmir what India was doing to China in Doklam. None of this is to say that India should have been a spectator to the advancing PLA workers on its crucial frontiers. It is to say that a face-off with potentially calamitous consequences should be underwritten by a great deal more than vague notions of camaraderie or the 'resolve' of a leader. The early confidence exuded by India, hinting at the existence of a plan, collapsed into a desperate face-saving exercise when it became apparent that Modi had all along been improvising. What his supporters called 'Modi doctrine' was pure bluster. India did not even have a full-time defence minister as its soldiers, holding off the Chinese for more than two months, exchanged blows with the enemy. By some accounts, Delhi had ammunition for a ten-day shooting war.[33] The two sides eventually disengaged. But the Chinese returned just as quickly to resume the construction work that had been interrupted by Modi.[34]

Having presided over a major debacle, Modi adopted his fall-back position: selling falsehoods. Highly visible during the chest-thumping stage of the crisis, he swiftly retreated from public view once things deteriorated. It was left to his foreign minister to inform parliament that India had prevailed in its objective to push back the Chinese.[35] This was, needless to say, very far from being true. Modi's climbdown appeared all the more ignominious because he retreated after having begun from a position of strength. In the end, Modi, the strongman who set out to teach China a lesson, did what every leader too afraid to upset the Chinese does: he refused to meet the Dalai Lama and paid court to the Chinese president.[36] Voices in Bhutan have since wondered if their country should not deal directly with Beijing. Doklam, in the end, was an even greater failure in one sense than India's defeat at China's hands on Nehru's watch. In 1962, India had no history to guide it and was caught by surprise. In 2018, Modi, who presented himself as the anti-Nehru, elected to chasten the Chinese and had no cards when his bluff was called.

A democratic security alliance in Asia comprising India, Japan, Australia, and the United States is not only unavoidable: it is perhaps also necessary. Yet an alliance forged in the name of principle is meaningless if the allies themselves depart from that principle. Democracy, brandished as the humane alternative to communism, has seldom looked more discredited than it does in the age of Trump and Modi. India can scarcely be taken seriously as a 'democratic counterweight' to China by those exposed to Beijing's roughest edges as it itself transforms into a brutally exclusionary Hindu-supremacist state under Modi.

Some years ago, Belarus's greatest poet, paraphrasing Solzhenitsyn—'a poet doesn't adjust his treatment of a theme to a tyrant's taste'—told me that what had sustained him in tenebrous times was the knowledge that there were systems of government beyond the Soviet Union's artificial frontiers consecrated to preserving human dignity, not forcibly to remaking human beings. The poet, effectively imprisoned in his home by the dictatorship of Aleksandr Lukashenko when I met him, listed the greatest inspirations of his youth: America—and India. He had read Tagore, Nehru, and Gandhi. It occurred to me then that perhaps one way for India to undermine the ideology that animates China—an ideology that to Tibetans and Uighurs is as lethal today as it was when Mao was alive—is not to crow about 'values' but to honour them.

A year after I met the Belarusian dissident poet, the Indian police was dispatched to apprehend Tenzin Tsundue, another poet striving to overcome another kind of totalitarianism, to please China. As he was violently dragged away, Tsundue spoke his final words on behalf of his fellow Tibetan refugees: 'India gives us our strength, our confidence—India is our guru.'[37] Paying homage to the foundational ideals of India was the poet's way of shaming the Indians who were presiding over their demise. But an India run by bigots dedicated to destroying all that made it, despite its manifest flaws, something that so many beyond its borders—from W.E.B Du Bois and Martin Luther King, Jr., to Nelson Mandela and Nikol Pashinyan—once looked up to is perhaps incapable of being shamed. This is Modi's legacy.

9

SEIZURE

If you were to ask me to choose between democratic values, and wealth, power, prosperity and fame, I will very easily and without any doubt choose democratic values.

Narendra Modi

Narendra Modi did not stage a coup. He won in a free election. Unlike Indira Gandhi, he has exhibited a disciplined outward commitment to the norms of constitutional democracy while vandalising the organs that secure Indian democracy. It is certainly a miracle that institutions battered for decades by Congress have survived at all. Conceived to safeguard a pluralistic nationalism, and annealed in a climate of official adherence to secularism, they are, despite their defects, structurally inimical to the Prime Minister's brand of majoritarianism. Unable precipitously to remake all of India, Modi sought programmatically to subordinate India's institutional machinery to his political project. The poor health of the Republic—political dysfunction, bottomless corruption scandals, collapse in trust—is what propelled him into power. And it is in the name of resuscitating the ailing Republic that he has subverted and seized institutions indispensable to India's existence as a secular democracy.

India's modern military, a product of the Indo-British encounter, has always been its most respected institution. It never intruded in civilian matters, and politicians never sought to exploit it for electoral advantage. Modi betrayed no qualms in stamping on this sacred covenant. On 19 September 2018, the University Grants Commission instructed the vice chancellors of public universities across India to celebrate 29 September—the second anniversary of the day on which Indian armed forces staged a heavily publicised raid into Pakistan-held Kashmir on Modi's orders—as 'Surgical Strikes Day'. Authorities were directed to hold parades, press students to write letters of support to the armed forces, 'provide photo-ops for the students', and then compile the photos and letters for the public relations division of the defence ministry 'for publicity across various media'.[1] Shortly after the 'surgical strikes', hoardings of Modi's hirsute face, foregrounded against the silhouette of a lone soldier, went up in Uttar Pradesh.[2]

In 1999, when freelancers in the Hindu-nationalist movement sought to milk the brief war between India and Pakistan with political posters bearing photos of the military chiefs, the head of the army at the time complained to the Prime Minister and the posters vanished.[3] This time, 'surgical strikes' became a rallying cry in the BJP's political campaigns in every state where an election was being held. The army itself was reduced to a prop. As Amit Shah told the press, the soldiers were merely giving militaristic expression to the Prime Minister's 'determination and political intent'.[4] Religion, disavowed by the military, was injected into the propaganda built around its valour. One poster, for instance, showed Modi as the Hindu deity Rama and Pakistan's Prime Minister Nawaz Sharif as the ten-headed demon-king Ravana with the caption: 'We need another surgical strike by Modi to end a Ravana-like Pakistan.'[5] Many veterans were aghast at Modi's appropriation of the armed forces.[6] If the Prime Minister remained undaunted by criticism, it was because the Indian Army at the highest levels, infected by the chest-thumping nationalism exemplified by Modi, did not appear particularly discomfited.[7]

An institution fabled for its neutrality now counts a minister in Modi's government among its former chiefs—a man notorious for denouncing adversarial journalists as 'presstitutes'. Retired officers routinely appear on pro-Modi television news networks and direct lurid threats at Pakistan. And in the days leading up to the 'Surgical Strikes Day' celebrations, no less a figure than the chief of the army staff, Bipin Rawat, went on television and, echoing the BJP, spoke of the 'need for another surgical strike' against Pakistan.[8] Such a belligerent remark, unthinkable not so long ago, would have invited a severe rebuke from the civilian authorities in the pre-Modi years. But Rawat, appointed to his role after Modi discarded the seniority principle by which top posts in the armed forces have traditionally been filled, went without being censured. Installed in office by Hindu nationalists at home, Rawat expressed the view that Pakistan should 'develop as a secular state'.[9] His exhortation, gratuitous, was also laden with irony: he got his own job by superseding at least one colleague—Mohamadali Hariz—who was in line to become the first Muslim chief of the Indian Army until India's sectarian Prime Minister decided to depart from convention and appoint Rawat, who, promoted to the rank of the first Chief of Defence Staff in 2020, died in a helicopter crash the following year.[10]

There was a time when senior officers of the Indian military remained largely out of the public's view. They reported to their civilian bosses, confined themselves to the barracks, were always discreet and dignified in public, and never allowed themselves to be dragged into debates about Pakistan or China. In their professionalism, the defenders of India were almost a people apart. Modi, instead of preserving this culture, has thoroughly politicised the institution. Asked to account for his order of fighter jets from France, the Prime Minister accused his political opponents of having 'humiliated' the army.[11] A man who did not rise to acknowledge the widow of a fallen soldier at the

Republic Day parade in 2015 enjoined Indians a year later to 'show respect to our defence forces'.[12]

The armed forces, as it happens, have never needed anyone to whip up admiration for them: they enjoy it in abundance. Besides, the Prime Minister's specious rhetoric can scarcely conceal the fact that not since Krishna Menon—Nehru's disastrous defence minister during the Chinese invasion of 1962—has India known a leader more indifferent to the welfare of India's defence personnel than Modi. He places them in grave danger without a plan (as he did in Doklam), seeks to profit at home from their sacrifices (as he did after the 'surgical strikes'), and brags about what a tough guy he is to audiences of diasporic Indians abroad (as he did at one of his embarrassing concerts in London).[13] But other than arriving with camera crews on Hindu holidays to be filmed greeting troops amassed on borders, what has Modi done to improve the lives of soldiers and veterans? The day after the 'surgical strikes', as much of the Indian media was panegyrising Modi, the government quietly slashed the pensions of disabled veterans.[14] Indian forces still carry ancient equipment. So abysmal is the state of affairs under Modi that, as the former Indian Army officer Ajai Shukla has written, 'soldiers often choose to fight with Kalashnikov rifles taken from dead militants'.[15]

India's Byzantine bureaucracy can always be counted on to provide an alibi for Modi's failures. But no bureaucrat appears to have impeded Modi when he deployed the army in 2016 to lay down pontoon bridges at an environmentally sensitive site in Delhi for a private event hosted by a Hindu guru.[16] It is difficult to imagine a more egregious insult to the men in uniform than to outsource them to a pro-government religious impresario as providers of menial labour. The precedent he has established by pulling India's most venerable institution into the foetid political swamp he inhabits will become—has already become—the new norm. Attempting to reverse it will generate its own intractable problems. It will require the military to assert its independence; but can the military make such an assertion without appearing to defy civilian authority? And what happens when a politician who feels slighted by the khakis miscalibrates the counter-assertion of civilian authority and ends up unwittingly making the military feel belittled and demoralised? The wall which in the pre-Modi years separated the armed forces from politics hardened over long decades during which both sides (for the most part) unfailingly upheld in conduct and in speech the unwritten codes by which democracies survive. The consequences of Modi's eroding of that wall for immediate political gain will haunt India long after he has exited the scene.

The Reserve Bank of India, as one of its former governors correctly pointed out, 'figures only after the army in terms of perception as a custodian of society's trust'. How, then, did this esteemed institution, home to some of the country's most distinguished minds, become party to Modi's hare-brained decision in 2016 to void high-denomination notes? It is clear in retrospect that the bank's autonomy—its capacity to mount resistance—was methodically abraded in the months preceding demonetisation. The chairman of the RBI at the time, Raghuram Rajan, a cosmopolitan alumnus of the IMF whose faith in capitalism is seasoned with an appreciation for restraint and regulation, was subjected to vicious personal assaults by the BJP's apparatchiks. In the summer of 2016, Subramanian Swamy, a Harvard-trained economist and BJP parliamentarian notorious for his prescription to strip Muslims of their voting rights,[17] urged Modi to sack Rajan and deport him 'back to Chicago'—Rajan held an economics chair at the University of Chicago—because he was not 'appropriate for the country'.[18] An arresting figure originally from Tamil Nadu, Rajan is the closest to a celebrity occupant his office has ever had. Columnists likened him to James Bond. A Singh appointee, he used his fame and position to propagate defences of India's liberal traditions as saffron terror intensified across the country. There may in the future be a clamour by self-cherishing liberals to conscript Rajan into politics to play Manmohan II. But as things stood, Rajan became a bugbear for the BJP. Not only was he ideologically at odds with Modi ('publicly disparaging of the BJP government', in Swamy's words). He was also competing with the Prime Minister for the headlines. This was an affront to Modi's grandiosity. The silence of the Prime Minister—and the refusal of any cabinet minister or senior party functionary to issue even a perfunctory defence of the country's most senior banker as he was savaged by members of the ruling party—bespoke the fact that the bruising of Rajan in May 2016 was the farthest thing from a rogue operation. Rajan, nearing the end of his term, announced his decision to retire from the RBI and return to academia. His subsequent revelation to the press that he had expressed grave reservations about demonetisation to the Prime Minister 'in no uncertain terms' when the idea was put to him further clarifies the reasons behind the well-oiled campaign to maul him.[19]

Rajan's successor, Urjit Patel, an impressively educated economist of Gujarati descent from Kenya, had worked for the Modi-supporting Ambani family's Reliance Industries and served as a director of Gujarat State Petroleum Corporation when Modi was Gujarat's chief minister.[20] He became a naturalised Indian citizen only in 2013, when he was appointed deputy chairman of RBI. Under Patel's stewardship, the central bank not only remained mute about demonetisation—assuming the secretive idea hatched in the Prime Minister's residence was run past it—but also allowed itself to be used to provide retrospective cover to the Prime Minister when chaos ensued. In November 2016, a senior member of Modi's cabinet told parliament that the decision to demonetise had in fact been 'taken by the RBI board'.[21] The only way to verify this claim designed to exculpate Modi was to examine the minutes of the RBI's board meeting. But the bank refused to disclose them. Even enquiries submitted under the Right to Information Act did not yield a meaningful answer. A submission by the RBI to a parliamentary panel obtained by the press revealed that the government notified RBI of its decision to ban currency notes only hours before it was announced.[22]

Patel's docile acquiescence, shredding the RBI's credibility, emboldened Modi to make a push for its total subjugation. Lauded in 2014 by commentators who decried the welfare programmes of Congress as 'bribes' and 'handouts' for the votes of poor Indians, the Prime Minister announced a raft of exorbitantly expensive welfare schemes in 2018, fashioned specifically to lure poor voters. How was he going to pay for them? His needs, which arose as an afterthought as elections approached, were not going to be met by the portion of the 'profits'—interest accrued on bonds—that the central bank transferred annually to the government. So Modi decided to make yet another unprecedented move: raid the RBI's vast reserves of cash. The central bank, even from its position of shrunken autonomy, was alarmed. Expropriating those funds, retained by the RBI to provide stability in the event of unforeseen crises, would paralyse the bank in a time of genuine need.[23] Modi was making a demand that no previous government—even in wartime—had made.

Patel, having complied with Modi's whims for too long, attempted belatedly to withstand political intrusion. His deputy fired a warning shot in an impassioned speech in Mumbai in October 2018, telling Indians that 'the risks of undermining the central bank's independence are potentially catastrophic'.[24] The speech would have given pause to any responsible Prime Minister who placed the national interest above self-interest. But Modi, who values fealty above all else and is invested more than anything else in the perpetuation of himself and the entrenchment of his ideology, retaliated forcefully, packing the bank's board with loyal bureaucrats and RSS ideologues, and threatening to invoke legal clauses that had never before been used to compel the bank to turn over its reserves to the government.[25] Besieged at lightning speed, Patel offered at first to make some concessions. Then, realising perhaps that he would forever be memorialised as the governor who presided over the total demise of the RBI's independence, he abruptly resigned from his job. Two successive resignations at the pinnacle of the RBI in two years is its own testament to the destruction of one of India's most cherished institutions. Still, if any doubt remained, it was cleared up by the first major action by the RBI under Patel's handpicked successor: a solemn pledge to transfer a gargantuan dividend to the government.[26]

Some of India's finest public universities are also strongholds of subaltern activism. They are places where young Indians from all corners of the country—many of them from disadvantaged backgrounds—meet, mingle with, and discover compatriots unlike themselves. The solidarity forged in these places transcends the narrow identities around which the BJP mobilises voters. It was inevitable that Modi was going to pounce on them. The intervention was indirect, delegated to the foot soldiers of the movement in the student wing of the RSS, the Akhil Bharatiya Vidyarthi Parishad, or ABVP. Backed and safeguarded by the powers that be, its troops have acquired a chilling leverage on university campuses across the country. The blueprint for the takeover of universities, activated first at the University of Hyderabad in 2016, has, in the years since, hardened into a terrifying pattern sustained by the blessings of the government and the complicity of law-enforcement agencies.

Members of the ABVP sniff the air each morning for fresh offence, trace the origin of the offence to a Dalit scholar or a Muslim student or a liberal or left-wing student organisation, accuse the offenders of propagating 'anti-national' ideas, and trigger unrest and agitation until the university, shivering with dread, takes punitive action. At Hyderabad University, it was a Dalit scholar named Rohith Vemula, a gifted writer dependent for survival on a government scholarship, who came into their crosshairs. That he was Dalit, an irredeemable sin in Hinduism, already made him an objectionable figure. But Rohith also had opinions, and expressed them forcefully when the ABVP disrupted the university with protests against the screening, at another university campus in faraway Delhi, of a film on sectarian riots that showed its masters in an unflattering light. Being reproved by an outcaste must have been particularly mortifying. So the ABVP drafted a letter to a minister in the Modi government accusing Rohith of being an 'anti-national'. The minister, an immensely powerful man, forwarded the note to the university authorities. The authorities moved swiftly against Rohith. The scholarship of the bright, promising scholar, who idolised the prose of Carl Sagan and dreamt of emulating his hero in his own writings, was suspended.[27] That meagre stipend was vital for him. But more than deprivation, Rohith appears to have been tormented by the violation of his dignity—the continuation of a primeval caste-Hindu sport. 'Never was a man treated as a mind' in India, Rohith wrote in a note. 'As a glorious thing made up of stardust.'[28] He killed himself. The outcry that erupted in the weeks that followed elicited no corrective action from Modi. The minister who intervened on behalf of the men who drove Rohith to end his life kept his job and was later appointed to the governorship of Himachal Pradesh. It was Rohith who was posthumously maligned as an imposter, a caste Hindu who had been masquerading as a Dalit to get easy handouts.[29] After this early success, the ABVP, in line with the template trialled in Hyderabad, menaced campuses at the best-known institutions of higher education across India.

At Delhi University's Ramjas College—no one's idea of a bastion of left-wing radicalism—hoodlums of the ABVP nearly strangled to death a faculty member and roughed up students for the crime of organising a literary festival whose content the philistines found distasteful.[30] Official collusion became indisputably apparent when students at Delhi's Jawaharlal Nehru University were charged in early 2019 with sedition—one of the gravest offences on the statute books—on the basis of allegations that they had chanted, almost three years earlier, 'anti-national' slogans at a meeting to protest the execution, under Singh, of a Kashmiri man.[31] One student, a Muslim, was 'disappeared'; the police, busy abetting the foul men who rule India, have not been able to locate him. Some of the slogans heard at JNU were certainly repugnant. Indians who condone the Republic's sworn foreign adversaries and advance mitigations for those devoted religiously to the cause of the country's territorial mutilation are not easy to warm to; yet the measure of a democracy's self-belief is not only its capacity passively to tolerate speech that is objectionable but its determination actively to protect the speechmakers.

The Modi government's decision to invoke a statute from the nineteenth century—once used by the British to tame Mahatma Gandhi—to crush young students was worthy of a tinpot tyranny. At central universities from Delhi to Hyderabad, from Rajasthan to Bengal, students and staff have been terrorised for failing the test of nationalism devised by people pledging allegiance to the RSS, an organisation that once refused to recognise the Indian flag on the grounds that it was a totem of secularism.[32] And the police, instead of hauling the emergent native avatar of Boko Haram to prisons, instead carried away their victims into custody. The rule of law hasn't so much broken down as become inverted. The application of the official boot to the bodies of underprivileged students with a proclivity for dissent has been accompanied by the withdrawal of governmental support for their education: the Modi administration withheld more than a billion dollars earmarked for scholarships to students from disadvantaged communities.[33] And the persecution of the talented but destitute students resisting Modi's majoritarianism has itself occurred against the backdrop of a methodical desiccation of the handful of prestigious institutions that rear them.

Most of the 760 universities—and the 35,000 colleges affiliated with them—spread over India are in a state of advanced decline. In the name of improving higher education, Modi announced the creation of 'Institutes of Excellence'. Institutions invited to joint this new layer of hierarchy will be given millions of pounds of public money. The principal condition for admission to this club is a record of academic excellence. One of the colleges selected for inclusion in the category was Jio Institute. Founded by Modi's billionaire cheerleader Mukesh Ambani and named after his mobile phone network, Jio Institute existed only on paper: there was no campus, no curriculum, no faculty, no students. It was a phantom institute, decorated with the 'eminence' tag on instructions from the Prime Minister's office.[34]

A host of existing central universities, meanwhile, have been granted 'autonomy' by Modi. What this heralds in practice is the gradual elimination of governmental support and the inevitable introduction of exorbitant tuition fees by universities compelled to fend for themselves. The result: the most disadvantaged students—such as the students at JNU, a nightmare for Hindu nationalists—will become further marginalised.

The defence that Modi is devolving powers through the grant of autonomy to universities—that his tinkering is all part of a high-minded administrative streamlining uncontaminated by ideological imperatives—is belied by his own decision to dismantle the University Grants Commission and replace it with a new central body vested with heightened powers of oversight over the 'autonomous' institutions. Since 1976, education has been a concurrent subject: both the state and the union governments are responsible for it. The termination of the University Grants Commission will mark the most significant transfer of power in this area from the states to the centre in at least four decades. A single agency under the thumb of the union government will henceforth decide what is taught, how it is taught, and who teaches it. This is a major triumph for the BJP and the RSS, which have sought for decades to seize the commanding heights of education.[35]

In 2017, the government constituted a committee of scholars to produce, in the words of its chairman, a 'report that will help the government rewrite certain aspects of ancient history'.

According to the minutes of their secretive meetings reviewed by *Reuters*, which was the first to alert the world to its existence, they were labouring to 'establish a correlation' between Indian history and the vast body of Hindu mythology.[36] Doing so would confer legitimacy on the Hindu-nationalist belief that Vedic culture emanated from autochthonous inhabitants of India, and not migrants from western and central Asia. It is a bogus belief, debunked by DNA studies of ancient settlers in northern India, who originated, it is now clear, in central and western Asia.[37] The diligence with which the distant past was illuminated must also be applied to the task of revamping how the relatively recent past is filtered and taught. The previous millennium was a calamitous period for India. By papering it over with untenable tales, secularists infantilised Indians, insulted their memories, and rendered them susceptible to the piffle purveyed by Hindu nationalists.

But a corrective to the well-meaning distortions enshrined in the curricula by secularists cannot come from the luminaries of the current dispensation, who are beneficiaries of those distortions. They are bereft of the intellectual equipment and emotional equanimity essential to explicate the past sincerely without seeking to revenge it. Education to the Hindu nationalists is a vehicle for the transmission of a collection of risible fables fabricated from an admixture of insupportable superiority complex and incurable inferiority complex that is the trait of self-pitying ethno-religious nationalists everywhere. Indian schoolchildren, already at the mercy of an educational system that withholds from them an intelligibly forthright accounting of their country's disturbing past, now appear destined to be conditioned by the ludicrous yet lethal pseudo-history that Modi and his confreres—many of whom today sit atop India's most eminent institutions—internalised in the boot camps of the RSS. They are men consumed by resentments. Their cure is rage and fantasy.

One of Modi's appointees to the staff of the Indian Council of Historical Research, or ICHR, an august body created to oversee and disburse funding for historical research, began his job by publishing a demand for 'an unqualified apology' from India's 'most learned historians' for obscuring 'systematic anti-Hindu violence' that had gone on apparently 'for 1,400 years', and called time on the '"eminent" intellectuals and the "high-profile" and "sophisticated" media and their political patrons [who] are now so agitated and apprehensive that [their] sort of history might soon be replaced by authentic history'.[38] But the construction of an 'authentic history' requires a bare minimum of expertise that Modi's nominee for the ICHR's chairmanship—an obscure academician from Andhra affiliated with the RSS—patently lacked. The new chairman's most substantial body of work appeared not in distinguished peer-reviewed journals but on his blog, where he expounded, among other things, on the utility of the Hindu caste system ('working well in ancient times and we do not find any complaint from any quarters against it').[39]

Instead of 'authentic history', school textbooks in state governments run by the BJP are now congested with lies. In Madhya Pradesh, a state until recently in the BJP's pocket, students have been taught that India won the 1962 war against China. Textbooks in Rajasthan, omitting any mention of Nehru, teach children that the state's revered medieval chieftain, Maharana Pratap, who was trounced by a Mughal force in 1576, 'conclusively defeated Mughal emperor Akbar'.[40] As Rajasthan's education minister explained, the objective of this grotesque anti-history 'is to bring the true history, culture, philosophy, ancient science and heroes of [India] to the fore ... to evoke an emotional and spiritual sentiment in the society. This is required for [India] to become "Vishwa Guru" [world leader]'.[41] In Maharashtra, the Mughal period has been effaced from history textbooks.[42]

The intellectual poverty of the new regime has been on near-constant display since 2014. Satyapal Singh, who until 2019 was Modi's minister for human resources—the department responsible for education—believes that Darwin's theory of evolution is 'scientifically wrong' and 'needs to change in school and college curriculum'. How did he alight at this discovery? Because 'nobody, including our ancestors, have said they saw an ape turning into a man. No books we have read or the tales told to us by our grandparents had such a mention'.[43] Benightedness, alas, is not an isolated phenomenon in Modi's cabinet. The Prime Minister himself believes, as he told an audience in 2014, that ancient Indians had mastered 'genetic science'. Exhibit A of his evidence for the claim was Karna, the thwarted anti-hero in the ancient Hindu epic *Mahabharata*, who was 'born outside his mother's womb'. The elephant-headed Hindu deity Ganesha was adduced by Modi as Exhibit B to argue the case that 'our ancestors' had perfected 'the practice of plastic surgery'.[44]

Nehru had wanted to promote a 'scientific temper' in the Indian mind. Modi has fostered an anti-science outlook. At the Indian Science Congress of 2015, inaugurated by the Prime Minister himself, academicians from across the land that once produced boffins such as C.V. Raman and Jagadish Chandra Bose tabulated the scientific achievements of ancient Indians. Among other things, Indians, they said, had built jets capable of interplanetary travel and placed a man on Mars. Indian cows, meanwhile, converted the grass they ingested into '24-carat gold'.[45] As chief minister of Gujarat, Modi had written a preface to a 'history' book for school students which informed them that the Hindu god Rama had flown the first aircraft.[46] As Prime Minister of India, he oversaw the diminution of the country that not so long ago had acquired a global reputation as a 'knowledge power' into an international laughing stock. But what is a reputational loss for India is a psychological gain for Hindu ideologues. Indians' confusion about their past, the chronic mismanagement of education, the powers of patronage—Modi exploited every crack and opportunity to suffuse institutions erected to wash away ignorance with the unenlightenment necessary to hasten contemporary India's conversion into a modern avatar of the pristinely high-tech Hindu fairyland he and his Hindutva kith genuinely believe once flourished in the subcontinent.

In 2017, Modi made the most far-reaching power-grab in recent memory. He piled on, stealthily, to that year's Finance Bill—a special class of legislation exempted from the traditional checks of the upper house of parliament, where the BJP sits in the opposition benches—a stack of amendments tailored to expand dramatically the executive's power.[47] The government gave itself extensive authority to make appointments to appellate tribunals, regulate the terms of service of the appointees, and to terminate them. More disturbingly, it vested tax inspectors, who have a hoary history of being deployed to exact political vengeance, with the power to raid any property without the need to disclose the purpose of the raid—not just to the person being raided but even to the tax tribunals. The law, moreover, could be applied retrospectively. Having campaigned on the promise to clean up politics, Modi introduced provisions in the same bill allowing any individual or private company incorporated in India to make potentially unlimited donations to political parties through the purchase of 'electoral bonds'—promissory notes issued at state banks in multiples of up to ten million rupees—and scrapped the prohibition that prevented corporations from giving more than a small portion of their net profits. The most extraordinary part was that the donors' and recipients' identities were to be kept confidential from the public. If all this were not outrageous enough, a year later, the government amended, without debate, a law that banned foreign donations to Indian political parties. Enacted ex post facto, the change not only emancipated the BJP and Congress from legal sanction—both parties were found guilty by a Delhi court of violating the law in its previous incarnation—but also opened the sluice gates to (anonymous) overseas money. A foreign company with an Indian subsidiary can now effectively channel unlimited amounts of cash to India's legendarily venal political parties.

The baleful effects of Modi's legislative power-grab on institutional autonomy have already become apparent.

The Election Commission of India is a marvel to behold. It has overseen the conduct of largely free and fair elections for decades in a nation riven by violence and awash with illicit money during the polls. The behaviour of this illustrious institution in the age of Modi betokens a distressing attrition of its autonomy. When the slippery device of 'electoral bonds' was first announced by the government, the ECI reacted furiously, denouncing it as a 'retrograde step as far as transparency of donations is concerned' and demanding its immediate withdrawal.[48] But when Modi pretended not to notice and pressed ahead with his plan, the ECI performed an about-turn and endorsed the scheme as 'a step in the right direction'.[49] What exactly prompted this change of mind is not known. What is known is that, in the intervening period, the ECI made another unusual decision to Modi's advantage when it delayed, by a whole month, state-wide elections that were scheduled to be held in Gujarat in November 2017. The official reason for the postponement—that the BJP government in Gujarat needed more time to carry out 'relief work' following heavy flooding earlier in the year—was shaky for two reasons. First, there had been far worse flooding in Jammu and Kashmir in 2014—300 people were killed—and yet the ECI had refused to adjourn the vote there. Second, the one month by which the ECI deferred the election in Gujarat was filled with electoral rather than relief activity by the BJP government. As the *Indian Express* outlined, 'a slew of financial sops were announced, big-ticket projects were launched across the state, and several [union] ministers and BJP chief ministers travelled [to Gujarat] to address election rallies'.[50] After casting his own vote when the elections finally were held, Modi proceeded to stage an improvised campaign march in flagrant violation of the ECI's codes. No action was taken against the Prime Minister.[51]

In the end, the only beneficiaries of the 'relief work' for which the election was delayed were Modi—intent on not losing face in his native state—and the BJP. The ECI's uncharacteristic decision generated, in the judgement of one of its own former chiefs, a credible 'ground of suspicion' that it had helped enable an outcome favourable to the ruling party.[52] If the perception of the ECI's integrity is the basis of its credibility, the submission of political parties to the ECI's authority is the condition of its viability. Modi's immediate political gain was predicated, as always, on the violation of conventions critical to the survival of Indian democracy. The enormity of the ECI's accommodation of the BJP, having gone largely unnoticed in a country distracted by the theatrics of the ruling dispensation, will become painfully clear when other parties clamour for the leeway generously extended to Modi—and, when denied it, defy the ECI exactly as Modi did.

Rewriting the Constitution is the highest ambition of Hindu nationalists.[53] The greatest obstacle in realising that ambition are the courts. At the lower levels of the judiciary in India, there is malfeasance and incompetence. At the apex, there is integrity and rectitude. Debilitated during Indira's dictatorship, the Supreme Court, unlike the lower courts, rebounded with fury and gradually created for itself a role that has often exceeded its original purpose. The court has effectively arrogated to itself legislative powers. For the most part, the decisions of its justices have been in accordance with liberal social mores—which explains the institution's international prestige—but they have also on occasion been reactionary and majoritarian: such as when a former chief justice restored a criminal law notorious for being used to persecute gays on the basis that 'the orifice of the mouth is not, according to nature, meant for sexual or carnal intercourse', or when the capital punishment awarded to a Kashmiri man was upheld on the grounds that 'the collective conscience of society will only be satisfied' if he was executed. Judicial trespass was always a symptom of the sickness that courses through the other branches of the government. In a Republic ravaged by a succession of subversive executives empowered by supine legislators, the Supreme Court attained popular legitimacy as the crusading custodian of constitutional democracy *because* of its overreach. Indians demoralised by political dysfunction have come to regard the Supreme Court as the Republic's deus ex machina, its saviour, and, like a hypochondriac who swallows antibiotics to fight off a common cold, become habituated to petitioning it to resolve matters that ought to remain the business of the executive and the legislature. This dependency is profoundly unhealthy, but what necessitated it is the poor health of Indian democracy.

The Supreme Court was the one institution that put up the stiffest resistance to Modi's rise to national leadership. After the bloodletting in Gujarat, it excoriated him as a 'modern-day Nero' who was 'looking elsewhere when ... innocent children and helpless women were burning' and 'probably deliberating how the perpetrators of the crime can be protected'.[54] That Modi survived such a bruising indictment and wormed his way into the Republic's highest political office is a reminder that institutions are not self-animating creatures. What they do is contingent upon those who people them. The exoneration Modi was granted in the run-up to the general elections by a special probe deputed by the apex court to investigate his complicity in one of the many massacres of 2002 appears, in retrospect, almost foreordained. Tasked with gathering facts in a state whose entire administrative machinery functioned as Modi's marionette, it produced a report held in place by fiction, as the distinguished lawyer and journalist Manoj Mitta, who followed the inquiry more closely than just about anyone else, has observed.[55] The solitary interview one of its officers held with Modi 'was more to place Modi's defence on record rather than to ferret out any inconsistency or admission of wrongdoing' on his part.[56] The advice of the Supreme Court's amicus to the special probe that criminal charges could reasonably be framed against Modi based on his alleged instructions to the police to 'go soft on Hindu rioters' was rejected.

Despite this clean bill, Modi's history in Gujarat threatened to generate legal jeopardy for him in the future. The fate of his closest ally, Amit Shah, was still uncertain when Modi became Prime Minister: a special court constituted by the Supreme Court in 2012 was deciding whether to put Shah on trial for the murder of a Muslim man. A month after Modi took office, the presiding judge in that case was removed from his job. Six months later, his successor, an upstanding judge named B.H. Loya, died in the most mysterious of circumstances the morning after spending a night at a government guest house. Loya's replacement, M.B. Gosavi, dropped the charges against Shah within three weeks of being given charge of the case.[57] The sequence of events could have been dismissed as a coincidence were it not for the allegations of foul play advanced in 2017 by Loya's family. The judge, his family said, had withstood fierce pressure to deliver the correct verdict before he died. The opposition then alleged that two of Loya's friends, with whom the judge had apparently shared his ordeal, had also dropped dead: one from the top of a building, another on a train.[58] Even as details of Loya's puzzling death were slowly trickling forth and a clearer picture of a criminal conspiracy to choke the lower judiciary was beginning to congeal, the Supreme Court became embroiled in what seemed like the most apocalyptic crisis in its history since Indira's dictatorship.

In January 2018, four of the top court's most senior justices made history by staging an unprecedented press conference to issue a direct warning to Indian citizens that 'unless this institution is preserved ... democracy will not survive in this country'.[59] The integrity of the highest court in the land, they explained, was being imperilled by the manner in which important cases were being assigned by the chief justice to benches of his choice with 'no rationale'. Loya's death was not an unimportant factor in the justices' decision to alert the public to the threat to the court's independence, as Ranjan Gogoi, the man then next in line to be chief justice, admitted.[60] It was abundantly clear from what was left unsaid that the insulation between the executive and the Supreme Court—the final court of appeal, the last hope of the Republic's endangered Constitution—was rapidly dissolving under Modi.

Given the Prime Minister's unsettling past, there was a tragic inevitability to all this. What looked like the beginning of an outright revolt momentarily startled him and stirred an inert opposition into action. But rescuing institutions from authoritarian assaults in a democracy is like administering heavy doses of radiation to a cancer patient: it seeds fresh risks. Smelling blood, the opposition mobilised to impeach the chief justice in parliament. But by seeking to activate a process that had never before been put to use—and that too not so much to preserve the court's independence as to magnify Modi's perceived influence on it—the democratic arrangement was being reconfigured drastically. Impeachment proceedings, put on to generate a public spectacle to embarrass the government, would have ripened the procedure for future abuse. What averted the trial, ironically, was the decay of parliament itself. India's Modi-worshipping vice-president, who chairs the upper house of parliament, refused to authorise the impeachment in spite of the fact that all the procedural conditions for it had been satisfied.[61] The Supreme Court, split within, found itself in an embarrassingly difficult position: to be seen to be going against the Prime Minister would open it up to accusations that it was seeking to allay the perception that its chief justice was biased. Having admitted a petition by activists demanding an independent inquest into Loya's death, a bench of the Supreme Court headed by the chief justice threw it out and upbraided the petitioners—none of whom could reasonably be called a busybody—for wasting the court's time. This was a baffling denouement. In the background, Loya's son held his own press conference to announce that he no longer had any 'suspicions' about how his father died. After a brief tremor, Shah and Modi won decisively.

In India, a country with thousands of newspapers and hundreds of television channels dedicated exclusively to news, there is, with some notable exceptions, a strange absence of dissenting voices. Instead, primetime shows on the most-watched television networks—almost all of them pro-Modi—are packed with panellists who trip over one another to praise the Prime Minister. 'Influential owners, anchors, editors across the nation', as the dauntless journalist Krishna Prasad has observed, serve as an 'advance party to quell dissent, manufacture consent, set the agenda, drum up support, and spread fear, venom, hatred and bigotry—sometimes through sheer silence'.[62] Prasad, eased out of his job editing one of India's finest English-language newsmagazines for the offence of scrutinising Hindu nationalists too vigorously, was not exaggerating when he wrote that the Indian media today is 'gasping under pressure not felt even during Emergency's darkest nights'. Indira Gandhi shackled the press. Modi co-opted it.

Outliers have found themselves relentlessly harried and harassed. In 2017, officers from the CBI, India's top investigative agency known as the 'caged bird' of governments, raided the residence of Prannoy Roy, the founder of NDTV, one of India's last remaining bulwarks of independent broadcast journalism, and the offices of his television channel. The reason for the swoop was an alleged 'loss' to a private bank arising from a loan of 3.5 billion rupees taken, almost a decade before, by Roy and his wife. The investigative agency's energetic effort to recoup such a tiny sum apparently due to a private lender in a country whose state banks are owed more than a hundred billion dollars by the country's oligarchs was mystifying on the face of it.[63] What made it all the more bizarre was the fact that the Roys had repaid the debt in full in 2009, and produced a letter from the bank attesting to this fact. A former head of the CBI questioned the agency's motive. But Modi's fixation with NDTV— and prominent journalists in the English-language media who covered the anti-Muslim pogrom of 2002 when he was chief minister of Gujarat, or questioned him about it—is all-consuming. A year before the raid on the Roys, NDTV's Hindi station was accused of imperilling India's national security for having reported on a terrorist attack, something virtually every other station did, and forced off the air for a day.

2017 was the year in which Modi consolidated his hold over the media. Karan Thapar was perhaps the only journalist who unnerved Modi with his direct questioning in a television interview after the violence in Gujarat. Modi walked out of the show within minutes of sitting down. But the payback came in 2017 when Thapar, among the best in his trade anywhere in the world, found himself out of a job after his employer, India Today TV, refused to renew his contract.[64] A few months later, Bobby Ghosh, the editor of *Hindustan Times* who distinguished his publication with an online 'Hate Tracker' to keep tabs on sectarian violence in the era of Modi, was shown the door the day after the broadsheet's owner had a meeting with Modi.[65] In between, a newly launched Marathi-language show hosted by Nikhil Wagle, another fiercely independent-minded broadcast journalist, was cancelled by TV9 despite its soaring ratings.[66] A year later, the recently empowered tax authorities raided the properties of Raghav Bahl, a media proprietor whose publications are not worshipful of Modi.[67]

The harassment and ostracisation of Modi's critics have been complemented by the introduction into the media landscape of a new television news channel, Republic, backed by an investor from southern India whom the BJP nominated to the upper house of parliament.[68] The star of Republic, Arnab Goswami, is an unabashed pro-government bully with an outsize pulpit. Times Now, the channel Goswami vacated to seek his own fortune, chases ratings by out-shouting and out-doing the polarising theatrics of its erstwhile leader. Careers of Modi's critics have tapered away. The Prime Minister's champions have prospered.

There is a pervasive atmosphere of self-censorship in newsrooms. Four hundred pairs of eyes and ears monitor every news channel in India from the offices of the government's Information and Broadcasting Ministry.[69] What they see and hear, for the most part, are shrill theatrics camouflaging the ethical and intellectual destitution of India's news media in the age of Modi. In America, legacy publications such as the *Washington Post* and the *Atlantic* have been able to rediscover and pursue vigorously (if with a touch of American self-righteousness and self-unawareness) a lofty purpose—the defence of democracy from the assaults of Trump—with the resources placed at their disposal by their billionaire proprietors. In India, with some exceptions, the proprietors of most of the once great and trusted brands in journalism have degenerated into hustlers. An extensive undercover operation in 2018 by the website *CobraPost* exposed the depths of the rot: a reporter posing as a deep-pocketed Hindu nationalist was able to obtain enthusiastic assent from virtually every major print and electronic news entity for his proposal to air anti-opposition, pro-Hindutva propaganda in return for cash.[70] They are all on tape—owners and top executives of the *Times of India*, *India Today*, the *New Indian Express*, *Radio One*—discussing the details of this cancerous idea. Vineet Jain, the owner of the *Times of India*, the world's largest-selling English-language newspaper that was also one of the principal cheerleaders of Modi's demonetisation, gave advice to the fake reporter on ways to launder hundreds of millions of rupees into legal cheques.[71] In 2022, NDTV, the last bastion of relatively independent broadcast journalism in English, was acquired by Gautam Adani, the businessman closest to Modi, against the wishes of its employees.

There are still exceptionally talented journalists at these titles. But their skill is fated to become insupportable just when it is most needed as what remains of India's fourth estate is repurposed into a PR service by the knaves, scoundrels, and bootlickers who own it. Practitioners of adversarial, public-interest journalism in India are to be found in greater numbers in the 'regions'—in small towns, villages, non-English languages—men and women such as Gauri Lankesh, Sandeep Sharma, Vijay Singh. Their circumstances were not glamorous, but the impact of their work can be judged from the gruesomeness of their kill-ings. The linguistic diversity of India, sadly, means that country-wide outrage against the localised murders of journalists can only be produced by extensive coverage in the 'national'—that is, English-language—media. And this is the sector that is also the most compromised and craven.

Many well-heeled 'national' media personalities in Delhi and Mumbai, incapable of extending their gaze beyond their own navels, were appalled when India was ranked 138 in the 2018 World Press Freedom Index published by Reporters Without Borders.[72] The fact that the 'world's largest democracy' was placed at such an insultingly low rank was proof to them of an international conspiracy to discredit Modi.[73] What their fulmina-tions did not take into account was all that was happening around them: the sacking of critics, the hacking apart of intrepid reporters in the regions, the deep corruption at media houses in the metropolises. The democratic content of the Republic was being gutted in the Modi era, but the people believing them-selves to be the guardians of democracy were concerned most of all with image. India, you see, had become Modified.

10

DISUNION

Unity in diversity is India's strength ...
Narendra Modi

India is an improbable nation. Inheriting the continental diversity consolidated into an elaborate colonial holding by the British and their native collaborators, it constructed its sovereignty by bypassing all the traditional determinants of nationhood—language, ethnicity, religion—long adduced to sift human beings into exclusionary silos. The polyglot, poly-ethnic, poly-religious political union envisaged by the founders of India was ratified in a free vote, held in 1951, in which every adult from Kashmir to Kanyakumari and Kutch to Kibithu, regardless of his or her origins, was for the first time enfranchised. But the democratic Republic consecrated by that astounding pageant of political participation could only be sustained by a creed that honoured the heterogeneity of India's human cast. Secularism, it turns out, was a great deal more than the private fetish of a deracinated post-colonial elite. It was, with all its defects, the condition of India's unity.

Only a citizenship premised on the repudiation of the procrustean presumptions of the phrase 'national identity' could fuse the variegated peoples of India into a nation. Indianness was a catholic category: you could speak any language, practise any faith, belong to any ethnicity—and still be able to call yourself Indian. Distinctions of language were overcome with relative ease; ethno-religious insularity was the fount of ungiving intransigence. The business of squashing it was phenomenally ugly. But force and chicanery alone could never have worked against the variety of resistance ranged against Indian integration. In the end, India could generate support for the union among Christians in Nagaland, Muslims in Kashmir, Sikhs in Punjab, and Buddhists in Sikkim because their faith was immaterial to full membership of it. But as India moves under Modi from defective secularism to *de facto* Hindu supremacism, it can no longer invoke the foundational arguments of the state to retain non-Hindus within its fold. Delhi can hold on to them only by force—as second-tier subjects of a Hindu imperium, not equal citizens of an inclusive non-confessional state.

Nowhere is the hazard of disunion more apparent than in Jammu and Kashmir. India's sole Muslim-majority state was a moral blot and a criminal enterprise long before Modi appeared on the scene and abolished its statehood. But his Hindu nationalism is not even theoretically equipped to defuse the crisis of legitimacy that stalks the state in Kashmir. Modi's presence in the Prime Minister's office is, if anything, a dream-come-true for Kashmir's radical Muslim separatists—and their sponsors in Pakistan—who have long preached to the brutalised local majority that India is a Hindu state and they its subjects. The fillip Modi has given their cause has an inescapable ring of finality to it. Two segregationist forms of nationalism are clashing, complementing, and fortifying each other in Kashmir. On the quartering block is a brittle unity forged in the dream of emancipating Indians from the malign thrall of small identities.

The crisis of modern Kashmir began at the birth of India. When the British partitioned and quit the subcontinent in 1947, Jammu and Kashmir was one of hundreds of 'princely states'—

tributaries of the crown of various sizes—faced with the choice of accession to either India or Pakistan, or independence from both. Most of these states, lorded over by unconscionably opulent maharajas and nawabs, transferred their loyalties to India to avert rebellions by their haggard subjects. Kashmir was Hyderabad in reverse: a Muslim-majority kingdom under the thumb of a Hindu king, Hari Singh, a dissolute despot. His forebears had received the territory in the nineteenth century as a token of gratitude for betraying Kashmir's Sikh rulers to Britain's advantage.[1] Now the dynasty faced an impossible choice. An Islamic Pakistan from which non-Muslims were fleeing *en masse* was as unthinkable for Singh as a secular state was for his counterpart in Hyderabad. Joining India, embarked on Nehruvian socialism, would mean relinquishing his privileges. So Singh temporised. Jinnah nonetheless felt confident in the beginning that, given its location and demography, Kashmir would end up in Pakistan. And it might have done had it not been for a major complicating factor in the form of Sheikh Abdullah. The wildly popular leader of Kashmir's largest political party, the secular National Conference, Abdullah was a close comrade of Nehru's. A socialist and secularist, he charged Jinnah with 'breath[ing] poison into the atmosphere' with his 'formula that Muslims and Hindus form separate nations'.[2]

Pakistan branded him a 'quisling and paid agent' out to 'disrupt the Mussalmans',[3] but it could not take chances: Kashmir's accession to India would instantly debunk the argument for Pakistan's invention—that Muslims and Hindus could not coexist in one state—and obliterate Pakistan's claim to be the authentic homeland of the subcontinent's Muslims that gave a gloss of purpose to its puzzling existence. Rattled, Jinnah authorised a war to seize Kashmir by force in October 1947. The American journalist Margaret Bourke-White interviewed the 'irregulars' setting out from Pakistan to 'liberate' Kashmir, which at that stage was an independent and sovereign state. 'We are going to help our Muslim brothers in Kashmir,' they told her.[4] There was barely any resistance as they crossed into Kashmir. Srinagar, the capital, was theirs for the taking. But then the men mobilised in the name of Islamic solidarity by the father of Pakistan distracted themselves for days by butchering the locals, razing a church, and raping and mutilating the nuns at a mission hospital.[5]

Belatedly taking notice of what was coming to him, Hari Singh appealed to India for help. But Kashmir was a foreign state. Nehru set conditions: Kashmir must accede to the Indian union and the accession must be approved by Sheikh Abdullah. Hari Singh, anxious to keep the Muslim socialist out of power, insisted on retaining some of his royal prerogatives. This was very far from ideal. But since the proposal had the assent of Kashmir's most popular politician, and since Kashmir was on the threshold of surrender to Pakistan, Indian troops were air-lifted to Srinagar on 27 October 1947.[6] The Instrument of Accession that gave Delhi juridical authority over the state, dated 26 October 1947, may have been an antedated document signed by Hari Singh on the day India initiated action. Whatever the case, Kashmir had acceded to the Indian union by the legal mechanism instituted under the terms of the sub-continent's partition. The matter was settled in law.

Inciting religious passions had yielded tremendous dividends for Jinnah in India. But the technique did not work in Kashmir. His emprise deepened Abdullah's revulsion for Pakistan's founder and horrified ordinary Kashmiris. When Bourke-White made her way into Kashmir—'heaped with rubble and blackened with fire'—she found that Kashmiri Muslims, far from yearning for Jinnah's Islamic state, were mourning the martyrdom of Mir Maqbool Sherwani, a local leader of Abdullah's National Conference, in the act of defending interfaith unity. Mir, who had led an heroic resistance against the invaders, was captured, tortured, and ordered to recite support for Pakistan. When he refused, he was crucified in the shade of a ransacked church and riddled with bullets. Mir's last words, relayed to

Bourke-White by the locals who now regarded him as a 'saint', were: 'Victory to Hindu–Muslim unity.'[7] That phrase, discredited in Kashmir since the late 1980s and even more thoroughly in India since 2014, was a poignant tribute to Kashmiri syncretism and a haunting indictment of Jinnah and his ideological kin in Hindu garb.

In the days leading up to the Pakistani invasion, Hari Singh's administration decommissioned and disarmed Muslim soldiers and abetted a massacre of their co-religionists in Jammu. Some 200,000 Muslims were killed and another 300,000 driven from their homes by Hindu nationalists embarked on a homicidal project to create a Hindu majority in the region. This crime, far exceeding anything perpetrated by the Nizam of Hyderabad, invited criminal prosecution.[8] Gandhi himself held Hari Singh culpable for the atrocities by Sikhs and Hindus who travelled to the kingdom to wipe out Muslims.[9] But having shrewdly shielded himself with the wording of the Instrument of Accession, Singh not only was not prosecuted but his criminality was airbrushed from history. Religion was a secondary concern for the Muslim Kashmiris who sought union with India. It was Singh and his Hindu-nationalist brethren—and their Muslim-nationalist counterparts in Pakistan—who injected the poison of religion into Kashmir.

A third of Kashmir had fallen to Pakistan by the time hostilities subsided. It should have been left to Indian forces to recover it. But Nehru, acting on British advice, referred Kashmir to the United Nations. It was a grievous mistake: it insulted the ordinary Kashmiris who had rallied behind India, created a costly diversion from the urgent task of rebuilding Kashmir, and made Pakistan a party to what now became a legal dispute. The UN devised a sequential prescription in 1948 for the resolution of the conflict: first, Pakistan would have to retreat from the Kashmiri territory it occupied; second, India would have to pare its troop levels down to numbers essential only for the maintenance of security; third, Kashmiris would have to be given a referendum to decide their future.[10] It is possible that Kashmiris may have voted for independence. But given that it was Kashmir's status as a sovereign independent state in 1947 that invited Pakistan's war of annexation, it is far more probable that they would have voted to ratify the Instrument of Accession backed by Abdullah and remain part of India. The plebiscite, however, never took place because the UN formula was sequent: the first condition had to be satisfied before the parties could move to meet the second, and the second before the third. Pakistan, rather than vacate the portion of Kashmir it took, continued a low-intensity fight to upend the status quo. And with Pakistani troops massed across the persistently violated ceasefire line, India maintained a strong military presence in Kashmir to deter a second invasion. A vote looked doomed from the beginning. The UN's plan, built on the preposterous presumption that a state that had just waged an illegal war would act in the interests of the victims of that war, effectively embalmed Kashmiris—divided between two powerful adversaries—in an intractable limbo.

The only elections held in Kashmir occurred on the Indian side. In 1951, the secular National Conference swept to power with all seventy-five seats in the constituent assembly (thirty-five were kept symbolically vacant for representatives from Pakistan-occupied Kashmir) in the state's first ever elections. Appointed prime minister in Hari Singh's emergency administration after the war, Abdullah had promulgated a radical redistribution programme that put Congress leaders elsewhere in India to shame. In a state where a small—mostly Hindu—coterie owned thousands of acres of land, he put the ceiling on individual landholdings at twenty-three acres. (Hari Singh, a crusty impediment to reform, was invited to Delhi in 1949 and never saw Kashmir again. Replanted in Bombay, he died in a wallow of monstrous self-pity, unrepentant to the end for his administration's role in the massacre of Muslims in Jammu, mourned beyond his bereaved family only by Hindu bigots.)

In his stirring inaugural speech to the first freely elected assembly of the people's representatives of Kashmir in 1951, Abdullah laid out the choices before Kashmiris. India's commitment to 'secular democracy based upon justice, freedom and modern democracy', he explained, negated the 'argument that the Muslims of Kashmir cannot have security in India, where the large majority of the population are Hindus'. 'The Indian Constitution,' Abdullah said, 'has amply and finally repudiated the concept of a religious state, which is a throwback to medievalism, by guaranteeing the equality of rights of all citizens irrespective of their religion, colour, caste and class.' Pakistan, on the other hand, 'is a feudal state' and its 'appeal to religion constitutes a sentimental and a wrong approach', because 'Pakistan is not an organic unity of all the Muslims in this subcontinent. It has, on the contrary, caused the dispersion of the Indian Muslims for whose benefit it was claimed to have been created.' He reminded those who spoke of independence 'that from 15 August to 22 October 1947 our State was independent and the result was that our weakness was exploited by the neighbour with invasion'.

Abdullah's speech was more than a litany of pros and cons. No leader of Congress—not even Nehru—had ever delivered a more eloquent defence of the secular nationalism of India or a more astringent confutation of the self-serving segregationism of Jinnah and his sybaritic sponsors. But Abdullah's rejection of Pakistan was also a reminder to India that secularism was the non-negotiable condition of Kashmir's place within India. Kashmiris, as he said, 'will never accept a principle which seeks to favour the interests of one religion or social group against another'.[11]

The sentence was aimed then at Pakistan. It applies now to India.

India's self-definition as a secular state was not contingent on the presence of Kashmir within its fold. India's inclusive nationalism, unlike Pakistan's exclusionary variant, was self-supporting: it was validated by the existing religious multiplicity of the land—India was home to 25 million more Muslims than West Pakistan—and did not require an additional legitimating garnish. The origins of India's entry into Kashmir were beyond legal and moral reproach. But having acquired Kashmir, India's capacity to hold on to what became the only Muslim-majority state in the Union was elevated by Nehru—who felt a special attachment to the place because it was his ancestral homeland—into a test of the Republic's secular identity. 'Kashmir', he told parliament in 1953, 'is symbolic as it illustrates that we are a secular state' with which 'a large majority of Muslims of [their] own free will wished to be associated'.[12] Having thus mortgaged its self-esteem to Kashmir, India became obsessively fixated on retaining Kashmir. The destruction of democracy and democratic institutions which began in the rest of India *after* Nehru's departure was inaugurated in Kashmir *by* Nehru.

After Nehru, Congress did to Kashmir what it did to every other state, but the consequences there were graver because Kashmir was unlike any other state in the union. In 1988, a substantial segment of Kashmiri Muslims, seething from the rigging of elections orchestrated by Congress the previous year, demanded independence for a state whose autonomy had progressively been eroded by a succession of Indian governments. The brazenness with which returns were doctored would have made a dictator wince. It was an affront to Kashmiris' intelligence, a devil-may-care display of contempt for their dignity.

The purely indigenous strand of the movement for Kashmiri independence appeared and fell by the wayside after a burst of ecstatic violence and retaliatory massacres. The cause, born of a just rage, was almost instantly hijacked by the vultures in Pakistan, who supplied arms, trained young men in terrorist camps on its soil, and diverted the veterans of the anti-Soviet jihad in Afghanistan to Kashmir. Hundreds of thousands of non-Muslims were cleansed from the valley at gunpoint as the call for an Islamic union with Pakistan eclipsed the clamour for freedom from India. India responded with extraordinary brutality, turning Kashmir into the most militarised zone on the planet and granting its troops total immunity from prosecution. Torture, murder, rape, mutilation, mass arrests became common tools of coercion.

Terrorism began to ebb in Kashmir in the 2000s. In the face of frequent mass protests, India spent the next decade ploughing money into the state—Kashmir is the largest recipient of government grants in the union—and holding transparent elections in the hope of winning back the hearts and minds of the people. But what the Kashmiris have seen they cannot un-see. Every generation carries in its bones a deeper trauma than the one before it, and India is now confronting a generation—a young, articulate, politically conscious, religiously perfervid generation—formed in the troubles of the 1990s. An acknowledgement of their torment, an apology for causing it, and a commitment to accountability by India are imperative, if woefully inadequate, for the rift to heal. But in the age of Modi, that is unthinkable. He campaigned on a reckless pledge to hold a debate on the future of Article 370—an entrenched provision of the Constitution that has been the legal basis of Kashmir's union with India for almost seven decades—and then detonated the moral basis of India's claim on Kashmir by initiating the Hinduisation of the state.

The appearance of calm in Kashmir began to crack in the second year of Modi's term in office, with the execution of Burhan Wani. An advocate of independence from India, Wani was a militant who lived by the gun. His exhortations for '*azadi*' from India, uploaded to the internet, expanded his reach to a vast new audience. In his last video, he called on Kashmiri officers to turn their weapons on India. He was hunted down and killed by the armed forces, who branded the operation the 'biggest success against militants' in decades. A twenty-one-year-old with a social media following had become the greatest nightmare for one of the most formidable security forces in the world, but not because he had the capacity to kill in large numbers. Wani's power lay in converting people to his cause. The men of his generation, unable to reconcile themselves with India, were receptive to his message.[13]

There was a public outpouring of grief to the news of Wani's death. A hundred thousand men and women marched behind his funeral cortege. Within days, Kashmir was paralysed by civil unrest. Dozens of protesters were killed by Indian forces. There were as many funerals for the dead, and every funeral occasioned a new protest, then fresh funerals, then more protest ... India, having imposed a curfew, initiated a 'non-lethal' crackdown. In practice, this meant firing 'pellet guns' at crowds of protesters. The 'pellets', loaded with lead and designed to penetrate the soft tissue of the body, mutilated and blinded hundreds of Kashmiris.

Since 1996, elections have been seen as the measure of Kashmiri allegiance to India. Kashmiris queuing to vote have routinely been heralded as proof of Indian nationalism's success. So what did the absence of voters in the by-election of April 2017 in Srinagar suggest, if not the near-death of the appeal of Indian nationalism? Only 7 per cent of the electorate voted. The poor showing was put down to violence. But when the vote was held again in thirty-eight polling stations the following week, voter turnout dropped to 2 per cent. In all, 702 people turned up to vote. Not a single vote was cast in many of the polling stations.[14] Voices in the government immediately blamed threats by Pakistan-backed separatists for the dismal turnout. But this excuse was a non-starter: the power of the separatists to disrupt elections was no match for the capacity of India's security apparatus to maintain order.

One Kashmiri who did defy the threats to cast his vote, a young man called Farooq Ahmad Dar, was picked up by the Army as he was returning home, tied to the bonnet of a jeep, and paraded through the streets as a 'human shield' against young Kashmiris pelting stones at security forces. Dar was done with India that day.[15] The officer who stamped on Dar's dignity instantly became a hero to Hindu nationalists, who rushed to his defence. Only three years before this squalid spectacle, Kashmiri voters had come out in impressive numbers, and the BJP, which swept the Hindu-dominated Jammu region, formed a coalition government headed by the pro-India Peoples Democratic Party in Kashmir. But Modi's inability to play the junior partner paralysed administration. And just when the place needed a stable government, the BJP pulled the rug from under the alliance and dissolved the government. At the end of 2018—the deadliest year in the state by the government's own records[16]—Kashmir was placed under President's Rule, ending even the pretence of representative government.[17]

To identify the failings of India is not to exonerate its adversaries. Pakistan has played a thoroughly ruinous role in Kashmir. Its quest for Kashmir is tied up with the identity crisis that has crippled Pakistan since its birth. The rationale behind Pakistan's foundation—that Muslims and Hindus could not coexist in one nation—was impeached when India refused to become a Hindu state and gave itself a secular Constitution. As long as Kashmir, a Muslim-majority region, remains part of the Indian union, Pakistan's self-conception as the authentic home of India's Muslims—the reason for its existence—will remain unfulfilled. But the Pakistan that was invented in 1947 ceased to exist in 1971. What conceivable moral right did the rump state that clung on to the neologism 'Pakistan' have to cast itself as the defender of Muslim destiny after having perpetrated the worst atrocities ever committed against a predominantly Muslim population in what is today Bangladesh?[18] If Pakistan was motivated by a sincere impulse to emancipate Kashmiris, it would not have signed away to its paymasters in China, as it did in 1963, large chunks of Kashmir over which it had no sovereignty.[19] Over the past three decades, Pakistan has created, trained, and armed militants in the Valley. It has treated Muslim Kashmiri human beings as weapons delivery systems.

None of those truths, however, negate the other truth: India's moral claim to Kashmir is now threadbare. Kashmiri separatists who labelled India a 'Hindu state' could once be dismissed as chauvinists. And India could credibly argue for Kashmir's place within its fold and promise a solution within the 'constitutional framework' because the religion of a majority of Kashmiris was irrelevant to full citizenship of the state. But now the separatists' claim against India has nearly as much substance and weight as Sheikh Abdullah's against Pakistan, while the argument of 'inclusive nationalism' deployed by Modi's predecessors to persuade Kashmiri separatists to participate in elections is not available to him, a religious nationalist, and nor is it available to India under him. When Kashmiri Muslims look at India, what they see is a Republic where Muslims are killed for eating beef, where Kashmiris are socially ostracised and physically brutalised by ordinary Indians for being Kashmiri, where the state licences murderous Hindu vigilantes. There will come a time, if this continues, when mainstream pro-India parties in Kashmir will not be able to show themselves in public or make a case for remaining in India. An India that has ceased to be secular has absolutely no basis to claim Kashmir.

Indian unity, even beyond Kashmir, is not divinely ordained. The founders recognised this and were consumed by the union's fragility. But the persistent anxiety about India's viability that haunted every Prime Minister dissolved in the solvent of the new wealth generated in the 1990s. And under Modi, the old divide between north and south has once again opened up. The Hindu-nationalist emphasis on Hindi has alienated non-Hindi speakers, especially in southern India. To be a non-Hindi speaker in today's India, Mihir Sharma has written, is 'to deal with a hundred little humiliations'.[20] These humiliations, compared to what the Kashmiris have endured, are really in the league of first-world problems.

The real trouble is not that Modi is antagonising the south. It is more serious than that: the south is imperceptibly inching

away from the north, and Modi's brand of nationalism is supplying a pretext for its acceleration. The fault is not the north's
because the true source of the deepening division is not culture
or language. It is wealth. India used to be lauded as an audacious experiment for being floated in a poor country, but
poverty may in fact have made it easier to bridge divides. An
impoverished India was also a more malleable India. A wealthier India, not so much: new money has already torn communities apart and incubated mercenary attitudes that make the
excesses of the pre-liberalisation era seem tame.

The south today is richer and more efficient than the north.
And it is the ideas being seeded by the stimulus of those riches
that pose perhaps the greatest threat to the Indian project. For
the first time, the grievances of the south are anchored in the
language of economics: their real complaint is not that they
aren't receiving enough from the union—it is that they are
giving too much away. If this trend continues, one parliamentarian from Andhra Pradesh threatened, 'all southern states
might have to come together to form a separate entity'.[21]
(Contrast the absolute silence with which this threat of secession was received with the howling outrage in 2012, when
Mustafa Kamal, a senior leader of Jammu and Kashmir's
National Conference party, upbraided Delhi for not bringing
down troop levels in Kashmir and said, ruefully, 'I feel our
enemy is our own country, not Pakistan'. Kamal was crucified
in the press and on TV for weeks.)[22]

Most states complain that they are not given much; southern
states complain that the north is sucking up their wealth. This is
a fatal line of argument, and it should be nipped before it blooms.
Contemporary politicians, from north and south, have responded
to it with the vocabulary of technocrats—and in the aridity of
their language can be detected a deep dread that this difference,
which seems a trifling matter now, could explode in the decades
ahead. If this crisis had come up forty years ago, or even during
the reign of P.V. Narasimha Rao, the national leadership of India

would almost certainly have responded by affirming the oneness of Indians—by reminding the cavillers that they are all children of India—but that is an argument Modi, headman of a narrow nationalism, cannot convincingly make. The south is not a victim—it never was—but Modi's politics have supplied a convenient fig leaf for the deplorably self-serving parochialism of southern politicians. The dispute over the division of resources has passed unnoticed. But it will re-emerge.

There is nothing natural or preordained about Indian unity. Indian civilisation is antique; Indian unity is rare and recent. And it is far from clear that it can be supported by a radical departure from the conditions in which it was forged. Others have been here. If you were a citizen of Yugoslavia in 1988 as the great Marshal Tito—whose achievement is hardly remembered today—boarded the train in Pristina after touring Kosovo, it would not have occurred to you that that is where post-war Europe's great experiment in multi-ethnic nationalism would unravel. Yugoslavs too believed they were special and supernaturally blessed until they realised they were not. And once the unravelling began, it was all over before people could catch their breath. Indira Gandhi once remarked that Yugoslavia was the one country most like India in the world. Today, Yugoslavia exists only in the nostalgias of those who took Yugoslavia for granted. It was devoured by its own version of Modi, its own vengeful variant of Hindu supremacism.

India, the protest goes, is a democracy. But there is no commandment that democracies are everlasting. Even Britain, which united India and is one of the oldest political unions on earth, is on the brink of disunion. It would behove us in India, seventy five years old, to be humbler. India survives as a union because most people within its frontiers see themselves as Indian first. And those who do not can be persuaded to see themselves as Indian because Indian nationalism is not premised on religion, or language, or ethnicity. But the terms of that nationalism are rapidly fading into obsolescence. In Kashmir, India holds on to the territory but fears and despises the people. In the south, the people increasingly wonder why they should underwrite the north. And there is no politician—no Nehru, no Tito—who can make the case for India without appealing to some sub-identity or surrendering to those who do. 'Separateness,' Nehru once said, 'has always been the weakness of India'. At no point since his departure has the Republic's political cast contained so few people capable of mounting an argument for *India*. The union is not dissolving. Not yet. But the dynamite of division that has always lain beneath the surface has never seemed so primed for detonation as it does under Modi.

CODA

RECLAMATION

When, finally, we reached the place,
We hardly knew why we were there.
The trip had darkened every face,
Our deeds were neither great nor rare ...

Nissim Ezekiel

India under Modi has undergone the most total transformation since 1991. Hindu chauvinism, ennobled as a healthy form of self-assertion, has become so untameable that it cannot be challenged on terms other than its own. Hindu rage that once manifested itself in localised violence has metastasised into a cancer of the national body politic. Anti-minority vitriol that once lurked on the peripheries of high politics has deluged the mainstream. Democratic institutions have been repurposed to abet Hindu nationalism. The military has been politicised, the judiciary plunged into the most existential threat to its independence since 1975. Kashmir has never more resembled a colonial possession. An incipient yearning for disaffiliation has crystallised in peninsular India.

The hoax of a technocratic moderniser crafted by an ensemble of intellectuals and industrialists collapsed early on under the

burden of Modi's incompetence, vainglory, and innate vicious-
ness. We now have more than a glimpse of the New India he has
spawned. It is a reflection of its progenitor: culturally arid, intellectually vacant, emotionally bruised, vain, bitter, boastful, permanently aggrieved, and implacably malevolent: a make-believe
land full of fudge and fakery, where savagery against religious
minorities is among the therapeutic options available to a self-
pitying majority frustrated by Modi's failure to upgrade its standard of living.

And it is only in its early stage. All those who believe they will
remain untouched by its wrath are delusional. If Ehsan Jafri, a
former member of parliament with a line to the deputy prime
minister's office, could be dragged out of his home and gashed
and burned alive, what makes anyone think he or she will
remain unharmed in a nation led by the man who did not go to
Jafri's aid? If Aamir Khan, one of India's biggest film stars, can
be unpersoned; if Gauri Lankesh, one of its boldest journalists,
can be shot dead; if Ramachandra Guha, its greatest living
historian, can be stopped from lecturing; if Naseeruddin Shah,
among its finest actors, can be branded a traitor; if Manmohan
Singh, the former Prime Minister, can be labelled an agent of
Pakistan by his successor; if B.H. Loya, a perfectly healthy
judge, can abruptly drop dead; if a young woman can be stalked
by the police machinery of the state because Modi has displayed an interest in her—what makes the rest of us think we
will forever remain untouched? Unless the Republic is
reclaimed, the time will come when all of us will be one incor-
rect meal, one interfaith romance, one unfortunate misstep
away from being extinguished by the furies released by Modi.
The mobs that slaughtered 'bad' Muslims will eventually come
for Hindus who are not 'good'.

India's tragedy is that just when it is faced with an existential
crisis, there exists no pan-Indian alternative to the BJP. What
remains of the opposition is bleached of conviction. The values of Hindu nationalism have become the default setting of

Indian politics. The centre has oscillated very far to the right. In 2014, Modi went to great lengths to manufacture the impression that he had shed his ideological baggage; over the next five years, Rahul Gandhi expended tremendous energies to give himself a religious makeover. As president of the Congress Party, he toured temples, brandished his Brahmin caste, and posted photos of himself on religious pilgrimages. In 2018, when the management of an ancient Hindu temple in southern India defied the Supreme Court's order to open its gates to female worshippers, the party of Nehru fell behind the faction of clerical reaction. Later that year, Congress stitched together a governing coalition in Madhya Pradesh, pushing the BJP from power in a state it had ruled for fifteen years. The change of guard was greeted as a new beginning, hailed as a blow to the Hindu-nationalist project. One of the first acts of the Congress-led government was to allocate fifty million pounds for cow shelters.[1] Its next act was to invoke the National Security Act against three Muslim men accused of slaughtering cows in the state.[2]

Fifty years before Modi became Prime Minister, the Congress leader Lal Bahadur Shastri, the Republic's second Prime Minister, was invited by a journalist to talk about his faith. Shastri's answer was curt: 'one should not discuss one's religion in public.'[3] Today's Congress has no such compunctions. Acquisition of power is the principal objective of a party that now seems to exist solely to provide subsistence to those who feed off it. It has taken slyly to mimicking the BJP and annexing its most explosive causes. In the Hindu heartlands of the north, its leaders accuse Modi of not evincing sufficient 'passion for Lord Rama'[4] and promise voters that a 'Rama temple will come up in Ayodhya only when the Congress comes to power'.[5] If a temple rises on the site of the Babri mosque, it will be as a tombstone for the secular state. When the party that claims to be the 'secular' alternative champions the temple, is it triangulation or treachery?

India will leap to a point from which return will become extremely difficult if Modi remains in power at the head of a government with an absolute majority in parliament. Indira Gandhi suspended the Constitution to brutalise Indians. Modi will seek to write his ideology into the Constitution to bisect them. If he succeeds, Hindu nationalism will become the official animating ideology of the Republic. There will be separate classes of citizens in law. Bigotry will not then be a deviation from the ideals of the Republic: it will be an affirmation of them. India will become Pakistan by another name.

The Hindu-nationalist project will neither dissipate nor die if and when Modi exits the scene. It will go into remission. Its leaders, cadres, believers will regroup and recrudesce. They are incompetent in government: they are peerless in opposition. Modi's pre-prime ministerial career is a lesson in how India's shameless elites can be co-opted to pimp for their cause: a commitment to the market is all they ask in return for their services. And on any given day, there are tens of thousands of activists of the RSS, spread out across India, preaching the gospel of Hindu nationalism and fomenting a revolution from the bottom-up. They believe in their cause; their adversaries long ago abandoned theirs.

That is why we are here.

We inhabit the most degraded moment in the history of the Indian Republic, the culmination of decades of betrayals, the eruption of a long-suppressed rage. But the good thing about bad times is that they force us to reflect, to see clearly. Modi's rule has shattered so many illusions, dispelled so much fog. We can begin to accept how we arrived here: a via Dolorosa lined with corruption, cowardly concessions to religious nationalists, demeaning bribes to the minorities, self-wounding distortions of the past, and wholesale abandonment of the many for the few.

Modi has drawn out the very worst in many Indians. But his reign has also smashed the complacency that governed the attitudes of many Indians and activated citizenly antibodies across the country. It has, as the nationwide uprisings in early

2020 against the Citizenship (Amendment) Act and the proposed National Register of Citizens demonstrated, belatedly awakened us to what we may be poised forever to lose. It has revealed to us that the Republic bequeathed by the founders was not a sham. It was an instantiation of ideals worth fighting for: rising from the inferno of Partition, it defiantly rejected the baleful idea that national unity could not be forged in the crucible of human multiplicity, that permanent political division was the only resolution to the predicament of religious variety. Modi, an affront to that idea, is also the result of the disfigurement of that idea. Those who preceded him fostered the conditions for his breakthrough; and he has dragged India, already heavy with the vices of yesteryear, to depths from which recovery may take generations.

Can we give up on India? Seven decades after the holocaust of Partition in the name of religious nationalism, can we throw away the improbable unity for which so many good people sacrificed their everything?

A year before Modi was born, at a time when Muslims were still fleeing or being driven from India for Pakistan, the poet Abdul Hayee, who wrote under the name Sahir Ludhianvi, made the contrariwise journey, leaving Pakistan for India. It was an audacious act of reclamation. One of my most cherished possessions for many years was an old cyclostyled copy of Sahir's poems, beautifully annotated by hand. I don't know from whom I inherited it but there was in it this verse, written after Pakistan had waged yet another war in the name of religion to validate the blasted logic of its birth, which its previous owner had underlined:

> *Wo waqt gaya, woh daur gaya jab do quamon ka nara tha,*
> *Woh log gaye is dharti se jinka maqsad batwara tha.*
> *Ab ek hain sab Hindustani,*
> *Ab ek hain sab Hindustani.*

> That time is past, that epoch is bygone,
> When there was the clamour of two nations;

From this land are gone the people whose dream was
segregation;
Now all Indians are one, now all Indians are one.

Sahir spoke for a generation of people who did more than believe in India. They placed their lives on the line for it. They willed India into existence merely by being present in it. Whenever I went to Bombay, I stopped by Sahir's final resting place to say a prayer. But there is no trace of Sahir today in his beloved city: some years ago, his grave was razed, its remains disinterred and destroyed, and a thick new layer of earth poured over it to create a fresh grave. If we delay the act of reclaiming it, no trace of his India will remain.

EPILOGUE TO THE PAPERBACK EDITION

PANDEMONIUM

[I]t can be said with pride that India not only defeated Covid-19 under the able, sensitive, committed and visionary leadership of Prime Minister Shri Narendra Modi but also infused in all its citizens the confidence to build an 'Atmanirbhar Bharat'. The party unequivocally hails its leadership for introducing India to the world as a proud and victorious nation in the fight against Covid-19

BJP Resolution, February 2021

To Narendra Modi, Covid-19 appeared not so much like a disease as a *deus ex machina*. Before he announced the largest lockdown in human history on 24 March 2020, the prime minister was floundering in a pool of self-engineered crises. Citizens' protests against his legislative disfigurement of Indian secularism via the Citizenship (Amendment) Act had erupted in every major city. More than four dozen lives were lost on his doorstep in February in the worst religious bloodletting in Delhi since 1984.[1] Unemployment was soaring. And the economy was to post the slowest pace of growth in a decade. Modi's 'New India' appeared about to implode because of the malevolence and incompetence of its own progenitor.

Then came the saviour from China in the guise of a pathogen.

Modi did not at first pay attention. In February 2020, as the coronavirus began claiming lives in India's neighbourhood, he was busy hosting a lavish reception for Donald Trump and toppling a democratically elected state government in Madhya Pradesh.[2] Nor did he do much by way of preparing India once casualties began mounting in Europe: in late March, there was only one isolation bed for every 84,000 people, one doctor for every 11,600 patients, and one hospital bed for every 1,826 Indians.[3] The first orders for personal protective equipment for front-line health care workers were made only hours before Modi appeared on television at 8 p.m. on 24 March to announce a total lockdown. It was an improvised performance: no thought appeared to have gone into it.

Within days, hundreds of thousands, if not millions,[4] of people who serve the needs of first-world India—as servants, cooks, cleaners, construction hands—set off on a homeward trek from the cities to the countryside. Modi had abandoned them. Their exodus on foot was redolent of the horrific migrations following India's partition in 1947. By mid-April, some 200 people had died as a consequence of the lockdown, and the number rose to a thousand weeks later.[5] Some dropped dead of exhaustion as they walked, others killed themselves as a way out of loneliness. The lockdown in India succeeded not only in suppressing the spread of the disease but also effectively in suspending the world's largest democracy. To criticise Modi's mismanagement was to invite accusations of *lèse-majesté* in a national emergency. To obey and exalt him was to qualify as a dutiful citizen.

Repression became the principal pursuit of the state during the pandemic. The coronavirus was invoked early on to sanctify a brazen attempt by the government to muzzle the press. A week after imposing the lockdown, Modi sought a directive from the Supreme Court of India requiring the press to self-censor and turn itself into a bulletin board for government propaganda.[6] The court, meeting Modi halfway, directed the media to publish the 'official version' of events alongside independent coverage.

That was the warm-up act. In the weeks following, police departments up and down the country began properly harrying journalists. In Kashmir, cases were filed under an oppressive piece of anti-terrorism legislation against Gowhar Geelani, the author of *Kashmir: Rage and Reason*, for apparently 'indulging in unlawful activities' by posting on social media content 'prejudicial to the national integrity, sovereignty, and security of India', as well as Masrat Zahra, an internationally acclaimed photojournalist, for publishing 'anti-national posts' on her Facebook page.[7] In New Delhi, the distinguished journalist Siddharth Varadarajan was summoned to appear at a police station 435 miles from his home in Delhi at the peak of the lockdown because a quote in an article in the *Wire*, the independent publication he edits, had been misattributed to the chief minister of Uttar Pradesh.[8] The mistake had been corrected almost instantly, but Hindu supremacists evidently take journalistic accuracy extremely seriously. The coronavirus exposed Modi's shortcomings. It also, tragically, created the conditions for him to quicken the conversion of the world's largest democracy into something akin to a plebiscitary autocracy. Police across India proceeded to lodge cases or open investigations against at least fifty-five journalists since March 2020—the worst pandemic-era record of any democracy.[9]

Despite a shutdown that ravaged the economy and ruined the livelihoods of millions of people across the nation[10]—estimates suggest one in four Indians lost their jobs in March and April—India found itself in the uppermost ranks of countries most severely stricken by the coronavirus. At more than half a million, its known caseload in the first wave of the pandemic was exceeded only by the numbers in Brazil and the United States. India's big cities abounded with horror stories of crowded hospitals turning away critically ill patients, congested wards stacked with dead bodies, and worn-out doctors and paramedics striving to operate in unfathomable conditions.[11]

Contrast the feeble planning that preceded the enforced isolation of 1.3 billion people with the attention that went into burnishing the cult of Modi once the lockdown came into effect. Days into the lockdown, Modi began soliciting tax-deductible donations for an opaque trust established, he said, for the purpose of aiding 'the poorest of the poor'.[12] With a brazenness that would have made Papa Doc Duvalier blush, he christened the fund 'PM CARES'. Nearly a billion dollars flowed into it in the first week. Staff at government departments were 'encouraged' by circulars to give a portion of their salary to it. Private corporations paid tens of millions into it while denying salaries to their low-wage workers.[13] One company sacked a thousand employees days after pouring more than half a million dollars of its cash reserves into PM CARES.[14]

Where has all that money gone? That question is impossible to answer to this day because PM CARES is structured as a private trust and cannot therefore be reviewed by the state auditor.[15] The flagrancy of the enterprise catches the breath: while his counterparts abroad panicked, fumbled, growled and pleaded with their people, Modi utilised the worst public health crisis in more than a century as an opportunity to stage the most audacious swindle in the democratic world. The fact that the cash he has collected will not be stashed away in Swiss bank accounts is hardly comforting for anybody who cares about the future of democracy. Some have speculated that the cash will likely be put to more sinister uses: to corrupt others, to shop for elected officials who have not yet capitulated to the prime minister's sectarian ideology, to outspend his rivals in an already extortionately expensive electoral market, to vandalise the residues of checks on his power.[16]

And what of the 'poorest of the poor'? Modi's myrmidons began discovering important uses for them immediately after the government extended the countrywide lockdown for another two weeks on 1 May. In Bangalore, emergency train services were cancelled to prevent labourers from going home.

The decision to terminate the rudimental rights of the most destitute Indians was explained away by one of Modi's MPs as a 'bold and necessary move' to 'help migrant labourers who came [to Bangalore] with hopes of a better life to restart their dreams'.[17] The local government, lobbied by construction barons, had intended to put the absconding labourers to work on construction sites. The ensuing public outcry prompted the government to let them go. But the regime that had been so eager to 'help migrant labourers'—some of the poorest people not only in India but also the world—could not bring itself to pay the cost of their train tickets. In a grotesque irony, the publicly owned Indian Railways, which insisted on collecting the full fare, had days before given more than fourteen million pounds to PM CARES.[18]

At the same time, at least two state governments run by Modi's party in central and northern India sought to regenerate the economy by revoking the elementary legal protections accorded to workers.[19] To get a sense of what this means in practice, consider their proposal to make factories in Bhopal—the scene of the worst industrial disaster in history—exempt from safety checks.[20] If bringing up that past seems alarmist, then consider this: a week before the recommendation, at least eleven people were killed in a gas leak from a polymers factory on the Coromandel coast in southern India.

Covid-19 rapidly became an alibi for the formalisation of the squalid social arrangement that has always flourished under the surface in India. And it wasn't just saffron-robed Hindu nationalists who were setting fire to labour laws. The high priests sanctifying the technocratic endeavour were liberal economists.[21] They are, like the Brahmins of old India who withheld liturgical knowledge from the lower castes by conducting their services in unintelligible Sanskrit, incomprehensible. Their language is freighted with jargon and euphemism because their business is selling as economic prudence the political disenfranchisement of the poor.

Covid-19 briefly resurrected Modi as their redeemer. Raised in poverty, the prime minister radiated the arriviste's disdain for the poor. The 2020 budget set aside more than Rs 8,000 crore for a pair of bespoke Boeing aircraft to fly the 'poor man's son'.[22] The intensifying distress of Indians did nothing, however, to provoke him to redirect the tens of billions he earmarked for projects conceived with the sole ambition of burnishing his personality cult. His megalomaniacal plan to erect a *new* New Delhi as a monument to his rule progressed even as life in India came to a halt.[23] For six years, Modi's malice, hubris and ineptitude ravaged India in every conceivable way. Instituting indentured servitude was his idea of healing it.

On 28 January 2021, Modi had declared victory against Covid-19. Addressing a virtual summit of the World Economic Forum, he sought applause for saving 'humanity from a big disaster by containing the coronavirus effectively'. Three months later, India became the epicentre of the pandemic. The country's health care system effectively imploded. In New Delhi, patients suffocating to death, relatives scrambled for beds, the most advanced hospitals were reduced to begging the government for emergency supplies of oxygen, and crematoriums—blazing non-stop—ran out of room and wood.[24] Social media became inundated with agonising pleas for help.

Some buried their dead in their gardens.[25] Others cremated them on makeshift pyres erected on pavements. In the neglected countryside, to use the unforgettable phrase of a local reporter in southern India, people dropped 'like flies'. Hardly anybody knew anyone who hadn't been ravaged by the contagion. The official death toll, which has surpassed 529,000, is a scandalous undercount. By some estimates, the true figure could be between 4 and 6 million.[26] A thriving black market for oxygen and essential medicine materialised, and a nation acclaimed in 2015 by the International Monetary Fund as an economic powerhouse poised to overtake China was forced to beg the world for emergency foreign aid.

What unfolded in India was more than a crisis triggered by a pathogen. It was a carnage precipitated by the conduct of its self-enamoured leader. After Modi's Davos speech, his administration went out of its way to lull Indians into the suicidal belief that the worst was behind them. In February, the BJP passed a florid resolution praising his 'leadership for introducing India to the world as a proud and victorious nation in the fight against Covid-19'. '[I]t can be said with pride,' the resolution declaimed, that India 'defeated Covid-19 under the able, sensitive, committed, and visionary leadership of Prime Minister Narendra Modi'.

Then, in early March, Modi's health minister announced that India was 'in the endgame' of the pandemic. That same month, thousands of unmasked cricket fans poured into a stadium in Gujarat named after Modi to watch matches between India and England. Many thousands more were bused to crowded political rallies for elections in four states in eastern and southern India. The Kumbh Mela—a Hindu festival and the world's largest religious gathering that ordinarily convenes every twelve years—was allowed to be brought forward by a year in deference to priests who decreed that 2021 was an auspicious year for it. On 12 April alone, more than three million pilgrims took a communal dip in the Ganga in the holy city of Haridwar.[27]

Five days later, just as India's reported daily new infections surged past 230,000, Modi bragged to a swarm of supporters in West Bengal that he had 'never seen such crowds at a rally'.[28] The pandemic, as far as Modi was concerned, was over. The hectic electioneering doubled as a victory lap. Just as he had feted Donald Trump a month before the first wave of the virus washed over India, Modi was eagerly preparing to host Boris Johnson, the then British prime minister, for a summit. Johnson's abrupt decision to cancel his tour in response to the rising infections in India jolted Modi. Denying reality was no longer feasible. But by the time he acknowledged what was happening, it was too late.

Modi had claimed in January that he had equipped India with 'Covid-specific infrastructure'. Where was it as Indians began perishing in record numbers? The man who had seduced voters in 2014 with promises of smart cities and abundant jobs had once again hoodwinked the country with a rhetorical Potemkin village: behind its lustrous façade, there was only desolation and death.

India might have been spared this humanitarian crisis had Modi not neglected his duties and vilified those who had offered him constructive counsel. He had the time, means and access to expertise to proof the country against this inferno.[29] As early as November 2020, a parliamentary committee had issued warnings of a second wave and urged the government to stockpile oxygen. On 3 May, the government of India, confronted by a calamity that was devouring the country, set a deadline for the completion of a palatial new residence for Modi in the heart of New Delhi. In that moment, as bodies piled up on pavements, floated in rivers and washed up on their banks, it was no longer tenable to measure Modi against the performance of previous prime ministers: he had broken into the malign ranks of India's British colonial overlords who went hunting as Indians starved in mass famines.

India's dire condition during the pandemic was inseparable from Modi's methodical demolition of the institutional safeguards bequeathed by the country's founders. Concentrating authority in his own hands and erecting a cult of personality unmatched in the democratic world, he had dismantled virtually every institution that might have impelled him to react swiftly and responsibly to the catastrophe around him. The Indian Supreme Court, one of the most interventionist in the world, is habituated to upbraiding governments for failing the people. Yet it did not utter a word against the Modi regime's appalling mishandling of the pandemic. India's most popular news media, co-opted early on by Modi, provided him cover by demonising his critics as traitors. The state broadcaster,

Doordarshan, devoted itself to portraying Modi as India's saviour. India's diplomats, meanwhile, exhibited their fealty to the prime minister by dashing off furious letters to editors of foreign newspapers for failing to recognise Modi's 'universally acclaimed approach' to Covid-19. Twitter and Facebook were ordered to take down posts critical of the government. Even in that apocalyptic hour, safeguarding the cult of Modi was the most pressing priority of his government.[30] And so deep was Modi's contempt for common decency that, even as foreign governments airlifted aid to India, his own party persisted with mass political congregations. Indians, lest we forget, have no means of confronting Modi—he has not held a single press conference since his first election in 2014.[31]

Modi, having botched India's inoculation drive by failing to order a sufficient number of doses in advance, devolved the responsibility of vaccinating Indians to financially strapped state governments, leaving them to negotiate prices and purchase shots on the open market. Most Indian states were in no position to execute the task. And there was, as a consequence, a scarcity of lifesaving jabs in a country that has the reputation of being the world's largest vaccine-maker. The government agreed to play a dominant role in the procurement process only after an intervention by the Supreme Court.[32] Covid-related mortalities exceeded the combined fatalities from all the wars India fought since its independence. If India survived at all, it was due entirely to the civic commitment of its front-line workers and ordinary citizens, who stepped in to do the duties of a government that, lost in the worship of Modi, had abandoned its people.

The pandemic also incinerated the vanities that have animated India's ruling elites since the 1990s—the vanities that could somehow abide a state of affairs in which the richest 1 per cent of Indians hoarded nearly half the national wealth while the government committed a trifling 0.34 per cent of GDP to health care.[33]

But how will it affect Modi? Will the despair coursing through India ultimately bring him down? Modi has a long record of surviving backlashes against him. As we have seen, the riots in Gujarat in 2001 appeared to spell the end to his political career. Yet not only did Modi absorb the outrage directed at him; he even succeeded in recruiting India's industrialists to deodorise his reputation and recast him as a modernising technocrat. Similarly, his decision in 2016 to abolish high-denomination currency notes detonated the economy and destroyed the prospects of countless Indians. But it did nothing to diminish his hypnotic hold on the minds of a sizeable number of voters. Months after the debacle of demonetisation, his party swept to power in India's largest state—an achievement it replicated again in the aftermath of the second wave of the pandemic.

For all the blood they shed to settle ancient historical scores, Indians are a forgetful people when it comes to the misdeeds of politicians. Modi will count on their forgetfulness at the next election. If the past is a guide, the possibility of losing power eventually will not demoralise or weaken him; it will energise him and make him more dangerous. He is the first Hindu nationalist to govern with untrammelled authority, the most formidable Hindu ruler of India in many centuries, and the father of what his ideological acolytes call 'New India'. If he departs the scene, that idea, hollow as it is, will suffer a setback. It was the prospect of being removed from office that prompted another prime minister, Indira Gandhi, to declare a state of internal emergency, suspend the Constitution and rule as a dictator almost half a century ago. What will Modi, who has never tasted electoral defeat in his life, do if he believes his defeat is on the horizon?

ACKNOWLEDGEMENTS

Michael Dwyer of Hurst invited me to lunch one afternoon and asked if I might consider writing an overview of India under Narendra Modi. The presence of Modi, the worst human being ever elected Prime Minister, in the office hallowed by Nehru and Shastri was a source of debilitating distress for me. But as I began writing I realised that to quarantine Modi from the reasons for his rise was to reinforce the self-comforting lie that he was an aberration. So I decided to begin before Modi. As the book evolved, I received only encouragement from my publishers. At Hurst, Michael has done more than identify and champion exceptional writing. He has created a repository of knowledge that is indispensable to arriving at a deeper understanding of the world. His service to India will someday receive the wide recognition it merits. For now, I record my gratitude to him for his years of friendship, counsel, and faith. If it is a special privilege to publish with Hurst in the fiftieth year of its journey, it truly is an honour to publish, in India, with Amazon Westland's Kathika V.K., the doyenne of South Asian publishers. I am tremendously grateful for her resolute support. Working with Ajitha G.S.—keen-eyed, cool-headed, superlative, and subtlest of editors—has been a thoroughly edifying experience. I cannot adequately thank her for her labour.

Nick March of *The National* gave me generous space to prospect some of the ideas that I have plumbed in the preceding pages. I acknowledge my debt to him for his many years of friendship and encouragement. Sections of the Prologue, which I have slightly fictionalised to conceal identities, first appeared in the *Daily Beast* under a pseudonym. I thank Constantin Roman for allowing me to use his lively translation of Paunescu's puckish tribute to the cult of Ceausescu, the Ezekiels of Bombay for granting me permission to use verses from the great Nissim Ezekiel's poem 'Enterprise' in the opening and closing chapters of the book—and Ramachandra Guha, Amitav Ghosh, and my dashing friend Andrew Anthony for their early encouragement.

The writing of this book was punctuated by too many departures. In early 2019, my beloved grandmother exited the scene. The distance between the world of antique horrors she once inhabited and the world she willed into existence for me is beyond my ability to measure. Widowed in extreme youth in the hell that was Hyderabad before the Indian Republic—before rights—existed, she managed and expanded her late husband's estate, raised a family, survived the ravages of Partition, and *never* brooked bigotry. She took me on Sufi pilgrimages as a boy and spent a severe English winter easing me and my brothers into London. She was the most outstanding person I knew.

I thank my dad and brothers—from Hyderabad to California—for their affection and support over the years. To my mother and father, this book is dedicated.

One of the great boons of my life has been the mentorship of David Frum. He was one of the first people to pay me to write after I left law school without a clear idea of what I wanted to do. In a world swarming with sciolists, David is that rarest of creatures: an authentically erudite man. He has read *everything*. And his generosity as a mentor, loyalty as a friend, and unabashed uxoriousness as a husband to his wonderful wife, Danielle, have always struck me as touchstones every man must strive to emulate. Our politics are different; but this book, in some ways a culmination of the many conversations I have had with him over the years, is also a tribute to him.

ACKNOWLEDGEMENTS

I'd be remiss if I did not mention the friends who, sustaining me over the years, played a part in this project: Laura John, Katie Earnshaw, Colleen Coalter, Edward Martin, Helen Burnell, Zarir Cama, Joel Jackson, Miranda Frum, Prashant Maske, Mahesh Soni, Jude Hart, Charanjit Singh Dhillon, William Kell, Sabeen Siddiqui, Andrew Anthony, Mehr Husain, Darryl Stein, Emily Fisher, Issam Ahmed, Purushottam Gautam, Anupam Kaushish, and Rose Sullivan. Peter Taheri, dearest of friends, stole time from his clients and constituents to read every word and offer invaluable suggestions. The existence of Nina 'Chino' Tumanishvili, Georgia's atonement for Stalin and Saakashvili, is one of the blessings of my life. Cleo, running behind schedule, arrived like a mistral of life-affirming air— and brought with her the gift of Lore and Gunther Hoffstead.

I thank Andrew, Sabeen, Peter (and others I cannot name) for reading and offering comments on various drafts of chapters. If there is anything that you, dear reader, find especially egregious, the fault, it goes without saying, is entirely theirs and not mine.

NOTES

PROLOGUE: RUPTURE

1. Savarkar, *Hindutva: Who is a Hindu?*, Popular Prakashan, Bombay, 1969 (first published 1923), p. 113.
2. Abraham Lincoln, 'The Perpetuation of Our Political Institutions: Address Before the Young Men's Lyceum of Springfield, Illinois, January 27, 1838': http://www.abrahamlincolnonline.org/lincoln/speeches/lyceum.htm.
3. Srinath Raghavan, *War and Peace in Modern India*, Hyderabad, Orient Blackswan, 2013, p. 75.
4. 'India: Anchor for Asia', *Time*, 17 October 1949.
5. 'Social, Economic and Educational Status of the Muslim Community of India', *Prime Minister's High Level Committee*, November 2006: www.mhrd.gov.in/sites/upload_files/mhrd/files/sachar_comm.pdf.
6. Sandeep Unnithan and Amarnath K Menon, 'Mecca blast leaves 9 dead and 40 injured', *India Today*, 4 June 2007.
7. 'Swami's confession', *Frontline*, Vol. 28, 3 Jan–29 Feb 2011; The US National Counterterrorism Centre said in a 2010 report that the attack was in fact the work of a Pakistan-based group, but Indian investigators have maintained otherwise: Abhishek Sharan, 'Huji, not Hindu group, behind Mecca Masjid blast', *Hindustan Times*, 23 September 2010.

1. EROSION

1. Lee Hall, 'A Man Who, with All His Heart and Mind, Loved India', *Life Magazine*, Vol. 56, No. 23, 5 June 1964.

225

2. Jawaharlal Nehru, 'Rashtrapati Jawaharlal Ki Jai', *Modern Review*, 5 October 1937.

3. Stanley Wolpert, *Zulfi Bhutto of Pakistan*, Oxford University Press, Karachi, 2007, pp. 79–80.

4. Ramachandra Guha, *India After Gandhi: The History of the World's Largest Democracy*, Macmillan, London, 2007, p. 399.

5. Wolpert, p. 91.

6. Ramachandra Guha, 'The forgotten prime minister', *Hindu*, 2 January 2005.

7. He accused India of buying 'Jewish influence' and wrote in 1965 that 'Israel is actively working on behalf of India' to influence the US, an ally of Pakistan's: Wolpert, p. 97.

8. Joseph Lelyveld, 'Rajiv the Son', *New York Times*, 2 December 1984.

9. Krishna Nehru with Alden Hatch, *We Nehrus*, Holt, Rinehart and Winston, New York, 1967, p. 144.

10. Pran Nevile, *Lahore: A Sentimental Journey*, Penguin, New Delhi, 2006, p. 2.

11. Kuldip Nayyar, *India: The Critical Years*, Weidenfeld & Nicolson, 1971, pp. 19–20.

12. Ramachandra Guha, 'An Indian fall', *Prospect*, Dec 2005.

13. Vinod Mehta, *The Sanjay Story: From Anand Bhavan to Amethi*, Jaico, 1978, p. 29.

14. Nayar, *India*, p. 44.

15. Ibid., p. 46.

16. Ibid., p. 36.

17. Kuldip Nayar, *The Judgement: Inside the Story of the Emergency in India*, Vikas, Delhi, 1977, p. 197.

18. Appeal by C.K. Daphtary, *Indian Advocate*, Bar Association of India, Vol. 13, 1973, p. 124.

19. John P. Thorp, 'Genocide in Bangladesh', in Israel W. Charny (ed.), *Encyclopaedia of Genocide: Volume I*, Jerusalem, 1999, p. 115. Geoffrey Davis, the Australian physician appointed by the UN to Bangladesh, concluded that 400,000 was a low estimate for the number of East Pakistani women raped by the Pakistani army: Lorraine Boissoneault, 'The Genocide the U.S. Can't Remember, but Bangladesh Can't Forget', *The Smithsonian Magazine*,

16 December 2016. Violence against women was fundamental to the military campaign. Susan Brownmiller, one of the first to study the violence against women, noted that 'Girls of eight and grandmothers of seventy-five had been sexually assaulted during the nine-month repression. Pakistani soldiers had not only violated Bengali women on the spot; they abducted tens of hundreds and held them by force in their military barracks for nightly use. The women were kept naked to prevent their escape': Susan Brownmiller, *Against Our Will*, Simon and Schuster, New York, 1975, p. 82.

20. 'Pakistan: Ali Bhutto Begins to Pick Up the Pieces', *Time* magazine, 3 Jan 1972.

21. Guha, pp. 452, 461.

22. Arun Shourie, 1974. 'India: An Arrangement at Stake', *Economic and Political Weekly*, Vol. IX, No. XXV, 22 June 1974, p. 985.

23. Ved Mehta, 'Letter from New Delhi', *New Yorker*, 14 October 1974.

24. Nayar, *The Judgement*, pp. 1–2.

25. Ibid., p. 8.

26. Ibid., p. 31.

27. Ibid., p. 25.

28. Ibid., p. 36.

29. J. Anthony Lukas, 'Indira is as Indira Does', *New York Times*, 4 April 1976.

30. John Dayal and Ajoy Bose, *Delhi Under Emergency*, Ess Ess Publications, 1977, p. 47.

31. Robert McNamara, *Notes of Visit to India*, 6–12 November 1976, World Bank Archives: http://pubdocs.worldbank.org/en/694201391199447554/wbg-archives-1771080.pdf.

32. Vinod Mehta, *The Sanjay Story*, p. 119.

33. Nayar, *The Judgement*, p. 135.

34. Ibid., p. 136.

35. Michael Henderson, *Experiment with Untruth: India Under Emergency*, Macmillan, 1977, p. 159.

36. William Borders, '"Rising Star" in Indian Politics', *New York Times*, 20 November 1976.

37. Henderson, *Experiment with Untruth*, p. 119.

38. Vinod Mehta, *The Sanjay Story*, p. 146.

39. Ibid., p. 144.

40. William Borders, 'India's Crown Prince', *New York Times*, 13 February 1977.

41. J. Anthony Lukas, 'Indira is as Indira Does', *New York Times*, 4 April 1976.

42. Ved Mehta, 'Letter from New Delhi', *New Yorker*, 14 October 1974.

43. J. Anthony Lukas, 'Indira is as Indira Does', *New York Times*, 4 April 1976.

44. Nayar, *The Judgement*, p. 108.

45. Ibid., p. 158.

46. Ibid.

47. Cited in Lewis M. Simmons, 'Gandhi Apologists Now Criticizing Emergency Rule', *Washington Post*, 3 July 1977.

48. Soutik Biswas, 'India's dark history of sterilisation', BBC News, 14 November 2014: https://www.bbc.co.uk/news/world-asia-india-30040790.

49. Ved Mehta, 'Letter from New Delhi', *New Yorker*, 14 October 1974.

50. Ibid.

2. SURRENDER

1. P.V. Narasimha Rao, meditating anonymously on Rajiv's rule in a Delhi magazine, predicted a descent for Congress and the country: 'The Great Suicide', *Mainstream*, 27 January 1990.

2. Ved Mehta, *Rajiv Gandhi and Rama's Kingdom*, New Haven, Yale University Press, 1994, p. 71.

3. Ramachandra Guha, *India After Gandhi: The History of the World's Largest Democracy*, Macmillan, London, 2007, p. 553; Rasheed Kidwai, *Ballot: Ten Episodes that Shaped India's Democracy*, Hachette, 2018, p. 73.

4. Ved Mehta, *Rajiv Gandhi*, pp. 70–71.

5. Pupul Jayakar, *Indira Gandhi: A Biography*, Penguin, Delhi, 1992, p. 486.

6. Mehta, *Rajiv Gandhi*, pp. 36–37.

7. Guha, *India After Gandhi*, pp. 559–561.

8. Uma Paroha, 'Terrorism in Punjab: Origins and Dimensions', *Indian Journal of Political Science*, Vol. 54, No. 2, April–June 1993, pp. 283–250.

9. Ibid.

10. Cynthia Keppley Mahmood, *Fighting for Faith and Nation: Dialogues with Sikh Militants*, University of Pennsylvania, 2010, p. 91.

11. Andrew Major, 'From Moderates to Secessionists: A Who's Who of the Punjab Crisis', *Pacific Affairs*, Vol. 60, No. 1, Spring, 1987, pp. 57–58.

12. Randeep Ramesh, 'Jagjit Singh Chauhan: Campaigner for a separate Sikh state', *Guardian*, 10 April 2007.

13. For a detailed documentation of the anti-Sikh violence, see Manoj Mitta, H.S. Phoolka, *When a Tree Shook Delhi: The 1984 Carnage and its Aftermath*, Lotus, Delhi, 2007.

14. Ibid., pp. 25–30.

15. This is the figure arrived at by the Nanavati Commission in 2000, p. 17: https://mha.gov.in/sites/default/files/Nanavati-I_eng_0.pdf; the actual figure is almost certainly many times that: at the peak of the horror, one Sikh is estimated to be have been killed every minute for 48 hours: see Harinder Baweja, "Manmohan Singh's pledge to Sikh riot-hit unfulfilled", *Hindustan Times*, 3 Nov 2012

16. Mary McGrory, 'Rajiv Gandhi: Carrying On Gracefully', *Washington Post*, 16 June 1985.

17. Mitta and Phoolka, *When a Tree Shook Delhi*, p. 213.

18. 'Modi 'puppy' remark triggers new controversy over 2002 riots', Reuters, 12 July 2013: www.in.reuters.com/article/narendra-modi-puppy-reuters-interview/modis-puppy-remark-triggers-new-controversy-over-2002-riots-idINDEE96B08S20130712

19. Mitta and Phoolka, *When a Tree Shook Delhi*, p. 69.

20. James Manor, 'Rajiv Gandhi and Post-Election India: Opportunities and Risks', *The World Today*, Vol. 41, No. 3, March 1985, p. 52.

21. Rao, 'The Great Suicide'.

22. 'When India became the first country to ban "The Satanic Verses" much before the Iranian fatwa', *Scroll*, 4 October 2015: www.scroll.in/article/758288/when-india-became-the-first-country-to-ban-the-satanic-verses-much-before-the-iranian-fatwa.

23. David Brewster, *India's Ocean: The Story of India's Bid for Regional Leadership*, Routledge, London, 2014, p. 52.

24. Pradeep Nayak, *The Politics of the Ayodhya Dispute*, Commonwealth Publishers, New Delhi, 1993, p. 120.

3. DECADENCE

1. Population: India Census, 1991 (it did not include Jammu and Kashmir). Telephone statistic: Arvind Panagariya, *India: The Emerging Giant*, Oxford University Press, New York, 2008, p. 371.

2. Atul Kohli, 'Politics of Economic Growth in India, 1980–2005, Part II: The 1990s and Beyond', *Economic & Political Weekly*, Vol. 41, No. 14, 8 April 2006, pp. 1361–1370.

3. Ved Mehta, 'Letter from New Delhi', *New Yorker*, 19 August 1991.

4. G.S. Bhargava, *Star Crossed India*, Gyan Books, Delhi, 2005, pp. 153–154.

5. Shobha Tsering Bhalla, 'No Ifs, Please, I'm PM', *Straits Times*, 30 June 1991.

6. Rao, 'The Great Suicide'.

7. 'His Own Man', *Economist*, 29 June 1991.

8. An excellent guide to the reforms of 1991 is Atul Kohli, *Poverty Amid Plenty in the New India*, Cambridge University Press, New York, 2012.

9. Edward A. Gargan, 'India's New Premier Challenges the System, and the Reaction is Predictable', *New York Times*, 6 August 1991.

10. For an interesting perspective, see Manju Parikh, 'The Debacle at Ayodhya: Why Militant Hinduism Met with a Weak Response', *Asian Survey*, July 1993, pp. 673–684.

11. Edward A. Gargan, 'Hindu Militants Destroy Mosque, Setting Off a New Crisis in India', *New York Times*, 7 December 1992.

12. Speech by K.R. Narayanan, President of India, 18 September 1998, www.krnarayanan.in/html/speeches/others/bilkent18sept 98.htm.

13. H.M. Eliot (ed.), *The History of India as Told by Its Own Historians: Vol III*, London, 1872, pp. 42–45.

14. Romila Thapar, *Medieval India: History Textbook for Class VII*, NCERT, Delhi, 1988, p. 26.

15. Ibid., p. 83.

16. Ibid., pp. 2–3.

17. Ibid., p. 66.

18. Octavio Paz, *In Light of India*, Harcourt, New York, 1995, p. 37

19. For an outstanding study of colonial India that compli-cates dominant post-colonial perspectives of the period, see Peter L. Schmitthenner, *Telugu Resurgence: C.P. Brown and Cultural Consolidation in Nineteenth-century South India*, Manohar, Hyderabad, 2001.

20. M.C. Shah, *Consensus and Conciliation: PV Narasimha Rao*, Shipra Publications, Delhi, 1992, pp. 80–83.

21. 'Negating Nehru', editorial, *Christian Science Monitor*, 14 August 1991.

22. 'Economic Reforms Make Deng Man of the Year', *South China Morning Post*, 30 December 1992.

23. M.C. Shah, *Consensus and Conciliation*, p. 85.

24. Minutes from the Liebler–Rao meeting can be found here: http:// jcpa.org/article/a-1991-meeting-with-prime-minister-narasimha-rao/; the best account of the India–Israel relations during PV's tenure is P.R. Kumaraswamy, *India's Israel Policy*, Columbia University Press, New York, 2010.

25. For a fascinating account of Rao's engagement with East Asia, see Sunanda Datta-Ray, *Looking East to Look West: Lee Kuan Yew's Mission India*, Institute of Southeast Asian Studies, Singapore, 2009. For a brisk summary of Rao's hectic foreign tours before his US visit, see Sanjaya Baru, 'Mr Rao Goes to Washington', *Times of India*, 29 April 1994.

26. For an interesting account, see Strobe Talbott, *Engaging India*, Viking, New Delhi, 2004, and C. Raja Mohan, *Crossing the Rubicon: The Shaping of India's New Foreign Policy*, Viking, New Delhi, 2003.

27. Editorial, *Wall Street Journal*, 25 May 1994.

28. 'The President's News Conference with Prime Minister Rao of India, 19 May 1994', Clinton Presidential Documents: www.gov-info.gov/content/pkg/WCPD-1994–05–23/pdf/WCPD-1994–05–23.pdf.

29. John Burns, 'India Now Winning US Investment', *New York Times*, 6 February 1995.

30. Pavan Varma, *The Great Indian Middle Class*, Viking, New Delhi, 1999, p. 180.

31. Ibid., p. 177.

32. For a vibrant account of the changes that occurred, see Varma, *The Great Indian Middle Class*, pp. 170–185.

33. Ibid., p. 182.

34. Atul Kohli, 'Politics of Economic Growth in India'.

35. Varma, *The Greater Indian Middle Class*, pp. 198–199.

36. 'Raise Him Up', *Economist*, 3 September 2016.

37. Sunanda K. Datta-Ray, 'The unsung genius of India's reforms', *New York Times*, 29 December 2004.

38. Vinay Sitapati, *The Man Who Remade India: A Biography of P.V. Narasimha Rao*, Oxford University Press, New York, 2018, p. 5.

4. DISSOLUTION

1. John F. Burns, 'Sonia Gandhi, the "Foreigner", Startles the Political Pundits', *New York Times*, 27 December 1998.

2. "Singh: Reform with 'human face'", *CNN*, 20 May 2004.

3. Vinod Jose, 'Falling Man', *Caravan*, 1 October 2011.

4. Sanjiv Shankaran, 'World Bank clears $4.3 bn loan package', *Mint*, 24 September 2009.

5. 'Banks may have to shell out another up to $5.6 billion for bad debt: India Ratings', *Reuters*, 5 February 2019: www.reuters.com/article/us-india-banks-indiaratings/banks-may-have-to-shell-out-another-up-to-56-billion-for-bad-debt-india-ratings-idUSKCN-1PU1GN.

6. 'Income, Expenditure, Productive Assets and Indebtedness of Agricultural Households in India', National Sample Survey Office, New Delhi, 2013: http://mospi.nic.in/sites/default/files/publication_reports/nss_rep_576.pdf

7. P. Sainath, 'Farm suicide trends in 2012 remain dismal', 29 June 2013: www.psainath.org/farm-suicide-trends-in-2012-remain-dismal/.

8. P. Sainath, 'How right you are, Dr. Singh', *Hindu*, 14 September 2010.

9. Kapil Komireddi, 'Blood runs in India's red corridor', *Guardian*, 23 April 2009: https://www.theguardian.com/commentisfree/2009/apr/23/india-elections-protest.

10. Amit Bhaduri, *The Face You Were Afraid to See*, Penguin, New Delhi, 2009, p. 181.

11. Sandeep Pandey, 'Reports on police firing in Dumka, Jharkhand', *Sanhati*: www.sanhati.com/news/1255/.

12. Nandini Sundar, 'Bastar, Maoism and Salwa Judum', *Economic and Political Weekly*, Vol. XLI, No. 29, 22 July 2006, p. 3187.

13. Freny Manecksha, India: Sexual Violence and Impunity, *CETRI*, 14 April 2016.

14. 'Dangerous Duty Children and the Chhattisgarh Conflict', *Human Rights Watch*, 5 September 2008: www.hrw.org/report/2008/09/05/dangerous-duty/children-and-chhattisgarh-conflict.

15. Sujan Dutta, 'Triveni in air, Green Hunt on ground', *Telegraph*, 4 October 2010.

16. Steve Coll, 'Manmohan Singh', *New Yorker*, 24 November 2009.

17. 'Pak backtracks on sending ISI chief to India', *Hindustan Times*, 29 November 2008.

18. 'What kind of story do you want?', *Open Magazine*, 20 November 2010.

19. Pavan Varma, *The Great Indian Middle Class*, p. 87.

20. Sagarika Ghose, 'A Raja says Vinod Rai was part of a political conspiracy against UPA 2', *Times of India*, 19 January 2018.

21. For a full list of the schemes, see: www.asuryaprakash.com/annexure1.html.

22. 'Our moral universe is shrinking: Sonia Gandhi', *Deccan Herald*, 19 Nov 2010.

23. 'IAS officer Ashok Khemka transferred three days after he asked for Robert Vadra-DLF inquiry', *NDTV*, 16 October 2012: www.ndtv.com/india-news/ias-officer-ashok-khemka-transferred-three-days-after-he-asked-for-robert-vadra-dlf-inquiry-501872.

24. Tushar Srivastava, 'Quattrocchi goes home, CBI watches', *Hindustan Times*, 16 August 2007.

25. Narendra Modi's Open Letter to Anna Hazare, 11 April 2011: www.narendramodi.in/narendra-modi's-open-letter-to-anna-hazare-3922.

26. Dean Nelson, 'Fear and intimidation in Anna Hazare's "model" village', *Daily Telegraph*, London, 25 August 2011.

27. Technically, there were nine Indian citizens on the Forbes list of the world's richest: Ruth David, 'Welcome To The Trillion Dollar

Club', *Forbes*, 26 April 2007; 'Indian millionaires zoom by 42,800', *Hindustan Times*, 29 September 2010.

28. Edward Gordon, *Future Jobs: Solving the Employment and Skills Crisis*, Praeger, Santa Barbara, 2013, p. 59.

29. P.V. Narasimha Rao, *A Long Way: Selected Speeches*, D.C. Books, Kottayam, 2002, pp. 146–154.

30. 'Montek Singh Ahluwalia rules out 9 pc growth, says India doing well', *India Today*, 4 October 2011.

12. T.R. Andhyarujina, 'An execution most foul', *Hindu*, 19 February 2013.

32. 'Budget speech of Manmohan Singh', 24 July 1991: www.indiabudget.gov.in/bspeech/bs199192.pdf.

33. Amitava Kumar, 'Central India's Ugly Fight for Environmental Justice', *New Yorker*, 10 February 2017.

34. Kohli, 'Politics of Economic Growth in India'.

5. CULT

1. Nicolae Ceausescu, *In memoriam*. Translated by Constantin Roman.

2. 'Birth of 2nd republic under Modi: Sanjaya Baru', the *Times of India*, 27 July 2014.

3. 'Modi can never become PM, can sell tea: Mani Shankar Aiyar', *Indian Express*, 17 January 2014.

4. Vinod Jose, 'The Emperor Uncrowned', *Caravan*, 1 March 2012.

5. Ross Colvin and Satarupa Bhattacharjya, 'The remaking of Narendra Modi', Reuters, 12 July 2013: https://in.reuters.com/article/india-modi-gujarat-bjp/special-report-the-remaking-of-narendra-modi-idINDEE96B00Y20130712.

6. Jose, 'The Emperor Uncrowned'.

7. Human Rights Watch, 'We Have No Orders to Save You: State Participation and Complicity in Communal Violence in Gujarat', Vol. 14, No. 3(c), 2002, pp. 15–17.

8. Jose, 'The Emperor Uncrowned', p. 3.

9. Ibid.

10. Celia Dugger, 'Religious Riots Loom Over Indian Politics', *New York Times*, 27 July 2002.

11. http://www.gujaratindia.com/whos-who/chief_ministers_gujara2.htm.

12. Christophe Jaffrelot, *Religion, Caste, and Politics in India*, Hurst, London, 2010, p. 408.

13. Ibid., p. 402.

14. Jose, 'The Emperor Uncrowned'.

15. Manas Dasgupta, 'All accused acquitted in Pandya murder case', *Hindu*, 29 August 2011.

16. 'Amit Shah headed extortion gang, CBI tells SC', *Hindustan Times*, 9 March 2011.

17. 'The Stalkers: Amit Shah's Illegal Surveillance Exposed', *Outlook*, 15 November 2013.

18. 'Ex-CJI Sathasivam is Governor, jurists say it may lead to more "political intervention"', *Indian Express*, 4 September 2014.

19. Binoy Prabhakar, 'How an American lobbying company Apco Worldwide markets Narendra Modi to the world', *Economic Times*, 9 December 2012.

20. Sam Asher, Paul Novosad, Charlie Rafkin, 'Intergenerational Mobility in India: Estimates from New Methods and Administrative Data', Sep 2018: www.dartmouth.edu/~novosad/anr-india-mobility.pdf.

21. 'Why India Needs Narendra Modi', *Financial Express*, 20 October 2008.

22. 'Modi locks adoring business in bear hug—Tata leads the charge in showering praise', *Telegraph*, 13 January 2009.

23. 'Modi PM material for Anil Ambani, Sunil Mittal', *Economic Times*, 15 January 2009.

24. 'Vibrant Gujarat: India Inc Invokes Gandhi to Praise Modi', *Outlook*, 12 January 2011.

25. 'Modi is king of kings: Anil Ambani', *Hindustan Times*, 11 January 2013.

26. Ashutosh Varshney, 'Modi the moderate', *Indian Express*, 27 March 2014.

27. Ashis Nandy, 'Obituary of a Culture', *Seminar*, May 2002.

28. David Pilling, 'Lunch with FT: Jagdish Bhagwati', 17 April 2014.

29. Gurcharan Das, 'Secularism or Growth? The Choice is Yours', *Times of India*, 6 April 2014.

30. 'Vote for BJP if you want revenge: Amit Shah at Muzaffarnagar', *Times of India*, 5 April 2014.

31. K. Balchand, 'Modi fears a "pink revolution"', *The Hindu*, 3 April 2014.

32. 'Gandhi's iconic charkha pose replaced by Modi's in Khadi Gram Udyog calendar, diary', *India Today*, 12 January 2017.

33. 'Catch them young?', *Business Standard*, 4 September 2014.

34. 'Should we run relief camps? Open child producing centres?', *Outlook*, 30 September 2002.

35. Narendra Modi, *Exam Warriors*, Penguin, New Delhi, 2018.

36. 'Delhi University tells High Court it cannot disclose details of Narendra Modi's degree', *Scroll*, 28 February 2018: https://scroll.in/latest/870370/delhi-university-tells-high-court-it-cannot-disclose-details-of-narendra-modis-degree.

37. Gaurav Vivek Bhatnagar, 'RTI Activists Bat for Information Commissioner', *Wire*, 19 January 2017: https://thewire.in/politics/rti-activists-bat-for-sridhar-acharyulu.

38. 'Modi-Obama "Mann ki Baat" to be available in e-book format', *Rediff*, 28 January 2015: news.rediff.com/commentary/2015/jan/28/modiobama-mann-ki-baat-to-be-available-in-ebook-format/7ec9e071e97c3c4649733d148f9c5158.

39. Andy Marino, *Narendra Modi: A Political Biography*, HarperCollins, New Delhi, 2014, p. x.

40. Ami Kazmin, 'Narendra Modi's mystery biographer', *Financial Times*, 1 April 2014.

41. Francis Elliott, 'Spin doctor was paid for India book', *Times*, 9 November 2015.

42. Swati Mathur, 'Mann ki Baat now in regional languages', *Times of India*, 2 June 2017.

43. For a deep investigation of Modi's digital army, see Swati Chaturvedi, *I Am a Troll: Inside the Secret World of the BJP's Digital Army*, Juggernaut, New Delhi, 2016.

44. 'How WhatsApp Fuels Fake News and Violence in India', *Wired*, 12 December 2018: https://www.wired.com/story/how-whatsapp-fuels-fake-news-and-violence-in-india.

45. Charu S. Kasturi, 'Discovery of Nehru, staged by Sushma', *Telegraph*, 4 August 2017.

46. Liz Matthew, 'Narendra Modi is God's gift for India, messiah of the poor: Venkaiah Naidu', *Indian Express*, 21 March 2016.

47. 'Sycophancy bug bites BJP leaders, hail Modi as "god's gift" and "messiah"', *Business Standard*, 21 March 2016.

48. 'Delhi election 2015: BJP launches 'Selfie with Modi' to woo young voters', *Times of India*, 25 January 2015

49. Poonam Mahajan, *Twitter*, 29 July 2018: https://twitter.com/poonam_mahajan/status/1023561279212990469.

50. Suresh Prabhu, *Twitter*, 29 July 2018: https://twitter.com/sureshprabhu/status/1023516637436280833.

51. Suresh Fadnavis, *Twitter*, 28 July 2018: https://twitter.com/Dev_Fadnavis/status/1023284207882264576.

52. Barack Obama, 'Remarks by President Obama at India State Dinner', 25 January 2015: obamawhitehouse.archives.gov/the-press-office/2015/01/25/remarks-president-obama-india-state-dinner.

6. CHAOS

1. Number of Branches and ATMs in India: www.gktoday.in/gk/number-of-branches-and-atms/.

2. Anto Antony and Iain Marlow, 'ATMs, banks run out of cash as people grapple to replace Rs500, Rs1000 notes', *Mint*, 11 November 2016.

3. 'Businessman dies of heart-attack after ban on Rs 500, Rs 1000 notes', *Financial Express*, 10 November 2016.

4. Abdul Jadid, 'Stunned over new Rs 1,000 rule woman dies of shock outside bank in Gorakhpur', *Hindustan Times*, 10 November 2016.

5. Hamza Khan, 'Jaipur: Infant dies, father says no cash for ambulance', *Indian Express*, 20 Aug 2018.

6. 'Baby dies as parents had no cash to buy medicines in Vizag', *Times of India*, 14 November 2016.

7. 'Demonetisation: Cash-starved farmer ends life in frustration in Raigarh', *First Post*, 14 November 2016: https://www.firstpost.com/india/demonetisation-cash-starved-farmer-ends-life-in-frustration-in-raigarh-3105098.html.

8. 'SBI cashier dies of heart attack in Bhopal amid rush to exchange notes', *Hindustan Times*, 14 November 2016.

9. Siva G., 'Baby dies as parents had no cash to buy medicines in Vizag', *Times of India*, 14 November 2014.

10. '3-yr-old dies as father waits at bank; no cash for fee, student commits suicide', *Hindustan Times*, 23 November 2016.

11. Jatin Gandhi, Give me 50 days over scrapped notes, punish me if problems persist: Modi', *Hindustan Times*, 13 November 2016.

12. Reserve Bank of India Annual Report, 29 August 2018: https://rbi.org.in/Scripts/AnnualReportPublications.aspx?Id=1235.

13. PTI, '99.30% of demonetised money back in the system, says RBI report', *Economic Times*, 30 August 2018.

14. Manas Chakravarty, 'Household savings grow highest in 7 years, but it's mainly in cash', *Mint*, 30 August 2018.

15. Gayatri Nayak, 'Cash still the king. Cash savings highest in a decade', *Economic Times*, 30 August 2018.

16. 'India's Economic Growth Slows Down in Fourth Quarter', *Wire*, 31 May 2017: https://thewire.in/economy/q4-gdp-growth-india.

17. Ananth Krishnan, 'China media mocks India's "GDP own goal", criticises PM Modi's demonetisation', *India Today*, 2 June 2017.

18. Shilpa Shaji, 'Here are the 105 people who died in 45 days of demonetisation', *Narada News*, 22 December 2016: naradanews.com/2016/12/here-are-the-97-people-who-died-in-37-days-of-demonetisation/.

19. B. Baskar, 'After the demonetisation tsunami', *Hindu Business Line*, 16 April 2017.

20. Sagar, "Beef-Eaters and Politicians Hire Labourers to Create Fake Bank Queues: RSS Officials Discuss Demonetisation", *The Caravan*, 2 December 2016: www.caravanmagazine.in/vantage/beef-eaters-politicians-hire-labourers-create-fake-bank-queues-rss-officials-discuss-demonetisation.

21. Tushar Dhara, 'Narendra Modi Mocks Harvard Economists, Manmohan and Quotes GDP Figures at UP Election Rallies', *News18*, 1 March 2017: www.news18.com/news/politics/pm-modi-mocks-harvard-economists-manmohan-and-quotes-gdp-stats-in-up-1354898.html.

22. 'Demonetisation "bitter medicine" to treat corruption', *Times of India*, 20 November 2018.

23. 'Agriculture ministry says farmers were unable to buy seeds after demonetisation: Report', *Scroll*, 21 November 2018: https://scroll.

in/latest/902905/agriculture-ministrys-report-says-farmers-were-unable-to-buy-seeds-after-demonetisation-report.

24. 'Behind Notes Ban, Team Of 6 Worked Secretly At PM Narendra Modi's Home: Report', *NDTV*, 9 November 2016: https://www.ndtv.com/india-news/who-knew-pm-narendra-modis-black-money-move-kept-a-closely-guarded-secret-1635822.

25. 'RTI: Bank With Amit Shah as Director Collected Highest Amount of Banned Notes Among Coop Banks', *Wire*, 22 June 2018: https://thewire.in/banking/bank-with-amit-shah-as-a-director-collected-highest-amount-of-banned-notes-among-dc-cbs-rti-reply.

26. 'What demonetisation? BJP revenue grew 81% to Rs 1034 crore in 2016–17; Congress, others earned this much', *Financial Express*, 11 April 2018.

27. 'RBI data isn't enough to argue if demonetisation was a success or failure', *Print*, 7 November 2017: www.theprint.in/opinion/premature-argue-demonetisation-success-failure/9195/.

28. Sharad Raghavan, 'Demonetisation a massive, draconian, monetary shock: Arvind Subramanian', *Hindu*, 29 November 2018.

7. TERROR

1. Aditi Vatsa, 'In Dadri, a daughter asks: "If it is not beef, will they bring back my dead father?"', *Indian Express*, 26 December 2015.

2. 'BJP MP Sakshi Maharaj says ready to kill and get killed for our mother, calls SP's Azam Khan a "Pakistani"', *News18*, 6 October 2015: https://www.news18.com/news/politics/bjp-mp-sakshi-maharaj-says-ready-to-kill-and-get-killed-for-our-mother-calls-sps-azam-khan-a-pakistani-1143939.html.

3. Aditi Vatsa, 'Dadri lynching: One BJP leader calls for a maha-panchayat, another blames victim, family', *Indian Express*, 2 October 2015.

4. Salman Ravi, 'Why India man was lynched over beef rumours', *BBC News*, 1 October 2015, www.bbc.co.uk/news/world-asia-india-34409354.

5. Kai Schultz, 'Murders of Religious Minorities in India Go Unpunished, Report Finds', *New York Times*, 18 February 2019.

6. Nandy, 'Obituary of a Culture'.

7. 'Bihar election is a fight between jungle raj and vikas raj, says Narendra Modi', *Mint*, 8 October 2015.

8. The six states—and one union territory—are Kerala, Arunachal Pradesh, Mizoram, Meghalaya, Nagaland, and Tripura.

9. Amar Diwarkar, 'How "Cow Vigilantes" Launched India's Lynching Epidemic', *New Republic*, 26 July 2017, newrepublic.com/article/144043/cow-vigilantes-launched-indias-lynching-epidemic.

10. 'Violent Cow Protection in India', *Human Rights Watch*, 18 February 2019, www.hrw.org/report/2019/02/18/violent-cow-protection-india/vigilante-groups-attack-minorities#.

11. Muzaffar Raina, 'Cow-carcass rumour fuels J&K flare-up', *Telegraph*, 11 October 2015.

12. 'Violent Cow Protection in India', *Human Rights Watch*.

13. 'Dalit Family Stripped, Beaten As "Gau Raksha" Vigilantism Continues', *Wire*, 13 July 2016: https://thewire.in/politics/dalit-family-stripped-beaten-as-gau-raksha-vigilantism-continues.

14. 'The Indian Dalits attacked for wearing the wrong shoes', BBC News, 19 June 2018, www.bbc.co.uk/news/world-asia-india-44517922.

15. Ibid.

16. In March 2020, two minors were sentenced to three years in a juvenile correctional facility after being convicted in the lynching case again Pehlu Khan: Rajendra Sharma and Yeshika Budhwar, '2 minors get 3 years in juvenile home in Pehlu Khan case', The Times of India, 14 March 2020

17. For a fascinating and detailed history of the effect of Indian vegetarianism on European thought, see Tristram Stuart, *The Bloodless Revolution: Vegetarians and the Discovery of India*, Harper Collins, London, 2006.

18. Kapil Komireddi, 'Mercy Towards Animals', *Aeon*, 26 June 2013: https://aeon.co/essays/mercy-toward-animals-runs-deep-in-asian-cultural-traditions.

19. Saba Naqvi, 'The Hawk in Flight', *Outlook*, 24 December 2007.

20. R.D. Thornton, *William Maxwell to Robert Burns*, John Donald Publishers Ltd, Edinburgh, 1979, p. 70.

21. 'Rate of Unemployment in India Highest in 20 Years: Report',

HuffPost, 25 September 2018, www.huffingtonpost.in/2018/09/
25/rate-of-unemployment-highest-in-india-in-the-20-years-says-
report_a_23541136/.

22. 'Hindutva Jihad: "If They Kill One Hindu, 100 Will Be..."',
Outlook, 27 Aug 2014.

23. Amy Kazmin, 'Yogi Adityanath, a firebrand cleric polarising politics in India', *Financial Times*, 4 March 2017.

24. 'Who will be the next CM of Uttar Pradesh? Ahead of BJP
announcement, here are a few names', *First Post*, 15 March 2017,
www.firstpost.com/politics/who-will-be-the-next-cm-of-uttar-
pradesh-ahead-of-bjp-announcement-here-are-a-few-names-
3335414.html.

25. 'Yogi: Cows no less important than humans', *Tribune*, 25 July 2018.

26. Basit Malik, '"Say, Pakistan Murdabad!": A Reporter Recounts
How a Mob in Delhi Assaulted Him When They Identified Him
As Muslim', *Caravan*, 19 June 2017.

27. Hari Kumar and Nida Najar, 'Police in India Arrest Fans
Celebrating Pakistan's Cricket Victory', *New York Times*, 21 June
2017.

28. Vidhi Doshi, '"How can they hate us so much?" asks father of
Muslim teen brutally killed in attack on train in India', *Washington
Post*, 24 June 2017.

29. Tweet posted by @NarendraModi, 25 June 2017: https://twit-
ter.com/narendramodi/status/879082577730035713?lang=en.

30. Annie Gowen, 'A Muslim and a Hindu thought they could be a
couple. Then came the 'love jihad' hit list', *Washington Post*, 26 April
2018.

31. 'BJP Leader, Activists Disrupt Hindu-Muslim Wedding Celebration
in Ghaziabad', *Wire*, 23 December 2017: https://thewire.in/com-
munalism/hindutva-activists-disrupt-wedding-ghaziabad-clash-
police-love-jihad.

32. V. Kumara Swamy, 'Mob attack aborts inter-faith wedding',
Telegraph, 25 July 2018.

33. Sukrita Baruah, 'Sent to protect her, UP cops beat woman, mock
her for Muslim friend', *Indian Express*, 26 September 2018.

34. Deep Mukherjee, 'Rajasthan hacking: 516 people from across
India donate Rs 3 lakh to Shambhulal Regar's wife', *Indian Express*,
14 December 2017.

35. 'Rajasthan government wants students, teachers to learn about love jihad; here is how', *Financial Express*, 19 November 2017.

36. Jeffrey Gettleman, 'An 8-Year-Old's Rape and Killing Fuels Religious Tensions in India', *New York Times*, 11 April 2018.

37. Piyasee Dasgupta, 'What Happens To The People Arrested For Insulting Modi?', HuffPost, 24 April 2018, www.huffingtonpost. in/2018/04/23/what-happens-to-the-people-arrested-for-insult-ing-modi_a_23417412/.

38. 'India's ruling party ordered online abuse of opponents, claims book', *Guardian*, 27 December 2016.

39. 'After Incredible India snub, Snapdeal to cut ties with Aamir Khan', *DNA*, 5 February 2016.

40. Vir Sanghvi, 'Dilemma of an Indian Muslim', *Hindustan Times*, 11 August 2007.

41. Raghu Karnad, 'Indian Liberals Must Die', *NPlusOne*, 12 September 2017.

42. 'PM Modi follows 4 Twitter accounts that trolled #GauriLankesh', *Newslaundry*, 6 September 2017, www.newslaundry.com/2017/ 09/06/modi-trolls-gauri-lankesh.

43. Raghu Karnad, 'It's Not What Modi Is Tweeting—It's What He Is Reading', *Wire*, 9 February 2017: https://thewire.in/politics/ narendra-modi-twitter-trolls.

44. 'Same group behind killings of Dabholkar, Kalburgi, Gauri Lankesh; members linked to Sanatan Sanstha: Police', *Hindustan Times*, 16 September 2018.

8. VANITY

1. 'The world is looking at India with renewed respect and immense enthusiasm, says PM Modi', *Business Standard*, 21 Nov 2014.

2. Iain Marlow, 'Modi's Trips Around the World Cost Indian Taxpayers $280 Million', *Bloomberg*, 13 December 2018.

3. 'FPIs stay bearish on India; pull out $5-bn in Oct so far', *Hindu Business Line*, 28 October 2018.

4. Yuji Kuronuma, 'India foreign direct investment growth slowest in 5 years', *Nikkei Asian Review*, 5 July 2018.

5. Modi is currently fending off allegations that he struck the deal to

help his cheerleader Anil Ambani. '4 puzzling questions about the Rafale deal', *Rediff News*, 4 December 2017.

6. Saumitra Dasgupta, 'Modi uncovers China e-visa surprise', *Telegraph*, 16 May 2015.

7. Mahesh Vijapurkar, 'Nehru declined offer of permanent U.N.', *The Hindu*, 10 January 2004.

8. Ameet Dhakal, 'Has Modi's "Neighbourhood First" model forgotten about Nepal?', *Scroll*, 24 September 2015, www.croll.in/article/757547/has-modis-neighbourhood-first-model-forgotten-about-nepal.

9. 'UN: Nepal blockade puts millions of children at risk, *BBC News*, 30 Nov 2015: www.bbc.co.uk/news/world-asia-34968252.

10. Utpal Parashar, 'China announces fresh $146 million aid for Nepal', *Hindustan Times*, 29 March 2015.

11. Elizabeth Roche, Pretika Khanna, 'Pakistan JIT claims Pathankot attack staged, say reports', *Mint*, 5 April 2016.

12. 'Won't engage with talent from neighbouring country in future: Karan Johar', *Hindustan Times*, 19 October 2016.

13. 'Myanmar lodges protest with India over border raid', *Frontier Myanmar*, 17 September 2015.

14. Bernard Weinraub, 'Israel and India: Long–Unhealed Rift', *New York Times*, 22 December 1974.

15. Itamar Eichner, 'From India with love', *YNet*, 4 March 2009: https://www.ynetnews.com/articles/0,7340,L-3696887,00.html; 'BBC poll shows support for Palestinian state', *BBC News*, 19 Sep 2011: https://www.bbc.co.uk/news/world-middle-east-14946179.

16. Mustafa El Feki, 'An Indo-Arab blunder?', *Al Ahram Weekly*, 17–23 February 2005.

17. 'Israel-India Relations/Strong, but Low-key', *Haaretz*, 1 December 2008.

18. Smita Nair, 'Purohit planned Israel-based Hindu govt-in-exile, support from Thai contacts: ATS chargesheet today', *Indian Express*, 20 January 2009.

19. "American Jewish group takes Indian Muslims to Israel", 16 Aug 2007, *Indian Muslims*: www.indianmuslims.info/news/2007/aug/15/american_jewish_group_takes_indian_muslims_israel.html

20. Paul Marshall, 'Hinduism and Terror', *Hudson Institute*, 1 June 2004: https://www.hudson.org/research/4575-hinduism-and-terror.

21. Shrenik Rao, 'Hitler's Hindus: The Rise and Rise of India's Nazi-loving Nationalists', *Haaretz*, 14 December 2017.

22. James Legge, Faxian, *A Record of Buddhistic Kingdoms*, Cosimo, New York, 2005, p. 4.

23. Sunanda K. Datta-Ray, 'Lee Kuan Yew and the Indian Romance', *The Commonwealth Journal of International Affairs*, Vol. 104, No. 3, July 2015.

24. Sarvepalli Gopal, *Jawaharlal Nehru: A Biography, Vol. I*, Harvard University Press, 1976, p. 236.

25. Guha, *India After Gandhi*, p. 305.

26. Ranjit Kalha, 'There is No Tibet Card for India to Play. Here's Why', *Wire*, 13 January 2017: www.thewire.in/external-affairs/india-has-no-tibetan-card-to-play-heres-why.

27. Jesse Johnson, 'Japan, U.S., India to hold major naval drill off Okinawa starting Friday', *Japan Times*, 7 Jun 2016.

28. Harsh V. Pant, *Indian Foreign Policy: An Overview*, Manchester University Press, Machester, 2017, p. 2.

29. Calum MacLeod, 'China angry at Obama's meeting with Dalai Lama', *USA Today*, 21 February 2014.

30. 'Met defends behaviour of Chinese torch guards branded thugs by Coe', *Guardian*, 7 May 2008.

31. 'English Rendering of Transcript of the special episode of Mann ki Baat: PM Shri Narendra Modi and US President Shri Barack Obama share their thoughts on Radio', *Press Information Bureau*, 27 Jan 2015: http://pib.nic.in/newsite/mbErel.aspx?relid=114987.

32. 'Pakistan-Russia hold joint military drill', *Times of India*, 22 October 2018.

33. 'Indian Army's ammunition stock will exhaust after 10 days of war: CAG report', *India Today*, 21 January 2017.

34. 'China has quietly resumed its activities in Doklam', *Hindu Business Line*, 26 July 2018.

35. 'Status quo in Doklam: Sushma Swaraj', *Economic Times*, 8 February 2018.

36. 'India, with eye on China ties, bans Tibetans rally in New Delhi', *Reuters*, 7 March 2018: www.reuters.com/article/us-india-china-tibet/india-with-eye-on-china-ties-bans-tibetans-from-holding-new-delhi-rally-idUSKCN1GJ1HP.

37. Jim Yardley, 'India Tightens New Delhi's Tibetan Districts on Eve of Summit', *New York Times*, 28 March 2012.

9. SEIZURE

1. Letter from the University Grants Commission: https://www.ugc.ac.in/pdfnews/0726695_UGC-Letter-Surgical-Strike-29–09–18.pdf.

2. 'Surgical strike: Sena poster shows Modi as Ram, Sharif as Ravana', *Rediff News*, 5 October 2016: https://www.rediff.com/news/report/surgical-strike-sena-poster-shows-modi-as-ram-sharif-as-ravana/20161005.htm.

3. Ajai Shukla, 'Army silent as soldier, surgical strikes feature in BJP election posters', *Business Standard*, 8 October 2016.

4. 'Battle royale as political parties spar furiously over surgical strikes', *DNA*, 8 October 2016.

5. 'Surgical strike: Sena poster shows Modi as Ram, Sharif as Ravana', *Rediff News*, 5 October 2016: www.rediff.com/news/report/surgical-strike-sena-poster-shows-modi-as-ram-sharif-as-ravana/20161005.htm.

6. Prakash Katoch, 'Modi government politicized surgical strikes but did little for soldiers', *Asia Times*, 4 October 2018: http://www.atimes.com/modi-government-politicized-surgical-strikes-but-did-little-for-soldiers/.

7. Ajai Shukla, 'Army silent as soldier, surgical strikes feature in BJP election posters', *Business Standard*, 8 October 2016.

8. 'There is a need for another surgical strike: Army Chief Bipin Rawat', *Indian Express*, 25 September 2018.

9. Pankaj Khelkar, 'Army chief Bipin Rawat: Pakistan needs to be secular to stay together with India', *India Today*, 20 November 2018.

10. Sudhi Ranjan Sen, 'In an Unusual Move, Govt Supercedes Two Generals to Name Bipin Rawat Next Army Chief', *HuffPost*,

5 December 2016: https://www.huffingtonpost.in/2016/12/05/in-an-unusual-move-govt-supercedes-two-generals-to-name-bi-pin-r_a_21620874/.

11. 'Congress has humiliated CAG, Army and every democratic institution: PM Modi', *Times of India*, 19 December 2018.

12. Suchandana Gupta, 'Stand-up and clap when you see a soldier: PM Modi', *Times of India*, 14 October 2016.

13. Devika Bhattacharya, 'At 'Bharat ki Baat' event, PM Modi rips into 'terror export factory' Pakistan', *Times of India*, 19 April 2018.

14. Ajai Shukla, 'While "surgical strikes" were under way, govt cut Army's disability pensions', *Business Standard*, 10 October 2016.

15. Ajai Shukla, 'Surgical Strikes: As Modi plays politics with Indian army, soldiers pay with their lives', *South China Morning Post*, 29 September 2018: https://www.scmp.com/week-asia/geopolitics/article/2166132/surgical-strikes-modi-plays-politics-indian-army-soldiers-pay.

16. 'Defence ministry told army to build bridges for Sri Sri event', *Hindustan Times*, 9 March 2016.

17. In 2011, Swamy published an article calling for the disenfranchisement of Indian Muslims: 'Harvard writes off Swamy for anti-Muslim write-up', *Hindustan Times*, 9 December 2011.

18. 'Subramanian Swamy takes a swipe at Raghuram Rajan again; says rexit caused no effect on stock markets', *Financial Express*, 7 September 2016.

19. Rajesh Mahapatra, 'Raghuram Rajan breaks silence, says neither he nor RBI under him wanted demonetisation', *Hindustan Times*, 5 September 2017.

20. 'Who is Urjit Patel? Everything you need to know about the new RBI Governor', *Indian Express*, 20 August 2016.

21. Anand Mishra, 'Demonetisation: On Nov 7, it was Govt which "advised" RBI to "consider" note ban, got RBI nod next day', *Indian Express*, 10 January 2017.

21. A.D. Shroff Memorial Lecture by Dr Viral Acharya, deputy governor of the RBI: https://rbi.org.in/Scripts/BS_SpeechesView.aspx?Id=1066.

22. Ibid.

23. Mihir Sharma, 'Why RBI Is Suddenly Standing Up to Modi—

And What's At Stake', *NDTV*, 31 October 2018: https://www.ndtv.com/opinion/what-modi-vs-rbi-is-all-about-its-an-election-year-stupid-1940419.

24. A.D. Shroff Memorial Lecture.

25. Alasdair Pal, 'Maverick accountant Gurumurthy shaking up India's central bank', *Reuters*, 30 November 2018: https://www.reuters.com/article/us-india-cenbank-gurumurthy-newsmaker/maverick-accountant-gurumurthy-shaking-up-indias-central-bank-idUSKCN1NZ0IE.

26. 'RBI likely to pay bumper interim dividend to help Modi government', *Reuters*, 7 January 2019.

27. 'What happened at Hyderabad Central University that led to Rohith Vemula's suicide?', *India Today*, 18 January 2016.

28. 'My Birth is My Fatal Accident: Rohith Vemula's Searing Letter Is an Indictment of Social Prejudices', *Wire*, 17 January 2019: https://thewire.in/caste/rohith-vemula-letter-a-powerful-indictment-of-social-prejudices.

29. Chandra Bhan Prasad, 'But the Earth moves, and Rohith Vemula is a Dalit', *Indian Express*, 17 August 2017.

30. Prasanta Chakravarty, 'I Am a Professor. This Is How I Was Beaten Up at Ramjas', *NDTV*, 23 February 2017: https://www.ndtv.com/blog/at-ramjas-they-tried-to-use-a-muffler-to-strangle-me-a-professors-blog-1662740.

31. 'Delhi Police charges Kanhaiya Kumar, others in JNU sedition case', *Rediff News*, 14 January 2019: https://www.rediff.com/news/report/delhi-police-charges-kanhaiya-kumar-others-in-jnu-sedition-case/20190114.htm.

32. Pavan Kulkarni, 'History Shows How Patriotic the RSS Really Is', *Wire*, 15 August 2018: https://thewire.in/history/rss-hindutva-nationalism.

33. Shreya Roy Chowdhury, 'Scholarships owed to Dalit students: Rs 8,600 crore. What government has budgeted: Rs 3,000 crore', *Scroll*, 12 March 2018: https://scroll.in/article/871448/scholarships-owed-to-dalit-students-rs-8600-crore-what-government-has-budgeted-rs-3000-crore.

34. Ritika Chopra, 'Institutes of Eminence tag: HRD Ministry and PMO disagreed on crucial issues', *Indian Express*, 28 August 2018.

35. 'Does Modi want to hijack higher education?', *Rediff News*, 5 September 2018: https://www.rediff.com/news/interview/does-modi-want-to-hijack-higher-education/20180905.htm.

36. Rupam Jain and Tom Lasseter, 'By rewriting history, Hindu nationalists aim to assert their dominance over India', 6 March 2018: https://in.reuters.com/article/india-modi-culture-special-report/special-report-by-rewriting-history-hindu-nationalists-aim-to-assert-their-dominance-over-india-idINKCN1GI178.

37. Lizzie Wade, 'South Asians are descended from a mix of farmers, herders, and hunter-gatherers, ancient DNA reveals', *Science*, 18 April 2018.

38. Saradindu Mukherji, 'A Case Study of Progressive History Writing', *India Facts*, 19 June 2015: http://indiafacts.org/ncert-class-xii-textbook-a-case-study-of-progressive-history-writing/.

39. Akshaya Mukul, 'Ancient Caste system worked well, ICHR head says', *Times of India*, 15 July 2015.

40. Harish C. Menon, 'In the version of history found in India's new textbooks, China lost 1962 and Gandhi wasn't murdered', *Quartz India*, 16 August 2017: https://qz.com/india/1054692/in-the-version-of-history-found-in-indias-new-textbooks-china-lost-1962-and-gandhi-wasnt-murdered/.

41. Shoeb Khan, 'Devnani's "revisionist" ideas, NDA schemes guide NCERT books', *Times of India*, 3 June 2018.

42. 'Maharashtra Board drops Mughal, Western history from syllabi, claims it's "irrelevant"', *Indian Express*, 8 August 2017.

43. 'Darwin's theory wrong, nobody saw ape turning into man: Minister Satyapal Singh', *Hindustan Times*, 21 January 2018.

44. Maseeh Rahman, 'Indian prime minister claims genetic science existed in ancient times', *Guardian*, 28 October 2014.

45. 'Don't miss: 5 howlers from the Indian Science Congress', *India Today*, 5 January 2015.

46. John Elliott, 'Modi puts Hindu myths at centre of India politics', *Newsweek*, 30 October 2014.

47. Mihir Sharma, 'Modi's Alarming Power Grab', *Bloomberg*, 27 March 2017: https://www.bloomberg.com/opinion/articles/2017-03-27/modi-s-alarming-power-grab.

48. 'EC against state funding of polls', *Pioneer*, 22 May 2017.

49. 'EC hopes electoral bonds are step in "right direction"', *Hindu Business Line*, 24 January 2018.

50. Ritika Chopra, 'EC cited model code and flood relief to delay Gujarat polls—but for J&K, took another line', *Indian Express*, 7 December 2017.

51. 'EC probes complaints of poll code violation by Modi amid attack from Opposition', *Rediff News*, 14 December 2017: https://www.rediff.com/news/report/ec-acting-like-bjps-puppet-congress-on-modis-roadshow-gujarat-election/20171214.htm.

52. Vijaita Singh, 'ECI decision to not announce Gujarat poll dates surprises former CEC SY Quarishi', *Hindu*, 12 October 2017.

53. 'RSS Ideologue Govindacharya: "We Will Rewrite the Constitution to Reflect Bharatiyata"', *Wire*, 20 June 2016: https://thewire.in/politics/rss-ideologue-govindacharya-we-will-rewrite-the-constitution-to-reflect-bharatiyata.

54. 'Modi modern-day Nero: SC', *Times of India*, 12 April 2004.

55. See Manoj Mitta, *Modi and Godhra: The Fiction of Fact-Finding*, Harper Collins, New Delhi, 2014.

56. Manoj Mitta, 'Don't ask, don't tell', *Outlook*, 17 February 2014.

57. 'The Amit Shah files', *Outlook*, 16 February 2015.

58. Apoorva Mandhani, 'Judge Loya's Two Confidants Faced Mysterious Death: Congress Alleges and Demands Independent Probe', *Live Law*, 1 February 2018: https://www.livelaw.in/judge-loyas-two-confidante-faced-mysterious-death-congress-alleges-demands-independent-probe/. Also see *Caravan* magazine's sustained investigation into this matter: www.caravanmagazine.in/tag/bh-loya.

59. Michael Safi, 'India's top judges issue unprecedented warning over integrity of supreme court', *Guardian*, 12 January 2018.

60. 'India Supreme Court judges: Democracy is in danger', *BBC News*, 12 January 2018: https://www.bbc.co.uk/news/world-asia-india-42660391.

61. Rakesh Mohan Chaturvedi, 'Vice President Venkaiah Naidu rejects opposition notice for CJI impeachment', *Economic Times*, 24 April 2018.

62. Krishna Prasad, 'Is the media under siege?', *The Hindu*, 16 June 2017.

63. Ellen Barry, 'Raids in India Target Founders of News Outlet Critical of Government', *New York Times*, 5 June 2017.

64. Aayush Soni, 'How India's ace journalist was punished for confronting Prime Minister Modi', *TRT World*, 14 August 2018: https://www.trtworld.com/magazine/how-india-s-ace-journalist-was-punished-for-confronting-prime-minister-modi-19584.

65. Anuj Srinivas, 'Hindustan Times Editor's Exit Preceded by Meeting Between Modi, Newspaper Owner', *Wire*, 25 September 2017: https://thewire.in/media/hindustan-times-bobby-ghosh-narendra-modi-shobhana-bhartia.

66. Varsha Torgalkar, 'Nikhil Wagle Quits TV9, Says TV Show Dropped Due to "Political Pressure"', *Wire*, 21 July 2017: https://thewire.in/media/nikhil-wagle-quits-tv9-popular-tv-show-dropped-due-political-pressure.

67. 'Media Owner Raghav Bahl's Noida Home, "The Quint" Office Raided By Taxmen', *NDTV*, 11 October 2018: https://www.ndtv.com/india-news/media-baron-raghav-bahls-home-in-noida-raided-over-alleged-tax-evasion-say-officials-report-1930231.

68. Nikita Saxena and Atul Dev, 'No Land's Man', *The Caravan*, 1 December 2017.

69. Punya Prasun Bajpai, 'A 200-Member Government Team Is Watching How the Media Covers Modi, Amit Shah', *Wire*, 10 August 2018: https://thewire.in/media/narendra-modi-amit-shah-media-watch-punya-prasun-bajpai.

70. https://www.cobrapost.com/blog/Operation-136:-Part-1/1009.

71. https://www.cobrapost.com/blog/Press-Release-Operation-136-Part-II/1063.

72. 'RSF issues warning to India in first World Press Freedom Index Incident Report', *Reporters Without Borders*, 4 July 2018: https://rsf.org/en/news/rsf-issues-warning-india-first-world-press-freedom-index-incident-report.

10. DISUNION

1. For an historical overview, see Victoria Schofield, *Kashmir in Conflict: India, Pakistan, and the Unending War*, I.B. Tauris, London, 2003, pp. 1–25.

2. Navnita Chadha Behera, *Demystifying Kashmir*, Brookings Institution, Washington, DC, 2006, p. 27.

3. Ibid., p. 33.

4. Margaret Bourke-White, *Halfway to Freedom*, Asia Publishing House, New York, 1949, p. 207.

5. Ibid., pp. 206–7.

6. Abdullah's endorsement was instrumental in Nehru's decision to authorise military action: M.C. Mahajan, *Looking Back*, Asia Publishing House, Bombay, 1963, p. 152.

7. Bourke-White, *Halfway to Freedom*, pp. 210–211.

8. Praveen Swami, *India, Pakistan and the Secret Jihad: The Covert War in Kashmir, 1947–2004*, Routledge, Abingdon, 2007, p. 15.

9. Stanley Wolpert, *Gandhi's Passion: The Life and Legacy of Mahatma Gandhi*, Oxford University Press, New York, 2001, p. 251.

10. Full text of the UN Security Council Resolution 47: https://undocs.org/S/RES/47(1948).

11. Address to the Jammu and Kashmir Constituent Assembly, 5 November 1951: http://www.jammu-kashmir.com/documents/abdullah51.html.

12. Toru Tak, 'The Term Kashmiriyat: Kashmiri Nationalism of the 1970s', *Economic and Political Weekly*, Vol 48, No. 16, 20 April 2013, p. 28.

13. Piyasree Dasgupta, 'Who Was Burhan Wani and Why Is Kashmir Mourning Him?', *HuffPost*, 11 July 2016: www.huffingtonpost.in/burhan-wani/who-was-burhan-wani-and-why-is-kashmir-mourning-him_a_21429499/.

14. '702 votes cast in Kashmir by-election', *Statesman*, 13 April 2017.

15. Rayan Naqash, '"I will never vote again": Kashmiri man used as "human shield" describes his journey of humiliation', *Scroll*, 15 April 2017: www.scroll.in/article/834706/i-will-never-vote-again-kashmiri-man-used-as-human-shield-describes-his-journey-of-humiliation.

16. Joanna Slater, '2018 is the deadliest year in a decade in Kashmir. Next year could be worse', *Washington Post*, 23 December 2018.

17. 'After Governor's rule, President's rule comes into force in Jammu and Kashmir', *Economic Times*, 20 December 2018.

18. John P. Thorp, 'Genocide in Bangladesh', in Israel W. Charny

(ed.), *Encyclopaedia of Genocide: Volume I*, ABC-CLIO, Santa Barbara, 1999, p. 115.

19. Stanley Wolpert, *Zulfi Bhutto of Pakistan*, p. 73.

20. Mihir Sharma, 'Modi Government's Latest Move To Further North-South Divide', *NDTV*, 22 March 2018: www.ndtv.com/opinion/the-latest-humiliation-by-bjp-of-southern-states-by-mihir-swarup-sharma-1827296.

21. 'Bias may force South to secede from India: MP M Muralimohan', *New Indian Express*, 18 February 2018.

22. Kapil Komireddi, 'How India Mistreats Kashmir', *CNN*, 15 Nov 2012: http://www.globalpublicsquare.blogs.cnn.com/2012/11/15/how-india-mistreats-kashmir/.

CODA

1. 'Madhya Pradesh to get 1000 cow sheds for housing 1 lakh cows', *DNA*, 30 January 2019.

2. Shruti Tomar, '3 booked under NSA for cow slaughter in MP, first since Congress came to power', *Hindustan Times*, 6 February 2019.

3. Guha, *India After Gandhi*, Harper Collins, New Delhi, 2008, p. 813.

4. 'Congress never opposed Ram temple, even Muslims want it now: Raj Babbar', *Times of India*, 22 November, 2018.

5. 'Ram temple will be built only when Congress comes to power: Congress leader Harish Rawat', *India Today*, 18 January 2019.

EPILOGUE TO THE PAPERBACK EDITION: PANDEMONIUM

1. 'What Are Delhi Riots 2020?', *Business Standard*: https://www.business-standard.com/about/what-is-delhi-riots-2020.

2. Mukesh Rawat, 'MP govt crisis: Kamal Nath announces resignation, Congress falls and BJP rejoices', *India Today*, 20 March 2020.

3. Abantika Ghosh, 'One isolation bed per 84,000 people, 1 quarantine bed per 36,000: Govt data', *The Indian Express*, 22 March 2020.

4. This paper suggests as much: A. Nizam, P. Sivakumar & S.I. Rajan, 'Interstate Migration in India During the COVID-19 Pandemic: An Analysis Based on Mobile Visitor Location Register and Roaming Data', *Journal of South Asian Development*, Vol. 17, Issue 3, 25 September 2022: https://doi.org/10.1177/09731741221122000.

5. Dheeraj Mishra, 'RTI Shows the Government Did Collect Data on Deaths of Migrant Workers During Lockdown', *Wire*, 17 September 2020: https://thewire.in/rights/centre-indian-railways-lockdown-deaths-migrant-workers-shramik-special-rti.

6. 'Government Urges Supreme Court To Bar Media From Publishing Covid-19 Info Before Vetting Facts', Press Trust of India, 31 March 2020.

7. Shafaq Shah, 'It Just Got More Dangerous To Be A Journalist in J&K', *Article-14.com*, 22 April 2020: https://article-14.com/post/it-just-got-more-dangerous-to-be-a-journalist-in-kashmir.

8. 'UP Police Serve Notice on The Wire, Summon Founding Editor to Ayodhya Despite Lockdown', *Wire*, 11 April 2020: https://thewire.in/media/up-police-serve-notice-on-the-wire-summon-founding-editor-to-ayodhya-despite-lockdown.

9. *India: Media's Crackdown During COVID19 Lockdown*, Rights and Risks Analysis Group: http://www.rightsrisks.org/wp-content/uploads/2020/06/MediaCrackdown.pdf.

10. 'CMIE says 1 in 4 jobs have already been lost. Fighting Covid cannot justify continued destruction of businesses and livelihoods', *The Times of India*, 6 May 2020.

11. Joanna Slater and Niha Masih, 'A frantic search for scarce hospital beds as pandemic rages in India', *The Washington Post*, 13 June 2020.

12. Aditya Kalra and Alexandra Ulmer, 'Donations pour in but India's "PM CARES" coronavirus fund faces criticism', *Reuters*, 8 April 2020.

13. Roselet Sheena Merli, 'Larsen and Toubro migrant workers protest against the non-payment of wages', *Freshers Live*, 1 May 2020: https://news.fresherslive.com/articles/larsen-and-turbo-migrant-workers-protest-against-the-nonpayment-of-wages-126441.

14. Vatsal Bhandari, 'Indian companies are contributing lavishly to PM-CARES—even amid layoffs and pay cuts', *Scroll.in*, 9 May 2020: https://scroll.in/article/961383/indian-companies-are-contributing-lavishly-to-pm-cares-even-amid-layoffs-and-pay-cuts.

15. Sofi Ahsan, 'PM-CARES Fund not a fund of Government of India, Delhi HC told', *The Indian Express*, 23 September 2021.

Also see: 'PM Cares can't be brought under RTI: Centre to HC', *Hindustan Times*, 23 September 2021.

16. Take for instance: 'Mamata hits back, alleges misuse of PM Cares fund', *Hindustan Times*, 21 March 2021; Congress on Twitter: https://twitter.com/incindia/status/1383691769531957250; 'PM CARES Fund A "Sophisticated Way Of Corruption": Mehbooba Mufti', *NDTV.com*, 8 November 2021: https://www. ndtv.com/india-news/pm-cares-fund-a-sophisticated-way-of-cor-ruption-mehbooba-mufti-2603292.

17. Tejasvi Surya, 6 May 2020: https://twitter.com/tejasvi_surya/ status/1257941527386484736.

18. Shyamal Yada, 'Rs 157 crore from Central staff salaries for PM Cares; over 93% from Railways', *Indian Express*, 15 October 2020.

19. Samrat Sharma, 'India moves big labour law changes to limit coronavirus impact; UP, MP, Punjab, others make these changes', *Financial Express*, 8 May 2020.

20. 'MP: Trade Unions across Political Hues Unite Against 'Anti-Labour' Reforms', *Newsclick*, 9 May 2020: https://www.newsclick. in/Madhya-Pradesh-Trade-Unions-Political-Hues-Unite-Against-Anti-Labour-Reforms.

21. See, for instance, K.P. Krishnan, Anirudh Burman, Suyash Rai, 'Migrant Workmen Act, 1979, must be rationalised to remove requirements that disincentivise formalisation', *The Indian Express*, 9 May 2020; and also see Gautam Chikermane, 'COVID-19 could be Modi's reform moment', Observer Research Foundation, 6 June 2020: https://www.orfonline.org/research/india-covid19-modi-reform-moment-67354/.

22. Manu Kaushik, 'Two Boeing wide-body planes for Modi, Kovind, Naidu to cost Rs 8,458 crore', *Business Today*, 3 February 2020.

23. Vijayta Lalwani, 'Three workers at Central Vista contract Covid-19. Many complain of cramped living space, late wages', *Scroll. in*, 28 May 2021: https://scroll.in/article/995968/three-work-ers-at-central-vista-contract-covid-19-many-complain-of-cramped-living-space-late-wages.

24. Soumya Pillai, 'Delhi's crematoriums run out of wood, seek forest dept's help', *Hindustan Times*, 28 April 2021.

25. Debarshi Dasgupta and Rohini Mohan, 'Families allowed to bury

dead in backyards as India's Covid-19 surge overwhelms crematoriums', *Straits Times*, 30 April 2021.

26. 'Estimating excess mortality due to the COVID-19 pandemic: a systematic analysis of COVID-19-related mortality, 2020–21', *The Lancet*, 10 March 2022; and Somayeh Malekian, 'India's staggering COVID-19 death toll could be 6 million: Study', *ABC News*, 23 December 2021: https://abcnews.go.com/Health/indias-staggering-covid-19-death-toll-million-study/story?id=81897534.

27. Vivek Mishra, 'Kumbh amid COVID-19: Protocol sinks as over 3 million take a dip', *Down To Earth*, 12 April 2021: https://www.downtoearth.org.in/news/health/kumbh-amid-covid-19-protocol-sinks-as-over-3-million-take-a-dip-76435.

28. Moinideepa Banerjee, '"Have Witnessed Such A Rally For The First Time…": PM Modi In Bengal', *NDTV.com*, 18 April 2021: https://www.ndtv.com/india-news/west-bengal-assembly-election-2021-prime-minister-narendra-modi-in-west-bengal-have-witnessed-such-a-rally-for-the-first-time-2416162.

29. Mohamed Zeeshan, 'Prioritising image management over planning has led to India's Covid catastrophe', *The Telegraph* (UK), 27 May 2021.

30. Aditya Sharma, 'Is India's Modi too focused on his public image during COVID crisis?', *DW.com*, 26 May 2021: https://www.dw.com/en/is-indias-modi-too-focused-on-his-public-image-during-covid-crisis/a-57668355.

31. The May 2019 conference does not count for this reason: 'At his first news conference in India, PM Modi declines questions', Reuters, 17 May 2019: https://www.reuters.com/article/india-election-modi-idUSKCN1SN224.

32. Richard Mahapatra, 'Modi's COVID-19 vaccine turnaround: An answer for Supreme Court queries just in time', *Down To Earth*: https://www.downtoearth.org.in/news/governance/modi-s-covid-19-vaccine-turnaround-an-answer-for-supreme-court-queries-just-in-time-77326.

33. Dipa Sinha, 'Despite Govt Claims, India's Health Budget Only Around 0.34% of GDP', *TheWire.in*, 1 February 2021: https://science.thewire.in/health/union-health-budget-nirmala-sitharaman-covid-19-pmasby-allocation-gdp-expert-analysis/.

FURTHER READING

Aguiar, Benny. *Rajiv Gandhi: The Flight of the Scion*. Delhi: Vitasta, 2011.

Aiyar, Nilakanta Sastri. *A History of South India: From Prehistoric Times to the Fall of Vijayanagar*. London: Oxford University Press, 1966.

Andersen, Walter K., and Shridhar D. Damle. *The Brotherhood in Saffron: The Rashtriya Swayamsevak Sangh and Hindu Revivalism*. Delhi: Sage, 1999.

Baru, Sanjaya. *1991: How P.V. Narasimha Rao Made History*. Delhi: Aleph, 2016.

Basu, Tapan. *Khaki Shorts and Saffron Flags: A Critique of the Hindu Right*. Hyderabad: Orient Longman, 1993.

Behera, Navnita Chadha. *Demystifying Kashmir*. Washington DC: Brookings, 2006.

Bhaduri, Amit, and Deepak Nayyar. *The Intelligent Person's Guide to Liberalisation*. Delhi: Penguin Books, 1996.

Bhaduri, Amit. *The Face You Were Afraid to See: Essays on the Indian Economy*. Delhi, India: Penguin Books, 2009.

Bhushan, Prashant. *The Case That Shook India: The Verdict That Led to the Emergency*. Haryana, India: Penguin Random House India, 2018.

Bourke-White, Margaret. *Halfway to Freedom*. New York: Asia Publishing House, 1949.

Brar, K. S. *Operation Blue Star: The True Story*. Delhi: UBS Publishers Distributors, 2006.

Chacko, Priya. *Indian Foreign Policy: The Politics of Postcolonial Identity*. London: Routledge, 2011.

Chandrasekhar, C. P., and Jayati Ghosh. *The Market That Failed: Neoliberal Economic Reforms in India*. Delhi: LeftWord, 2009.

Chaudhuri, Rudra. *Forged in Crisis: India and the United States since 1947*. London: Hurst, 2013.

Datta-Ray, Sunanda K. *Looking East to Look Eest: Lee Kuan Yew's Mission to India*. Singapore: ISEAS Publishing, 2010.

Dhulipala, Venkat. *Creating a New Medina: State Power, Islam, and the Quest for Pakistan in Late Colonial North India*. Cambridge: Cambridge University Press, 2016.

Dua, B. D., and James Manor, eds. *Nehru to the Nineties: The Changing Office of Prime Minister in India*. Delhi: Viking, 1994.

Elliot, Henry Miers, and John Dowson. *The History of India: As Told by Its Own Historians*. Vol. 3. London: Trübner, 1871.

Frank, Katherine. *Indira: The Life of Indira-Nehru Gandhi*. Delhi: HarperCollins, 2005.

Gandhi, Arun. *Morarji Papers: Fall of the Janata Government*. Delhi: Vision Books, 1983.

Gidla, Sujatha. *Ants Among Elephants: An Untouchable Family and the Making of Modern India*. New York: Farrar, Straus, and Giroux, 2017.

Gopal, Sarvepalli. *Jawaharlal Nehru: A Biography*. London: Cape, 1984.

Guha, Ramachandra. *India After Gandhi: The History of the World's Largest Democracy*. London: Pan Macmillan, 2007.

Hall, Ian. *The Engagement of India: Strategies and Responses*. Washington DC: Georgetown University, 2014.

Harrison, Selig. *India: The Most Dangerous Decades*. Madras: Oxford Univ. Press, 1968.

Henderson, Michael. *Experiment with Untruth: India Under Emergency*. London: Macmillan, 1977.

Jaffrelot, Christophe. *The Hindu Nationalist Movement in India*. New York: Columbia University Press, 1998.

Kohli, Atul. *Democracy and Discontent: India's Growing Crisis of Governability*. Cambridge: Cambridge University Press, 1990.

Kohli, Atul. *Poverty Amid Plenty in the New India*. Cambridge: Cambridge University Press, 2013.

Liu, Xinru. *Ancient India and Ancient China Trade and Religious Exchanges AD 1–600*. Delhi: Oxford University Press, 1991.

Mankekar, D. R., and Kamla Mankekar. *Decline and Fall of Indira Gandhi*. Delhi: Vision Books, 1977.

Marino, Andy. *Narendra Modi: A Political Biography*. Delhi: HarperCollins, 2015.

Mehta, Ved. *The New India.* Harmondsworth: Penguin Books, 1978.

Mehta, Ved. *Rajiv Gandhi and Rama's Kingdom.* New Haven, CT: Yale University, 1994.

Mehta, Vinod. *The Sanjay Story: From Anand Bhavan to Amethi.* Bombay: Jaico, 1978.

Mitta, Manoj, and H. S. Phoolka. *When a Tree Shook Delhi: The 1984 Carnage and Its Aftermath.* Delhi: Lotus, 2007.

Mitta, Manoj. *Modi and Godhra: The Fiction of Fact-Finding.* Delhi: HarperCollins, 2014.

Mohan, C. Raja. *Crossing the Rubicon: The Shaping of India's New Foreign Policy.* Delhi: Penguin Books, 2005.

Moraes, Dom. *Indira Gandhi.* Boston: Little, Brown, 1980.

Moraes, Dom, and Sarayu Srivastava. *Out of God's Oven: Travels in a Fractured Land.* Delhi: Penguin Books, 2007.

Mukherji, Nirmalangshu. *The Maoists in India: Tribals Under Siege.* London: Pluto, 2012.

Mukhopadhyay, Nilanjan. *Narendra Modi: The Man, the Times.* Delhi: Westland, 2014.

Nayak, Pradeep. *The Politics of the Ayodhya Dispute: Rise of Communalism and Future Voting Behaviour.* Delhi: Commonwealth Publishers, 1993.

Nayar, Kuldip. *India: The Critical Years.* London: Weidenfeld & Nicolson, 1971.

Nayar, Kuldip. *The Judgement: Inside Story of the Emergency in India.* Delhi: Vikas, 1977.

Nehru, Jawaharlal. *The Discovery of India.* New York: John Day, 1946.

Omvedt, Gail. *Understanding Caste: From Buddha to Ambedkar and Beyond.* Hyderabad: Orient Blackswan, 2016.

Panagariya, Arvind. *India: The Emerging Giant.* New York, NY: Oxford University Press, 2008.

Paz, Octavio. *In Light of India: Essays.* Translated by Eliot Weinberger. New York: Harcourt Brace, 1997.

Price, Lance. *Modi Effect: Inside Narendra Modi's Campaign to Transform India.* London: Hodder & Stoughton, 2015.

Rao, K. N. *Chandra Shekhar: The Survivor.* Delhi: Manak Publications, 1991.

Sanyal, Meera H. *The Big Reverse: How Demonetisation Knocked India Out.* Delhi: Harper Business, an Imprint of HarperCollins Publishers, 2018.

Selbourne, David. *Through the Indian Looking-Glass: Selected Articles on India, 1976–1980*. London: Zed, 1982.

Shah, MC. *Consensus and Conciliation: PV Narasimha Rao*. Delhi: Shpra, 1992.

Sherwani, Harun. *History of Medieval Deccan (1295–1724)*. Hyderabad: Government of Andhra Pradesh, 1973.

Singh, K. Natwar. *One Life Is Not Enough: An Autobiography*. Delhi: Rupa, 2014.

Sitapati, Vinay. *The Man Who Remade India: A Biography of P.V. Narasimha Rao*. New York: Oxford University Press, 2018.

Srivastava, C. P. *Lal Bahadur Shastri: A Life of Truth in Politics*. Delhi: Oxford University Press, 2007.

Subramanian, Arvind. *Of Counsel: The Challenges of the Modi-Jaitley Economy*. Delhi: Penguin Random House India, 2018.

Talbot, Cynthia. *Precolonial India in Practice: Society, Region, and Identity in Medieval Andhra*. Oxford: Oxford University Press, 2001.

Thapar, Romila. *Past as Present: Forging Contemporary Identities Through History*. Delhi: Aleph, 2014.

Titus, Murray. *Indian Islam. A Religious History of Islam in India*. London: Oxford University Press, 1930.

Tully, Mark, and Satish Jacob. *Amritsar: Mrs. Gandhi's Last Battle*. Calcutta: Rupa, 1994.

Narasimha Rao, P.V. *The Insider*. Delhi: Penguin Books, 2000.

Varma, Pavan. *The Great Indian Middle Class*. Delhi: Penguin Books, 1999.

Wolpert, Stanley. *Zulfi Bhutto of Pakistan*. New York: Oxford Univ. Press, 1993.

INDEX

K.S. (Kapil Satish) Komireddi is an essayist, author, and journalist. He was born in India, and educated there and in England. His commentary, criticism, and journalism—from South Asia, Europe, and the Middle East—appear, among other leading publications, in the *The New York Times*, *The Washington Post*, *The Guardian*, *The Economist*, *The Spectator*, the *Daily Mail*, the *Los Angeles Times*, *TIME*, *Foreign Policy* and the *Jewish Chronicle*.

A sought-after speaker, Komireddi has delivered lectures at Yale, London, and Delhi. He has also advised, written speeches and published commentary for a number of high-profile public figures in Europe.

A columnist for *The Print* and a panellist on Monocle Radio, Komireddi appears frequently on ABC, CBC, the BBC and CNN, among others, to discuss international affairs. He lives in India, this is his first book.